# PRIMAL
# LEADERSHIP

D0166799

# PRIMAL LEADERSHIP

## UNLEASHING THE POWER OF EMOTIONAL INTELLIGENCE

DANIEL GOLEMAN

RICHARD BOYATZIS

ANNIE McKEE

HARVARD BUSINESS REVIEW PRESS
*Boston, Massachusetts*

Requests for permission to use or reproduce material from this book should be directed to permissions@hbsp.harvard.edu, or mailed to Permissions, Harvard Business School Publishing, 60 Harvard Way, Boston, Massachusetts 02163.

The web addresses referenced in this book were live and correct at the time of the book's publication but may be subject to change.

Library of Congress Cataloging-in-Publication Data

Goleman, Daniel.
  Primal leadership: learning to lead with emotional intelligence / Daniel Goleman, Richard Boyatzis, AnnieMCKee; with a new preface by the authors.
    pages cm
  Includes bibliographical references and index.
    ISBN 978-1-4221-6803-5
    1. Leadership—Psychological aspects. 2. Management—Psychological aspects. 3. Executive ability. 4. Emotional intelligence. I. Boyatzis, Richard E. II. McKee, Annie, 1955- III. Title.
    HD57.7.G664 2013
    658.4'092019—dc23

                                                                    2013018294

*To Tara, Sandy, and Eddy,*
*our respective spouses,*
*for helping us to learn*
*about resonance*
*and emotional intelligence*
*in a lifelong love*

# CONTENTS

# PREFACE, TENTH ANNIVERSARY EDITION

IN THE decade since *Primal Leadership* was first published, the world has changed in ways that make its message all the more timely. Leaders face ever-increasing pressures, including globalization and the economic roller coaster, the hyper-speed of evolving information technologies, the shortening of product life cycles, and the ratcheting up of competitive forces, to name just a few.

This whirlwind of change makes it more important than ever for leaders to be self-aware and composed, focused and high energy, empathic and motivating, collaborative and compelling—in short, resonant. A host of studies worldwide on emotions, emotional contagion, leader-follower relations, and coaching, as well as research on human behavior continue to confirm and clarify our understanding of why emotionally intelligent leaders get results. Our own research on brain imaging related to effective leaders also confirms what we proposed ten years ago.

That message has already shown its relevance to the million or so readers of *Primal Leadership*, in twenty-eight languages—a number that confirms the global appeal of emotionally intelligent leadership. And that appeal reaches beyond the business world. Our book is now used routinely in universities, business and medical schools, other professional training programs, and by a growing legion of leadership coaches.

Part of our message is "leadership at all levels." We each have spheres of influence where we lead, no matter our position or title. But the difficult reality so many organizations have faced in hard times has put leadership development on the back burner. Today, many people are seeking ways to develop their leadership skills on their own. Our work helps.

To build on the work of *Primal Leadership* and further support the hands-on application of our ideas, Richard Boyatzis and Annie McKee have written *Resonant Leadership* (Harvard Business School Press, 2005) and, with Frances Johnston, *Becoming a Resonant Leader* (Harvard Business Press, 2008). And for those who want a quick summary of the theory and research behind the practice, Daniel Goleman has compiled his key writings in *Leadership: The Power of Emotional Intelligence* (More Than Sound, 2011).

These books amplify the work of *Primal Leadership*, broadening its impact and adding to the toolkit of the thousands of individuals, coaches, and others who are applying its message in their own lives, work, and leadership.

In coming years we can expect increased interdependence— both within organizations and between them in new partnerships. And as the need increases to use resources more thoughtfully, efficiently, and with benign impacts, emotional and social intelligence will become even more critical to building and maintaining the working relationships needed to achieve these ends. The driving force in learning, adaptation, and change will continue to be resonant leadership and the personal renewal that accompanies it.

## Contacting the Authors

This book represents an ongoing exploration into the role of emotional intelligence in leadership. We welcome reactions from our readers—thoughts, stories, questions. Though we are not always able to respond to every e-mail, we enjoy hearing from (and always learn from) our readers.

To reach us via e-mail, use the following addresses:

Daniel Goleman: contact@danielgoleman.info

Annie McKee: amckee@teleosleaders.com

Richard Boyatzis: richard.boyatzis@case.edu

# PREFACE

W E'VE WRITTEN this book in large part because of the unprecedented, enormously enthusiastic reader response to the *Harvard Business Review* articles "What Makes a Leader?" and "Leadership That Gets Results." But this book goes far beyond those articles to advance a new concept: primal leadership. The fundamental task of leaders, we argue, is to prime good feeling in those they lead. That occurs when a leader creates *resonance*—a reservoir of positivity that frees the best in people. At its root, then, the primal job of leadership is emotional.

We believe this primal dimension of leadership, though often invisible or ignored entirely, determines whether everything else a leader does will work as well as it could. And this is why emotional intelligence—being intelligent about emotions—matters so much for leadership success: Primal leadership demands we bring emotional intelligence to bear. In this book we show not just why emotionally intelligent leadership drives resonance, and thus performance, but also how to realize its power—for the individual leader, in teams, and throughout entire organizations.

Perhaps uniquely among management theories, the primal leadership model builds on links to neurology. Breakthroughs in brain research show why leaders' moods and actions have enormous impact on those they lead, and shed fresh light on the power of emotionally intelligent leadership to inspire, arouse passion and enthusiasm, and keep people motivated and committed. Conversely, we sound a warning about the power of toxic leadership to poison the emotional climate of a workplace.

Each of us brings a different perspective to this task. For Daniel Goleman, the worldwide response to his books and his *Harvard Business Review* articles on leadership has brought invitations to speak with leaders around the world. In addition to his own worldwide speaking, Richard Boyatzis, as a professor at the Weatherhead School of Management, has the advantage of in-depth research from fifteen years of guiding thousands of MBAs and executives through the challenge of cultivating the essential competencies of emotionally intelligent (EI) leadership. And Annie McKee, on the faculty of the University of Pennsylvania Graduate School of Education, consults to business and organization leaders worldwide and brings practical insights gained from her hands-on work helping dozens of organizations transform to foster emotionally intelligent leaders. We have woven our collective expertise together to offer a perspective that takes advantage of our diverse backgrounds.[1]

Just what the many faces of primal leadership look like has become evident to us as we've talked with hundreds of executives, managers, and workers at companies and organizations around the world. We have encountered resonant leaders in organizations of every sort and at all levels. Some have no official leadership position, yet step forward to lead as needed, then fade back until another ripe moment arrives. Others head a team or an entire company, guide a start-up, catalyze change in their organization, or nimbly split away to start their own renegade venture.

We'll share stories of many such leaders in these pages (some of whom we name, while others who spoke to us in confidence we have disguised). And we've confirmed these personal observations with data on thousands of leaders.

We've been able to reap a rich harvest of data from other sources. Colleagues at the research arm of The Hay Group have shared with us two decades of analyses of leadership effectiveness done for their clients globally. In recent years, an expanding network of academic researchers has been gathering data with the ECI-360, our measure of the key emotional intelligence competencies for leadership. And from many other centers of research the body of findings and theory on emotional intelligence and leadership has been growing steadily.

From all these sources we've drawn answers to telling questions about primal leadership: What emotional resources do leaders need to thrive amidst chaos and turbulent change? What gives a leader the inner strength to be honest about even painful truths? What enables a leader to inspire others to do their best work and to stay loyal when other jobs beckon? How do leaders create an emotional climate that fosters creative innovations, all-out performance, or warm and lasting customer relationships?

For too long managers have seen emotions at work as noise cluttering the rational operation of organizations. But the time for ignoring emotions as irrelevant to business has passed. What organizations everywhere need now is to realize the benefits of primal leadership by cultivating leaders who generate the emotional resonance that lets people flourish.

Take, for example, the horrific catastrophe in New York, Washington, D.C., and Pennsylvania on September 11, 2001—which occurred in the final days of writing this book. That calamity underscores the essential role of emotional leadership, particularly in moments of human tragedy and crisis. And it brings home the point that resonance goes beyond positivity, to cover the range of emotions. Consider Mark Loehr, CEO of SoundView Technology, a technology brokerage in Connecticut. A handful of friends, colleagues, and family members of people there were lost in the tragedy. Loehr's first response was to invite all employees to come to the office the next day—not to work, but to share their feelings and talk over what to do. Over the following days Loehr was there as people wept together, and he urged people to talk about what they were going through. Every night at 9:45 he sent out an e-mail to the entire company about the personal side of the ongoing events.

Loehr went a step further, encouraging and guiding a discussion of how to find meaning in the chaos through an action they could all participate in to help out. Rather than just making a group donation, they decided to donate their company's proceeds from one day of trading to those victimized by the tragedy. On an average day, that might be more than half a million dollars; the most they had made in a day was around $1 million. But as they spread the word of what they wanted to do to their clients, it inspired an amazing response: They raised more than $6 million that day.

To continue the healing process, Loehr also asked employees to compile a "memory book" to record their thoughts, fears, and hopes, which could be shared with future generations. There was an outpouring of e-mails with poems, moving stories, reflections—people speaking from their hearts.

In such a grave crisis, all eyes turn to the leader for emotional guidance. Because the leader's way of seeing things has special weight, leaders manage meaning for a group, offering a way to interpret or make sense of, and so react emotionally to, a given situation. Mark Loehr courageously performed one of the most crucial emotional tasks of leadership: He helped himself and his people find meaning and sense, even in the face of chaos and madness. To do so, he first attuned to and expressed the shared emotional reality so that the direction he eventually articulated resonated at the gut level, putting into words what everyone was feeling in their hearts.

What would our lives look like if the organizations where we spent our working days were naturally places of resonance, with leaders who inspired us? In most parts of the developing world best practices for business have not yet formed. Imagine what an organization would be like if these concepts of resonant leadership were founding principles rather than—as is usually the case in highly developed settings—a corrective. Then from the start hiring would focus on recruiting those with the EI skills for leadership, as would promotions and development. Ongoing learning for these leadership skills would be part of everyday operations, and the entire organization would be a place where people flourished by working together.

And then what if we brought these qualities home to our marriages, families, children, and communities? Very often when we work with leaders to help them cultivate a greater range or depth in emotional intelligence competencies, they tell us that the payoff for them has been not just in their work as leaders, but in their personal and family lives as well. They find themselves bringing home heightened levels of self-awareness and empathic understanding, self-mastery, and attuned relationships.

Let's take that a step further. What would our schools—and children—be like if education also included those emotional intelligence abilities that foster resonance? For one thing, employers of every kind would have the pleasure of taking into their ranks new generations of leaders-to-be who were already adept at these key work skills. The personal benefits for young people themselves would also be reflected in a decline in those social ills—ranging from violence to substance abuse—that stem in large part from deficits in skills such as handling impulses and rocky emotions. Beyond that, communities would benefit from higher levels of tolerance, caring, and personal responsibility.

Given that employers themselves are looking for these capacities in those they hire, colleges and professional schools—particularly business schools—should be including the basics of emotional intelligence in the skill sets they offer. As Erasmus, the great Renaissance thinker, reminds us, "The best hope of a nation lies in the proper education of its youth."

The most innovative business educators will, we hope, recognize the importance of emotional intelligence in higher education for helping their graduates become leaders instead of mere managers. The most forward-thinking business people will encourage and support such business education, not just for added leadership strength in their own organizations, but for the vitality of an entire economy. And the benefits will accrue not just for a new generation of leaders, but for our families, communities, and society as a whole.

One final note: There are many leaders, not just one. Leadership is distributed. It resides not solely in the individual at the top, but in every person at every level who, in one way or another, acts as a leader to a group of followers—wherever in the organization that person is, whether shop steward, team head, or CEO. We offer these insights to leaders wherever they may be.

# ACKNOWLEDGMENTS

T HIS BOOK represents decades of our work on the themes that have culminated in the theory of primal leadership, each of us approaching the topic from a unique angle. Our indebtedness extends to many who have contributed to our thinking, research, and our ability to write this book.

For Richard Boyatzis and Daniel Goleman, many of those whose research has contributed to our thinking are colleagues on the Consortium for Research on Emotional Intelligence in Organizations, headed by Cary Cherniss of the Graduate School for Professional and Applied Psychology at Rutgers University. These include Lyle Spencer, Marilyn Gowing, Claudio Fernández-Aráoz, and Matthew Mangino, whose research has directly contributed to this book.

But our first inspiration was our main professor at Harvard during our graduate school years, David McClelland—his research and theories shaped much of our own work until his death in 1998. We also are indebted to colleagues from those early years who are now at The Hay Group and who have continued to share their research findings and explorations into the ingredients of excellence. These include Murray Dalziel, group managing director for worldwide practices at The Hay Group, who continues to be a fount of insights and analytic clarity in his thinking about leadership and organizational development; Mary Fontaine, senior vice president, and James Burrus, vice president, at the McClelland Center of The Hay Group in Boston; John Larrere, vice president and general manager, The Hay Group; and Paul Basile, formerly director of marketing, The Hay Group.

Among the many other colleagues at The Hay Group whose work has supported our own are Keith Cornella, Ginny Flynn, Patricia Marshall, Signe Spencer, and Bill Tredwell, all in Boston; Therese Jacobs-Stewart in Minneapolis; Connie Schroyer in Arlington, Virginia; Rick Lash in Toronto; Nick Boulter, Chris Dyson, Alison Forsythe, Katherine Thomas, and Peter Melrose in London; Sergio Oxer and Luis Giorgio in São Paolo; and Tharuma Rajah in Kuala Lumpur.

In the Boston office of The Hay Group, Ruth Jacobs has provided crucial data analyses, along with Michele Burckle. Fabio Sala, who continues to direct research with the ECI, has also done yeoman service with data analyses.

Richard Boyatzis gives special thanks to David Kolb, professor of organizational behavior at Case Western Reserve University, who introduced him to the model of behavior change and intrigued him to study it further. Also, he thanks the many colleagues who helped him in the research and building of the self-directed learning model, or who helped him teach it: Ann Baker, Robert F. Bales, Diana Bilimoria, Susan Case, Scott Cowen, Christine Dreyfus, Vanessa Druskat, Louella Harvey-Hein, Retta Holdorf, David Leonard, Poppy McLeod, Charalampos Mainemelis, Angela Murphy, Patricia Petty, Ken Rhee, Lorraine Thompson, Jane Wheeler, and Robert Wright.

Many others have contributed to the thinking about leadership in this book. Daniel Goleman wishes to acknowledge Deepak Sethi of Thomson Corporation; Naomi R. Wolf of the Woodhull Institute for Ethical Leadership; Richard Davidson, director of the Laboratory for Affective Neuroscience at the University of Wisconsin; Steve Kelner of Egon Zehnder International; and Robin Stern of the Program for Social and Emotional Learning at Teachers College, Columbia University. Rachel Brod provided resourceful literature searches, and Rowan Foster gave invaluable logistical support.

In addition, Annie McKee gives special thanks to Fran Johnston of the Gestalt Institute of Cleveland, whose keen insights
and coaching over the years have enriched her thinking and practice, and whose friendship is a treasure; Cecilia McMillen of the
University of Massachusetts, whose research and work with organizations has been enlightening; and Tom Malnight of IMD, for
creativity, collaboration, and fun. Also acknowledged is the
invaluable help of Barbara Reitano, Tracy Simandl, Neen Kuzmick,
Lezlie Lovett, Beulah Trey, Jonno Hanafin, MaryAnn Rainey,
Michael Kitson, Linda Pittari, Felice Tilin, David Smith, and
Carol Scheman.

At Harvard Business School Press, our thanks to Marjorie
Williams and Carol Franco, who guided us to the completion of
this work. A special thanks to our lead editor, Suzanne Rotondo,
for her keen insights and partnership, and to Lucy McCauley for
inspired aid in rewrites. Astrid Sandoval, Sharon Rice, and Gayle
Treadwell each lent invaluable help. As ever, Suzy Wetlaufer
advanced our own thinking even as she shaped an article for the
*Harvard Business Review*.

On a personal note, Annie McKee thanks her husband, Eddy
Mwelwa, who is her inspiration; her children, Becky Renio, Sean
Renio, and Sarah Renio, who through their own leadership
demonstrate the power of emotional intelligence and bring resonance to the family; her parents, Cathy MacDonald Wigsten and
Murray Wigsten, for intellectual and emotional support of this
work; her brothers, Rick, Matt, Mark, Jeff, and Robert; and her
sister, Sam.

Richard Boyatzis thanks his wife, Sandy, for tolerance of his
preoccupation over the months of writing, and her loving support and help in reacting to drafts; and his son, Mark Scott, and
late father-in-law, Ronald W. Scott, for reacting to drafts.

Daniel Goleman, as ever, appreciates the inspiration and
patience of his wife, Tara Bennett-Goleman, and hopes this book
will help create a better future for his granddaughters, Lila and
Hazel Goleman.

And finally, we'd each like to acknowledge the value of our
collaboration—and its resonance—in writing this book.

# PART ONE

# THE POWER OF EMOTIONAL INTELLIGENCE

### CHAPTER ONE

# PRIMAL LEADERSHIP

GREAT LEADERS move us. They ignite our passion and inspire the best in us. When we try to explain why they are so effective, we speak of strategy, vision, or powerful ideas. But the reality is much more primal: Great leadership works through the emotions.

No matter what leaders set out to do—whether it's creating strategy or mobilizing teams to action—their success depends on *how* they do it. Even if they get everything else just right, if leaders fail in this primal task of driving emotions in the right direction, nothing they do will work as well as it could or should.

Consider, for example, a pivotal moment in a news division at the BBC, the British media giant. The division had been set up as an experiment, and while its 200 or so journalists and editors felt they had given their best, management had decided the division would have to close.[1]

It didn't help that the executive sent to deliver the decision to the assembled staff started off with a glowing account of how well rival operations were doing, and that he had just returned from a wonderful trip to Cannes. The news itself was bad enough, but the brusque, even contentious manner of the executive incited something beyond the expected frustration. People became enraged—not just at the management decision, but also at the bearer of the news himself. The atmosphere became so threatening, in fact, that it looked as though the executive might have to call security to usher him safely from the room.

The next day, another executive visited the same staff. He took a very different approach. He spoke from his heart about the crucial importance of journalism to the vibrancy of a society, and of the calling that had drawn them all to the field in the first place. He reminded them that no one goes into journalism to get rich—as a profession its finances have always been marginal, with job security ebbing and flowing with larger economic tides. And he invoked the passion, even the dedication, the journalists had for the service they offered. Finally, he wished them all well in getting on with their careers.

When this leader finished speaking, the staff cheered.

The difference between the leaders lay in the mood and tone with which they delivered their messages: One drove the group toward antagonism and hostility, the other toward optimism, even inspiration, in the face of difficulty. These two moments point to a hidden, but crucial, dimension in leadership—the emotional impact of what a leader says and does.

While most people recognize that a leader's mood—and how he or she impacts the mood of others—plays a significant role in any organization, emotions are often seen as too personal or unquantifiable to talk about in a meaningful way. But research in the field of emotion has yielded keen insights into not only how to measure the impact of a leader's emotions but also how the best leaders have found effective ways to understand and improve the way they handle their own and other people's emotions. Understanding the powerful role of emotions in the workplace sets the best leaders apart from the rest—not just in tangibles such as better business results and the retention of talent, but also in the all-important intangibles, such as higher morale, motivation, and commitment.

## The Primal Dimension

This emotional task of the leader is *primal*—that is, first—in two senses: It is both the original and the most important act of leadership.

Leaders have always played a primordial emotional role. No doubt humankind's original leaders—whether tribal chieftains or shamanesses—earned their place in large part because their leadership was emotionally compelling. Throughout history and in cultures everywhere, the leader in any human group has been the one to whom others look for assurance and clarity when facing uncertainty or threat, or when there's a job to be done. The leader acts as the group's emotional guide.

In the modern organization, this primordial emotional task—though by now largely invisible—remains foremost among the many jobs of leadership: driving the collective emotions in a positive direction and clearing the smog created by toxic emotions. This task applies to leadership everywhere, from the boardroom to the shop floor.

Quite simply, in any human group the leader has maximal power to sway everyone's emotions. If people's emotions are pushed toward the range of enthusiasm, performance can soar; if people are driven toward rancor and anxiety, they will be thrown off stride. This indicates another important aspect of primal leadership: Its effects extend beyond ensuring that a job is well done. Followers also look to a leader for supportive emotional connection—for empathy. All leadership includes this primal dimension, for better or for worse. When leaders drive emotions positively, as was the case with the second executive at the BBC, they bring out everyone's best. We call this effect *resonance*. When they drive emotions negatively, as with the first executive, leaders spawn *dissonance*, undermining the emotional foundations that let people shine. Whether an organization withers or flourishes depends to a remarkable extent on the leaders' effectiveness in this primal emotional dimension.

The key, of course, to making primal leadership work to everyone's advantage lies in the leadership competencies of *emotional intelligence*: how leaders handle themselves and their relationships. Leaders who maximize the benefits of primal leadership drive the emotions of those they lead in the right direction.

How does all of this work? Recent studies of the brain reveal the neurological mechanisms of primal leadership and make clear just why emotional intelligence abilities are so crucial.

## The Open Loop

The reason a leader's manner—not just what he does, but *how* he does it—matters so much lies in the design of the human brain: what scientists have begun to call the *open-loop* nature of the limbic system, our emotional centers. A closed-loop system such as the circulatory system is self-regulating; what's happening in the circulatory system of others around us does not impact our own system. An open-loop system depends largely on external sources to manage itself.

In other words, we rely on connections with other people for our own emotional stability. The open-loop limbic system was a winning design in evolution, no doubt, because it allows people to come to one another's emotional rescue—enabling, for example, a mother to soothe her crying infant, or a lookout in a primate band to signal an instant alarm when he perceives a threat.

Despite the veneer of our advanced civilization, the open-loop principle still holds. Research in intensive care units has shown that the comforting presence of another person not only lowers the patient's blood pressure, but also slows the secretion of fatty acids that block arteries.[2] More dramatically, whereas three or more incidents of intense stress within a year (say, serious financial

trouble, being fired, or a divorce) triple the death rate in socially isolated middle-aged men, they have *no impact* whatsoever on the
death rate of men who cultivate many close relationships.[3]

Scientists describe the open loop as "interpersonal limbic regulation," whereby one person transmits signals that can alter hormone levels, cardiovascular function, sleep rhythms, and even
immune function inside the body of another.[4] That's how couples
who are in love are able to trigger in one another's brains surges
of oxytocin, which creates a pleasant, affectionate feeling. But in
all aspects of social life, not just love relationships, our physiolo-
gies intermingle, our emotions automatically shifting into the register of the person we're with. The open-loop design of the limbic
system means that other people can change our very physiology—
and so our emotions.

Even though the open loop is so much a part of our lives, we
usually don't notice the process itself. Scientists have captured this
attunement of emotions in the laboratory by measuring the physiology—such as heart rate—of two people as they have a good
conversation. As the conversation begins, their bodies each operate at different rhythms. But by the end of a simple fifteen-minute
conversation, their physiological profiles look remarkably similar—
a phenomenon called *mirroring*. This entrainment occurs strongly
during the downward spiral of a conflict, when anger and hurt
reverberate, but also goes on more subtly during pleasant interactions.[5] It happens hardly at all during an emotionally neutral discussion. Researchers have seen again and again how emotions spread
irresistibly in this way whenever people are near one another, even
when the contact is completely nonverbal. For example, when three
strangers sit facing each other in silence for a minute or two, the
one who is most emotionally expressive transmits his or her
mood to the other two—without speaking a single word.[6] The
same effect holds in the office, boardroom, or shop floor; people
in groups at work inevitably "catch" feelings from one another,
sharing everything from jealousy and envy to angst or euphoria.
The more cohesive the group, the stronger the sharing of moods,
emotional history, and even hot buttons.[7]

In seventy work teams across diverse industries, for instance, members who sat in meetings together ended up sharing moods—either good or bad—within two hours.[8] Nurses, and even accountants, who monitored their moods over weeks or every few hours as they worked together showed emotions that tracked together—and the group's shared moods were largely independent of the hassles they shared.[9] Studies of professional sports teams reveal similar results: Quite apart from the ups and downs of a team's standing, its players tend to synchronize their moods over a period of days and weeks.[10]

## Contagion and Leadership

The continual interplay of limbic open loops among members of a group creates a kind of emotional soup, with everyone adding his or her own flavor to the mix. But it is the leader who adds the strongest seasoning. Why? Because of that enduring reality of business: Everyone watches the boss. People take their emotional cues from the top. Even when the boss isn't highly visible—for example, the CEO who works behind closed doors on an upper floor—his attitude affects the moods of his direct reports, and a domino effect ripples throughout the company's emotional climate.[11]

Careful observations of working groups in action revealed several ways the leader plays such a pivotal role in determining the shared emotions.[12] Leaders typically talked more than anyone else, and what they said was listened to more carefully. Leaders were also usually the first to speak out on a subject, and when others made comments, their remarks most often referred to what the leader had said than to anyone else's comments. Because the leader's way of seeing things has special weight, leaders "manage meaning" for a group, offering a way to interpret, and so react emotionally to, a given situation.[13]

But the impact on emotions goes beyond what a leader says. In these studies, even when leaders were not talking, they were watched more carefully than anyone else in the group. When people raised a question for the group as a whole, they would keep their eyes on the leader to see his or her response. Indeed, group members generally see the leader's emotional reaction as the most valid response, and so model their own on it—particularly in an ambiguous situation, where various members react differently. In a sense, the leader sets the emotional standard.

Leaders give praise or withhold it, criticize well or destructively, offer support or turn a blind eye to people's needs. They can frame the group's mission in ways that give more meaning to each person's contribution—or not. They can guide in ways that give people a sense of clarity and direction in their work and that encourage flexibility, setting people free to use their best sense of how to get the job done. All these acts help determine a leader's primal emotional impact.

Still, not all "official" leaders in a group are necessarily the emotional leaders. When the designated leader lacks credibility for some reason, people may turn for emotional guidance to someone else who they trust and respect. This de facto leader then becomes the one who molds others' emotional reactions. For instance, a well-known jazz group that was named for its formal leader and founder actually took its emotional cues from a different musician. The founder continued to manage bookings and logistics, but when it came time to decide what tune the group would play next or how the sound system should be adjusted, all eyes turned to the dominant member—the emotional leader.[14]

## People Magnets

Regardless of who the emotional leader might be, however, she's likely to have a knack for acting as a limbic "attractor," exerting a palpable force on the emotional brains of people around her. Watch a gifted actor at work, for example, and observe how easily she draws an audience into her emotional orbit. Whether she's conveying the agony of a betrayal or a joyous triumph, the audience feels those things too.

# LAUGHTER AND THE OPEN LOOP

E MOTIONS MAY SPREAD like viruses, but not all emotions spread with the same ease. A study at the Yale University School of Management found that among working groups, cheerfulness and warmth spread most easily, while irritability is less contagious and depression spreads hardly at all.[15] This greater diffusion rate for good moods has direct implications for business results. Moods, the Yale study found, influence how effectively people work; upbeat moods boost cooperation, fairness, and business performance.

Laughter, in particular, demonstrates the power of the open loop in operation—and therefore the contagious nature of all emotion. Hearing laughter, we automatically smile or laugh too, creating a spontaneous chain reaction that sweeps through a group. Glee spreads so readily because our brain includes open-loop circuits, designed specifically for detecting smiles and laughter that make us laugh in response. The result is a positive emotional hijack.

Similarly, of all emotional signals, smiles are the most contagious; they have an almost irresistible power to make others smile in return.[16] Smiles may be so potent because of the beneficial role they played in evolution: Smiles and laughter, scientists speculate, evolved as a nonverbal way to cement alliances, signifying that an individual is relaxed and friendly rather than guarded or hostile.

Laughter offers a uniquely trustworthy sign of this friendliness. Unlike other emotional signals—especially a smile, which can be feigned—laughter involves highly complex neural systems that are largely involuntary: It's harder to fake.[17] So whereas a false smile might easily slip through our emotional radar, a forced laugh has a hollow ring.

In a neurological sense, laughing represents the shortest distance between two people because it instantly interlocks limbic systems. This immediate, involuntary reaction, as one researcher puts it, involves "the most direct communication possible between people—brain to brain—with our intellect just going along for the ride, in what might be called a "limbic lock."[18] No surprise, then, that people who relish each other's company laugh easily and often; those who distrust or dislike each other, or who are otherwise at odds, laugh little together, if at all.

In any work setting, therefore, the sound of laughter signals the group's emotional temperature, offering one sure sign that people's hearts as well as their minds are engaged. Moreover, laughter at work has little to do with someone telling a canned joke: In a study of 1,200 episodes of laughter during social interactions, the laugh almost always came as a friendly response to some ordinary remark like "nice meeting you," not to a punchline.[19] A good laugh sends a reassuring message: We're on the same wavelength, we get along. It signals trust, comfort, and a shared sense of the world; as a rhythm in a conversation, laughing signals that all is well for the moment.

---

How easily we catch leaders' emotional states, then, has to do with how expressively their faces, voices, and gestures convey their feelings. The greater a leader's skill at transmitting emotions, the more forcefully the emotions will spread. Such transmission does not depend on theatrics, of course; since people pay close attention to a leader, even subtle expressions of emotion can have great impact. Even so, the more open leaders are—how well they express their own enthusiasm, for example—the more readily others will feel that same contagious passion.

Leaders with that kind of talent are emotional magnets; people naturally gravitate to them. If you think about the leaders with whom people most want to work in an organization, they probably have this ability to exude upbeat feelings. It's one reason emotionally intelligent leaders attract talented people—for the pleasure of working in their presence. Conversely, leaders who emit the negative register—who are irritable, touchy, domineering, cold—

repel people. No one wants to work for a grouch. Research has proven it: Optimistic, enthusiastic leaders more easily retain their people, compared with those bosses who tend toward negative moods.[20]

Let's now take the impact of primal leadership one step further, to examine just how much emotions determine job effectiveness.

## How Moods Impact Results

Emotions are highly intense, fleeting, and sometimes disruptive to work; moods tend to be less intense, longer-lasting feelings that typically don't interfere with the job at hand. And an emotional episode usually leaves a corresponding lingering mood: a low-key, continual flow of feeling throughout the group.

Although emotions and moods may seem trivial from a business point of view, they have real consequences for getting work done. A leader's mild anxiety can act as a signal that something needs more attention and careful thought. In fact, a sober mood can help immensely when considering a risky situation—and too much optimism can lead to ignoring dangers.[21] A sudden flood of anger can rivet a leader's attention on an urgent problem—such as the revelation that a senior executive has engaged in sexual harassment—redirecting the leader's energies from the normal round of concerns toward finding a solution, such as improving the organization's efforts to eliminate harassment.[22]

While mild anxiety (such as over a looming deadline) can focus attention and energy, prolonged distress can sabotage a leader's relationships and also hamper work performance by diminishing the brain's ability to process information and respond effectively. A good laugh or an upbeat mood, on the other hand, more often enhances the neural abilities crucial for doing good work.

Both good and bad moods tend to perpetuate themselves, in part because they skew perceptions and memories: When people feel upbeat, they see the positive light in a situation and recall the good things about it, and when they feel bad, they focus on the downside.[23] Beyond this perceptual skew, the stew of stress hormones secreted when a person is upset takes hours to become reabsorbed in the body and fade away. That's why a sour relationship with a boss can leave a person a captive of that distress, with a mind preoccupied and a body unable to calm itself: *He got me so upset during that meeting I couldn't go to sleep for hours last night.* As a result, we naturally prefer being with people who are emotionally positive, in part because they make us feel good.

## Emotional Hijacking

Negative emotions—especially chronic anger, anxiety, or a sense of futility—powerfully disrupt work, hijacking attention from the task at hand.[24] For instance, in a Yale study of moods and their contagion, the performance of groups making executive decisions about how best to allocate yearly bonuses was measurably boosted by positive feelings and was impaired by negative ones. Significantly, the group members themselves did not realize the influence of their own moods.[25]

For instance, of all the interactions at an international hotel chain that pitched employees into bad moods, the most frequent was talking to someone in management. Interactions with bosses led to bad feelings—frustration, disappointment, anger, sadness, disgust, or hurt—about nine out of ten times. These interactions were the cause of distress more often than customers, work pressure, company policies, or personal problems.[26] Not that leaders need to be overly "nice"; the emotional art of leadership includes pressing the reality of work demands without unduly upsetting people. One of the oldest laws in psychology holds that beyond a moderate level, increases in anxiety and worry erode mental abilities.

Distress not only erodes mental abilities, but also makes people less emotionally intelligent. People who are upset have trouble reading emotions accurately in other people—decreasing the most basic skill needed for empathy and, as a result, impairing their social skills.[27]

Another consideration is that the emotions people feel while they work, according to new findings on job satisfaction, reflect most directly the true quality of work life.[28] The percentage of time people feel positive emotions at work turns out to be one of the strongest predictors of satisfaction, and therefore, for instance, of how likely employees are to quit.[29] In this sense, leaders who spread bad moods are simply bad for business—and those who pass along good moods help drive a business's success.

## Good Moods, Good Work

When people feel good, they work at their best. Feeling good lubricates mental efficiency, making people better at understanding information and using decision rules in complex judgments, as well as more flexible in their thinking.[30] Upbeat moods, research verifies, make people view others—or events—in a more positive light. That in turn helps people feel more optimistic about their ability to achieve a goal, enhances creativity and decision-making skills, and predisposes people to be helpful.[31] Insurance agents with a glass-is-half-full outlook, for instance, are far more able than their more pessimistic peers to persist despite rejections, and so they make more sales.[32] Moreover, research on humor at work reveals that a well-timed joke or playful laugher can stimulate creativity, open lines of communication, enhance a sense of connection and trust, and, of course, make work more fun.[33] Playful joking increases the likelihood of financial concessions during a negotiation. Small wonder that playfulness holds a prominent place in the tool kit of emotionally intelligent leaders.

Good moods prove especially important when it comes to teams: The ability of a leader to pitch a group into an enthusiastic, cooperative mood can determine its success. On the other hand, whenever emotional conflicts in a group bleed attention and energy from their shared tasks, a group's performance will suffer.

Consider the results of a study of sixty-two CEOs and their top management teams.[34] The CEOs represented some of the *Fortune*

500, as well as leading U.S. service companies (such as consulting and accounting firms), not-for-profit organizations, and government agencies. The CEOs and their management team members were assessed on how upbeat—energetic, enthusiastic, determined—they were. They were also asked how much conflict and tumult the top team experienced, that is, personality clashes, anger and friction in meetings, and emotional conflicts (in contrast to disagreement about ideas).

The study found that the more positive the overall moods of people in the top management team, the more cooperatively they worked together—and the better the company's business results. Put differently, the longer a company was run by a management team that did not get along, the poorer that company's market return.

The "group IQ," then—the sum total of every person's best talents contributed at full force—depends on the group's emotional intelligence, as shown in its harmony. A leader skilled in collaboration can keep cooperation high and thus ensure that the group's decisions will be worth the effort of meeting. Such leaders know how to balance the group's focus on the task at hand with its attention to the quality of members' relationships. They naturally create a friendly but effective climate that lifts everyone's spirits.

## Quantifying the "Feel" of a Company

Common wisdom, of course, holds that employees who feel upbeat will likely go the extra mile to please customers and therefore improve the bottom line. But there's actually a logarithm that predicts that relationship: For every 1 percent improvement in the service climate, there's a 2 percent increase in revenue.[35]

Benjamin Schneider, a professor at the University of Maryland, found in operations as diverse as bank branches, insurance company regional offices, credit card call centers, and hospitals that employees' ratings of service climate predicted customer satisfaction, which drove business results. Likewise, poor morale among

## GETTING TO SERVICE WITH A SMILE

O F ALL THE ASPECTS of business, superior customer care—that holy grail of any service industry—is perhaps affected most by mood contagion, and therefore by the open-loop aspect of the brain. Customer service jobs are notoriously stressful, with high emotions flowing freely, not just from customers to the front lines but also from workers to customers. From a business viewpoint, of course, bad moods in people who serve customers are bad news. First, rudeness is contagious, creating dissatisfied, even angry, customers—quite apart from whether or not a particular service matter was handled well. Second, grumpy workers serve customers poorly, with sometimes devastating results: Cardiac care units where the nurses' general mood was "depressed" had a death rate among patients four times higher than on comparable units.[36]

By contrast, upbeat moods at the front lines benefit a business. If customers find interactions with a counterperson enjoyable, they start to think of the store as a "nice place" to shop. That means not only more repeat visits, but also good word-of-mouth advertising. Moreover, when service people feel upbeat, they do more to please customers: In a study of thirty-two stores in a U.S. retail chain, outlets with positive salespeople showed the best sales results.[37]

But just what does that finding have to do with leadership? In all of those retail outlets, it was the store manager who created the emotional climate that drove salespeople's moods—and ultimately, sales—in the right direction. When the managers themselves were peppy, confident, and optimistic, their moods rubbed off on the staff.[38]

frontline customer service reps at a given point in time predicts high turnover—and declining customer satisfaction—up to three years later. This low customer satisfaction, in turn, drives declining revenues.[39]

So what's the antidote? Besides the obvious relationships between climate and working conditions or salary, resonant leaders play a key role. In general, the more emotionally demanding the work, the more empathic and supportive the leader needs to be. Leaders drive the service climate and thus the predisposition of employees to satisfy customers. At an insurance company, for instance, Schneider found that effective leadership influenced service climate among agents to account for a 3 to 4 percent difference in insurance renewals—a seemingly small margin that made a big difference to the business.

Organizational consultants have long assumed a positive link of some kind between a business unit's human climate and its performance. But data connecting the two have been sparse— and so, in practice, leaders could more easily ignore their personal style and its effects on the people they led, focusing instead on "harder" business objectives. But now we have results from a range of industries that link leadership to climate and to business performance, making it possible to quantify the hard difference for business performance made by something as soft as the "feel" of a company.

For instance, at a global food and beverage company, positive climate readings predicted higher yearly earnings at major divisions. And in a study of nineteen insurance companies, the climate created by the CEOs among their direct reports predicted the business performance of the entire organization: In 75 percent of cases, climate alone accurately sorted companies into high versus low profits and growth.[40]

Climate in itself does not determine performance. The factors deciding which companies prove most fit in any given quarter are notoriously complex. But our analyses suggest that, overall, the climate—how people feel about working at a company—can account for 20 to 30 percent of business performance. Getting the best out of people pays off in hard results.

If climate drives business results, what drives climate? Roughly 50 to 70 percent of how employees perceive their organization's climate can be traced to the actions of one person: the leader. More than anyone else, the boss creates the conditions that directly determine people's ability to work well.[41]

In short, leaders' emotional states and actions do affect how the people they lead will feel and therefore perform. How well leaders manage their moods and affect everyone else's moods, then, becomes not just a private matter, but a factor in how well a business will do.[42]

And that gets us to how the brain drives primal leadership, for better or for worse.

### CHAPTER TWO

# RESONANT LEADERSHIP

L ET'S RETURN to our example of the BBC division that was being shut down. The first executive who was sent to deliver the bad news—and who made people so angry that he almost needed to call security for an escort out—exemplifies what we call *dissonant* leadership: Out of touch with the feelings of the people in the room, he drove the group into a downward spiral from frustration to resentment, rancor to rage.

When such leaders fail to empathize with, or to read the emotions of, a group accurately, they create dissonance, sending needlessly upsetting messages. The resulting collective distress then becomes the group's preoccupation, displacing the attention they need to give to the leader's message—or to their mission. In any work setting, the emotional and the business impact of a dissonant leader can be gauged easily: People feel off-balance, and thus perform poorly.

The second executive, who got a round of applause from the laid-off employees, exemplifies *resonant* leadership: He was attuned to people's feelings and moved them in a positive emotional direction. Speaking authentically from his own values and resonating with the emotions of those around him, he hit just the right chords with his message, leaving people feeling uplifted and inspired even in a difficult moment. When a leader triggers resonance, you can read it in people's eyes: They're engaged and they light up.

The root of the word *resonance* is revealing: the Latin word *resonare*, to resound. Resonance, the *Oxford English Dictionary* states, refers to "the reinforcement or prolongation of sound by reflection," or, more specifically, "by synchronous vibration." The human analog of synchronous vibration occurs when two people are on the same wavelength emotionally—when they feel "in synch." And true to the original meaning of resonance, that synchrony "resounds," prolonging the positive emotional pitch.

One sign of resonant leadership is a group of followers who vibrate with the leader's upbeat and enthusiastic energy. A primal leadership dictum is that resonance amplifies and prolongs the emotional impact of leadership. The more resonant people are with each other, the less static are their interactions; resonance minimizes the noise in the system. "One team," as a business mantra proclaims, means "more signal, less noise." The glue that holds people together in a team, and that commits people to an organization, is the emotions they feel.[1]

How well leaders manage and direct those feelings to help a group meet its goals depends on their level of emotional intelligence. Resonance comes naturally to emotionally intelligent (EI) leaders. Their passion and enthusiastic energy resounds throughout the group. Even so, such leaders might sometimes project a more serious mood, when appropriate, using empathy to attune to the emotional register of the people they lead. For example, if something has happened that everyone feels angry about (such as the closing of a division) or sad about (such as a serious illness in a much-loved co-worker), the EI leader not only empathizes with those emotions, but also expresses them for the group. That kind of resonance reinforces synchrony just as much as enthusiasm does, because it leaves people feeling understood and cared for.

Under the guidance of an EI leader, people feel a mutual comfort level. They share ideas, learn from one another, make decisions collaboratively, and get things done. They form an emotional bond that helps them stay focused even amid profound change and uncertainty. Perhaps most important, connecting with others at an emotional level makes work more meaningful. We all know what it feels like to share in the excitement of a moment, the elation of completing a job well done. These feelings drive people to do things together that no individual could or would do. And it is the EI leader who knows how to bring about that kind of bonding.

On the other hand, if a leader lacks resonance, people may be going through the motions of their work but doing merely a "good enough" job rather than giving their best. Without a healthy dose of heart, a supposed "leader" may manage—but he does not lead.

## The Discordant Leader

*Dissonance*, in its original musical sense, describes an unpleasant, harsh sound; in both musical and human terms, dissonance refers to a lack of harmony. Dissonant leadership produces groups that feel emotionally discordant, in which people have a sense of being continually off-key.[2]

Just as laughter offers a ready barometer of resonance at work, so rampant anger, fear, apathy, or even sullen silence signals the opposite. Such dissonance, research finds, is all too common in the workplace. In a survey of more than a thousand U.S. workers, for example, 42 percent reported incidences of yelling and other kinds of verbal abuse in their workplaces, and almost 30 percent admitted to having yelled at a co-worker themselves.[3]

Consider the biological costs of such dissonance. Although surfacing genuine complaints can clear the air—and build resonance—when the person complaining does so with anger, the encounter can easily spiral into emotional toxicity. For example, rather than saying calmly, "When you're late for our meetings, it wastes our time—we'd all be more effective if you showed up on time," the complainer launches into a character attack.

He snarls, "I see His Highness has deigned to join us. I'm glad to see you could fit us into your busy schedule. We'll try not to waste too much of your time."

Such disturbing encounters wreak havoc emotionally, as demonstrated in studies in which physiological responses were monitored during arguments.[4] Such attacks—which send the painful emotional messages of disgust or contempt—emotionally hijack the person targeted, particularly when the attacker is a spouse or boss, whose opinions carry much weight.

John Gottman, a psychologist at the University of Washington, uses the term "flooding" to describe the intensity of the fight-or-flight reaction that such an extreme message of contempt can trigger: Heart rate can leap 20 to 30 beats per minute in a single heartbeat, accompanied by an overwhelming feeling of distress. When flooded, a person can neither hear what is said without distortion, nor respond with clarity; thinking becomes muddled and the most ready responses are primitive ones—anything that will end the encounter quickly. As a result, people will often tune out (or "stonewall") the other person by putting either an emotional or physical distance between them.

Although these studies were done with married couples, a dissonant encounter between boss and employee takes much the same emotional toll. In one study, employees were asked to recall times managers had lost their tempers at them and launched into a personal attack. Typically the employee became defensive, evaded responsibility, or stonewalled, avoiding contact with the manager. And when 108 managers and white-collar workers reported on the causes of conflict in their jobs, the number one reason was inept criticism by a boss.[5]

In short, dissonance dispirits people, burns them out, or sends them packing. There's another personal cost to dissonance: People who work in toxic environments take the toxicity home. Stress hormones released during a toxic workday continue to swirl through the body many hours later.[6]

## The Varieties of Dissonance

There are countless kinds of dissonant leaders, who not only lack empathy (and so are out of synch with the group) but also transmit emotional tones that resound most often in a negative register. Most of those leaders, we find, don't mean to be so discordant; they simply lack the critical EI abilities that would help them lead with resonance.

In the extreme, dissonant leaders can range from the abusive tyrant, who bawls out and humiliates people, to the manipulative sociopath. Such leaders have an emotional impact a bit like the "dementors" in the Harry Potter series, who "drain peace, hope and happiness out of the air around them."[7] They create wretched workplaces, but have no idea how destructive they are—or they simply don't care.

Some dissonant leaders, however, are more subtle, using a surface charm or social polish, even charisma, to mislead and manipulate. Those leaders don't truly hold their professed values, or they lack empathy, caring about little other than their own advancement. When followers sense that kind of insincerity— when a manipulative leader feigns friendliness, for instance—the relationship dissolves into cynicism and distrust.

Dissonant leaders sometimes may seem effective in the short run—they may get a coveted promotion, for instance, by focusing on pleasing their boss—but the toxicity they leave behind belies their apparent success. Wherever they go in an organization, the legacy of their tenure marks a telltale trail of demotivation and apathy, anger and resentment. In short, dissonant leaders are the bosses that people dread working for.

When we see someone leading an organization by stirring such negative resonance, we know that trouble lies ahead. Despite any short-term rise in performance, if a leader resonates exclusively in the negative emotional range, the effect will be to eventually burn people out. Such leaders transmit their own—often corrosive—emotions but don't receive; they neither listen to nor

## THE DEMAGOGUE

GIVEN THAT ADEPT LEADERS move followers to their emotional rhythm, we face the disturbing fact that, throughout history, demagogues and dictators have used this same ability for deplorable ends. The Hitlers and Pol Pots of the world have all rallied angry mobs around a moving—but destructive— message. And therein lies the crucial difference between resonance and demagoguery.

Compared with resonant leaders, demagogues spread very different emotional messages, ones that elicit negative emotions, particularly a mix of fear and anger: the threat to "us" from "them," and the dread that "they" will take what "we" have. Their message polarizes people rather than uniting them in a common cause. Such leaders build their platform for action on a negative resonance—on the disturbing fight-or-flight survival emotions that stream through the brain when people feel threatened or enraged. The Serbian leader Slobodan Milosevic, for example, was a master at fanning the flames of ethnic hatred, uniting his followers behind a banner of resentments, fears, and rage—to both his own and his nation's detriment.

Demagoguery casts its spell via destructive emotions, a range that squelches hope and optimism as well as true innovation and creative imagination (as opposed to cruel cunning). By contrast, resonant leadership grounded in a shared set of constructive values keeps emotions resounding in the positive register. It invites people to take a leap of faith through a word picture of what's possible, creating a collective aspiration.

Luckily, the demagogue is a rare type in business; politics seems the demagogue's more natural ecological niche. Still, some business leaders do resort to nefarious tactics. Workplace leadership built on negative resonance—for instance, cultivating fear or hatred of some "enemy"—amounts to a cheap trick, a quick and dirty way to mobilize a group toward a common goal. It may be relatively easy to get people to hate or fear something together; these emotions come readily, given the right threat. But from a biological perspective, these emotions were designed for short, intense bursts meant to prepare us to fight or run. If they last too long or are continually primed, they exhaust us or slowly burn us out. Anger or fear, then, may get a leader through the crisis of the day, but they are short-lived motivators.

care about other people. EI leaders, in contrast, follow the more lasting path to motivation by evoking positive resonance: rallying people around a worthy goal.

There are also the leaders we call "clueless," who try to resonate in a positive tone but are out of touch with the unpleasant fact that their subordinates are stuck in a negative emotional register. In other words, the organizational reality makes people angry or anxious or otherwise unhappy, but the leader remains oblivious and so sends an upbeat message that resonates with no one.

One executive we know describes his organizational vision this way: "We are nimbly moving into a complex future, leading our industry as we reach for new heights. Our leaders look for opportunities at every turn and our managers are blasting the competition. We delight in our customers' satisfaction."

At first glance it may sound pretty good—but on second thought, it's a string of empty platitudes. We don't know what he really meant (do you?), but when we began to look at the culture and the leadership practices, we couldn't find much flexibility; tolerance for ambiguity, risk taking, or innovation; or attunement to customers. We found groups of people focused on the same old routine and cynical about the vision their leader described. The sad fact is that business jargon can be a smokescreen, so that a leader never has a real conversation about what people are actually doing in the organization—and never has to change.

Self-absorbed leaders can often be clueless. For instance, a group of managers at a consumer goods company requested a meeting with their CEO because they were deeply troubled by what they saw happening at their company. Though the company was still ranked in the top ten compared with others in their industry, the trend lines pointed downward. These managers, so close to the work, wanted to help their CEO move things in the right direction.

But when the CEO met with the managers, he didn't seem to hear them. His reply to their concerns: "People want a hero—they need one—and that's what I am to the employees. I'm like a movie star—people want to see me and look up to me. That's why I thought it was a good idea for you to come here, so you can hear what I have to say and tell everyone what I'm really like."

There was a stunned silence in the room as he spoke—a silence that the CEO no doubt took as agreement. For him, this was not about "us" but about "me." The dark side of ambition is that it can focus a leader's attention on himself, leading him to ignore the worries of the people who he needs to make him successful—and breeding dissonance.[8]

By contrast, emotionally intelligent leaders build resonance by tuning into people's feelings—their own and others'—and guiding them in the right direction. To understand the mechanisms that drive emotionally intelligent leadership, and so create resonance, we look to new findings in brain research.

## Leadership and the Brain's Design

No creature can fly with just one wing. Gifted leadership occurs where heart and head—feeling and thought—meet. These are the two wings that allow a leader to soar.

All leaders need enough intellect to grasp the specifics of the tasks and challenges at hand. Of course, leaders gifted in the decisive clarity that analytic and conceptual thinking allow certainly add value. We see intellect and clear thinking largely as the

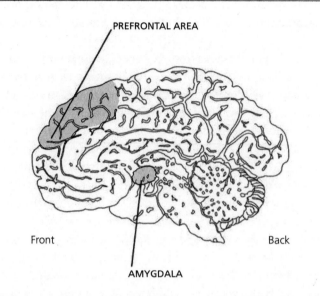

PREFRONTAL AREA

Front

Back

AMYGDALA

The crucial emotional regulatory circuitry runs from the prefrontal area to the amygdala, located on either side of the mid-brain as part of the limbic system.

characteristics that get someone in the leadership door. Without those fundamental abilities, no entry is allowed. However, intellect alone will not make a leader; leaders execute a vision by motivating, guiding, inspiring, listening, persuading—and, most crucially, through creating resonance. As Albert Einstein cautioned, "We should take care not to make the intellect our god. It has, of course, powerful muscles, but no personality. It cannot lead, it can only serve."

The neural systems responsible for the intellect and for the emotions are separate, but they have intimately interwoven connections.[9] This brain circuitry that interweaves thought and feeling provides the neural basis of primal leadership. And, despite the great value that business culture often places on an intellect devoid of emotion, our emotions are, in a very real sense, more powerful than our intellect. In moments of emergency, our emotional centers—the limbic brain—commandeer the rest of the brain.

There's good reason for this special potency of emotions. They're crucial for survival, being the brain's way of alerting us to something urgent and offering an immediate plan for action: fight, flee, freeze. The thinking brain evolved from the limbic brain and continues to take orders from it when we perceive a threat or are under stress. The trigger point for these compelling emotions is the amygdala, a limbic brain structure that scans what happens to us from moment to moment, ever on the alert for an emergency.[10] As our radar for emotional emergencies, the amygdala can commandeer other parts of the brain, including rational centers in the neocortex, for immediate action if it perceives a threat.

This arrangement worked well during the last 100 million or so years of evolution. Fear guided early mammals through the real dangers of predators; anger mobilized a mother to fight to protect her young. And social emotions such as jealousy, pride, contempt, and affection all played a role in the family politics of primate groups— just as they do in the underworld of organizational life today.

While emotions have guided human survival through evolution, a neural dilemma for leadership has emerged in the last 10,000 years or so. In today's advanced civilization, we face complex social realities (say, the sense someone isn't treating us fairly) with a brain designed for surviving physical emergencies. And so we can find ourselves hijacked—swept away by anxiety or anger better suited for handling bodily threats than the subtleties of office politics. (*Just who the hell does this guy think he is! I'm so mad I could punch him!*)

Fortunately, such emotional impulses follow extensive circuitry that goes from the amygdala to the prefrontal area, just behind the forehead, which is the brain's executive center. The prefrontal area receives and analyzes information from all parts of the brain and then makes a decision about what to do. The prefrontal area can veto an emotional impulse—and so ensure that our response will be more effective. (*Remember, he's giving your annual review—*

*just relax and see what else he says before you do something you might regret.*) Without that veto, the result would be an emotional hijack, where the amygdala's impulse is acted upon. This happens when the prefrontal zone circuitry fails in its task of keeping these emotional impulses in check.

The dialogue between neurons in the emotional centers and the prefrontal areas operates through what amounts to a neurological superhighway that helps to orchestrate thought and feeling. The emotional intelligence competencies, so crucial for leadership, hinge on the smooth operation of this prefrontal–limbic circuitry. Studies of neurological patients with damaged prefrontal–limbic circuitry confirm that their cognitive capacities may remain intact, while their emotional intelligence abilities are impaired.[11] This neurological fact clearly separates these competencies from purely cognitive abilities like intelligence, technical knowledge, or business expertise, which reside in the neocortex alone.

Biologically speaking, then, the art of resonant leadership interweaves our intellect and our emotions. Of course, leaders need the prerequisite business acumen and thinking skills to be decisive. But if they try to lead solely from intellect, they'll miss a crucial piece of the equation.

Take, for example, the new CEO of a global company who tried to change strategic directions. He failed, and was fired after just one year on the job. "He thought he could change the company through intellect alone, without moving people emotionally," a senior vice president at the company told us. "He made radical strategic changes without bothering to get buy-in from the people who would execute those changes. A storm of e-mails from employees to the board complained of his tuned-out leadership, and the CEO was finally ousted."

## How the Four Core EI Domains Interact

We are by no means the first to suggest that the main tasks of a leader are to generate excitement, optimism, and passion for the job ahead, as well as to cultivate an atmosphere of cooperation and trust.[12] But we wish to take that wisdom one step further and demonstrate how emotional intelligence enables leaders to accomplish those fundamental tasks. Each of the four domains of emotional intelligence—self-awareness, self-management, social awareness, and relationship management—adds a crucial set of skills for resonant leadership.

These domains are, of course, closely intertwined, with a dynamic relationship among them. For instance, a leader can't manage his emotions well if he has little or no awareness of them. And if his emotions are out of control, then his ability to handle relationships will suffer. Our research has found a system underlying this dynamic.[13] In short, self-awareness facilitates both empathy and self-management, and these two, in combination, allow effective relationship management. EI leadership, then, builds up from a foundation of self-awareness.

Self-awareness—often overlooked in business settings—is the foundation for the rest: Without recognizing our own emotions, we will be poor at managing them, and less able to understand them in others. Self-aware leaders are attuned to their inner signals. They recognize, for instance, how their feelings affect themselves and their job performance. Instead of letting anger build into an outburst, they spot it as it crescendos and can see both what's causing it and how to do something constructive about it. Leaders who lack this emotional self-awareness, on the other hand, might lose their temper but have no understanding of why their emotions push them around. Self-awareness also plays a crucial role in empathy, or sensing how someone else sees a situation: If a person is perpetually oblivious to his own feelings, he will also be tuned out to how others feel.

Social awareness—particularly empathy—supports the next step in the leader's primal task: driving resonance. By being attuned to how others feel in the moment, a leader can say and do what's appropriate, whether that means calming fears, assuaging anger, or joining in good spirits. This attunement also lets a leader sense the shared values and priorities that can guide the group.

By the same token, a leader who lacks empathy will unwittingly be off-key, and so speak and act in ways that set off negative reactions. Empathy, which includes listening and taking other people's perspectives, allows leaders to tune in to the emotional channels between people that create resonance. And staying attuned lets leaders fine-tune their message to keep it in synch.

Finally, once leaders understand their own vision and values and can perceive the emotions of the group, their relationship management skills can catalyze resonance. To guide the emotional tone of a group, however, leaders must first have a sure sense of their own direction and priorities—which brings us back again to the importance of self-awareness.

These dynamic relations among the four EI domains are of practical, not just theoretical, importance. They're the basic ingredients of effective primal leadership—of resonance. Next we'll explore the neural anatomy that underlies the EI abilities that allow leaders to prime resonance in the people they lead.

### CHAPTER THREE

# THE NEUROANATOMY OF
# LEADERSHIP

R ESONANCE, in terms of brain function, means that people's emotional centers are in synch in a positive way. One of the most powerful and most direct ways to make that resonant brain-to-brain connection, remember, is through laughter.

Consider the implications for the neuroanatomy of leadership of a difficult moment at a meeting of top management at a large retailer. Judging by the market research data that everyone held in their hands, the vice president for marketing had made a poor decision about a large advertising buy. As the group pored over the data, the silent consensus was clear: The marketing chief had goofed.

After a long, tense moment, the silence was broken by another executive in the room, who quipped, "Maybe you just didn't have your glasses on." Everyone laughed.

That small joke served two purposes: It implicitly affirmed for everyone that the marketing chief had indeed erred, while softening that critical message—bypassing the need to spend time disagreeing or arguing about it. The group seamlessly moved on to the next decision, which was how to remedy the predicament.

Everything known about the neurophysiology of humor and the open loop (as we saw in chapter 1) suggests that the quip by the executive pitched the management team's emotional centers into a positive range of activity. This, presumably, helped the group avoid becoming emotionally hijacked by fixating on the problem—the marketing chief's error—thus letting them swiftly move on to the solution. And the executive did all that without having to say anything explicitly about how he was keeping them on track in a positive mode.

As we have already noted, the artful use of humor typifies effective leadership. That doesn't mean that you should always avoid disagreements or conflicts. But the best leaders have a sense of when spending time airing grievances will be useful and when it will not.

People don't need a comedian's sense of timing or huge comic repertoire to use humor effectively. What may later seem a rather feeble joke can still be a powerful emotional prod in a tense moment—if it gets a laugh or smile. The data linking leadership effectiveness to laughter come from hundreds of actual incidents like the tension-relieving joke about the marketing chief.[1] Take, for example, one study of executives interviewing for leadership positions, which looked at how often each candidate got a laugh during the interview and then tracked the candidates' careers for two years to see which ones became stars. The finding was that outstanding leaders got the interviewer to laugh with them twice as often as the just-average executives. (The leaders' success was defined by two elements: They were in the top third of bonuses reflecting financial performance, and they were rated as "excellent" by 90 percent of their peers and bosses.)

The researchers also interviewed high-level leaders, almost half of whom were CEOs or general managers from the United States and abroad, about high and low points in their careers. During the interview, the outstanding leaders used *three* times more humorous comments—about one every four minutes—than the average leaders.

The most effective leaders, then, use humor more freely, even when things are tense, sending positive messages that shift the underlying emotional tone of the interaction. Although the words that leaders speak may deal with dry details—clauses in a contract, the numbers in a business plan—the good feelings that a laugh brings keep a leader's relationships simpatico.

## EI Competencies: The Vehicles of Primal Leadership

What's particularly telling, though, was that these successful leaders' use of humor strongly correlated with the very emotional intelligence competencies we have found to be key to a leader's superior performance.[2] These EI competencies are the vehicles of primal leadership.

To review our earlier work, a significant part of the competence research base we rely on stems from a then-radical proposal made back in 1973 by the late Harvard professor David McClelland.[3] Writing in the flagship psychology journal, McClelland proposed that if an organization wanted to hire or promote the best person for a specific job, such as a leadership position, it should discard what were then the standard criteria. Instead of testing people for their IQ, technical skills, or personality—or just looking at their résumés—McClelland proposed first studying employees who were already outstanding performers in that job and systematically comparing them with those who were just average at it.

That analysis yields not just the threshold abilities for the position (the basic skills everyone must have to do the job) but, more important, the *distinguishing* competencies: abilities that the stars exhibited and the average performers did not. Then, said McClelland, choose people who have those same competencies— or help your people develop those strengths. That proposal spawned what is today standard practice in world-class organizations: developing a leadership "competency model" to identify, train, and promote likely stars.

Take, for example, the leadership competence model developed by Lyle Spencer, a longtime associate of McClelland, for an industrial controls firm (a $2 billion global division of Siemens with 400 branches in fifty-six countries).[4] The first step was to identify the pool of star leaders, whose growth in revenues and return on sales put their performance in the top 10 to 15 percent.[5]

Next, the stars were compared with managers whose performance was only average, and the two groups underwent intensive interviews designed to assess their competencies. Four competencies of emotional intelligence—but not a single technical or purely cognitive competency—emerged as the unique strengths of the stars: the drive to achieve results, the ability to take initiative, skills in collaboration and teamwork, and the ability to lead teams.

Then, with a clear idea of which EI competencies to target, another pool of branch managers was trained to cultivate these same strengths. They became familiar with and were evaluated on each competence, and they set goals for improving those competencies—and thereby their business performance.

The result was that the leaders increased their effectiveness and reaped significantly improved profits. The revenue growth in their branches that year added an additional $1.5 million profit, double that of a comparison group who had no training.

## Leaders: The Next Generation

When we talk about the value of an emotionally intelligent leader, we do not intend to revive the discredited claim that an organization's—or nation's—success rises or falls on a single charismatic leader. As the sociologist Max Weber argued a century ago, institutions that endure thrive not because of one leader's charisma, but because they cultivate leadership throughout the system.

That's especially true when it comes to creating companies that are "built to last": The ones that thrive for decades know how to incubate generations of effective leaders.[6] Consider, for example, a compelling study on the future of leadership at Johnson & Johnson (J&J), the global pharmaceuticals company. Looking at the company's growth projections, CEO Ralph Larsen realized that J&J would need increasingly more leaders if it were to succeed; in fact, he considered such leadership development the organization's most critical business issue. His research team began by looking at 358 midcareer executives at J&J, half of whom had been identified as "high potentials," that is, managers who'd demonstrated early success; the rest comprised a less high-performing comparison group.[7] The 358 executives, 45 percent of whom were women and 55 percent men, were carefully chosen to reflect a global spread, representing the Americas, Europe, the Middle East, Africa, Asia, and Australia. Each was rated in confidence by three executives familiar with his or her work, using both the company's leadership model and the emotional intelligence competencies. The researchers evaluated this talent pool through the lens of the leadership competencies assessed in the ECI (Emotional Competence Inventory), a 360-degree measure of emotional intelligence in leadership.[8]

Managers in the high-potential group were found to exhibit virtually every one of the competencies, while the executives in the comparison group possessed few of those competencies.[9] In other words, EI competencies, the leadership capabilities that drive resonance, marked distinctive abilities of this select group. Moreover, the cross-cultural differences proved insignificant; EI competencies could be identified equally well throughout the world, indicating that these abilities matter and can be assessed anywhere a company operates.

## The Four Dimensions of Emotional Intelligence

Our thinking about the dimensions of emotional intelligence, and their accompanying competencies, has evolved and been streamlined as we've analyzed new data. Readers familiar with earlier versions of the EI model will notice some changes here. Where we formerly listed five main domains of EI, we now have simplified the model into four domains—self-awareness, self-management, social awareness, and relationship management—with eighteen competencies instead of the original twenty-five (see the chart).[10] For instance, an EI domain would be social awareness; a competency in that domain would be empathy or service. The result is an emotional intelligence model that more clearly links specific clusters of competencies to the underlying brain dynamics that drive them.

Recent findings about emotions and the brain make clearer the neurological basis of these competencies.[11] This lets us sketch their dynamics more thoroughly, while providing practical guidelines for building leadership skills.

An important note, which we will develop later in this book: These EI competencies are not innate talents, but learned abilities, each of which has a unique contribution to making leaders more resonant, and therefore more effective.

That fact speaks to an urgent business need, one with great impact on financial results: helping leaders to lead more effectively. Now, guided by the neurology underlying the emotional intelligence framework, we can make a sharp distinction between what works and what doesn't when it comes to learning the art of leadership—our topic in Part II of this book.

Our basic argument, in a nutshell, is that primal leadership operates at its best through emotionally intelligent leaders who create resonance. Underlying that proposition is a theory of performance, one that surfaces the links between the neurology of the four fundamentals of emotional intelligence and the EI competencies that build on those fundamentals. These EI competencies are in turn the building blocks of the modes of leadership that prime resonance in a group.[12]

Interestingly, no leader we've ever encountered, no matter how outstanding, has strengths across the board in every one of the many EI competencies. Highly effective leaders typically exhibit a critical mass of strength in a half dozen or so EI competencies.[13] Moreover, there's no fixed formula for great leadership: There are

## Emotional Intelligence Domains and
## Associated Competencies (see Appendix B for details)

**PERSONAL COMPETENCE:** These capabilities determine how we manage ourselves.

### SELF-AWARENESS
- *Emotional self-awareness:* Reading one's own emotions and recognizing their impact; using "gut sense" to guide decisions
- *Accurate self-assessment:* Knowing one's strengths and limits
- *Self-confidence:* A sound sense of one's self-worth and capabilities

### SELF-MANAGEMENT
- *Emotional self-control:* Keeping disruptive emotions and impulses under control
- *Transparency:* Displaying honesty and integrity; trustworthiness
- *Adaptability:* Flexibility in adapting to changing situations or overcoming obstacles
- *Achievement:* The drive to improve performance to meet inner standards of excellence
- *Initiative:* Readiness to act and seize opportunities
- *Optimism:* Seeing the upside in events

**SOCIAL COMPETENCE:** These capabilities determine how we manage relationships.

### SOCIAL AWARENESS
- *Empathy:* Sensing others' emotions, understanding their perspective, and taking active interest in their concerns
- *Organizational awareness:* Reading the currents, decision networks, and politics at the organizational level
- *Service:* Recognizing and meeting follower, client, or customer needs

### RELATIONSHIP MANAGEMENT
- *Inspirational leadership:* Guiding and motivating with a compelling vision
- *Influence:* Wielding a range of tactics for persuasion
- *Developing others:* Bolstering others' abilities through feedback and guidance
- *Change catalyst:* Initiating, managing, and leading in a new direction
- *Conflict management:* Resolving disagreements
- *Building bonds:* Cultivating and maintaining a web of relationships
- *Teamwork and collaboration:* Cooperation and team building

many paths to excellence, and superb leaders can possess very different personal styles. Still, we find that effective leaders typically demonstrate strengths in at least one competence from each of the four fundamental areas of emotional intelligence.

## Self-Awareness

Simply put, self-awareness means having a deep understanding of one's emotions, as well as one's strengths and limitations and one's values and motives. People with strong self-awareness are realistic—neither overly self-critical nor naively hopeful. Rather, they are honest with themselves about themselves. And they are honest about themselves with others, even to the point of being able to laugh at their own foibles.

Self-aware leaders also understand their values, goals, and dreams. They know where they're headed and why. They're attuned to what "feels right" to them. For example, they're able to be firm in turning down a job offer that's tempting financially but doesn't fit with their principles or long-term goals. Conversely, a person lacking self-awareness will likely make decisions that trigger inner turmoil by treading on buried values. "The money looked good so I signed on," someone might say two years into a job, "but the work means so little to me that I'm constantly bored." Because the decisions of self-aware people mesh with their values, they more often find their work energizing.

Perhaps the most telling (though least visible) sign of self-awareness is a propensity for self-reflection and thoughtfulness. Self-aware people typically find time to reflect quietly, often off by themselves, which allows them to think things over rather than react impulsively. Many outstanding leaders, in fact, bring to their work life the thoughtful mode of self-reflection that they cultivate in their spiritual lives. For some this means prayer or meditation; for others it's a more philosophical quest for self-understanding.

All of these traits of self-aware leaders enable them to act with the conviction and authenticity that resonance requires.

## A Sense of What Matters Most

In a technical sense, our guiding values are represented in the brain as a hierarchy of emotionally toned thoughts, with what we "like" and find compelling at the top, and what we loathe at the bottom. The strength and direction of those emotions determine whether a goal appeals to us or repels us. If the thought of helping disadvantaged children, for example, or of working with people at the top of their game, thrills us, it will be highly motivating.

All of this occurs in the brain's prefrontal areas—the seat of attention and hence of self-awareness—which monitor feelings about preferences. Circuits in that part of brain, then, harbor our positive feelings, quietly bringing them to mind over and over as we struggle toward a goal. Pleasant thoughts thereby operate as a sort of cheering section, urging us on over the long haul. From a neurological standpoint, what keeps us moving toward our goals in life comes down to the mind's ability to remind us of how satisfied we'll feel when we accomplish those things—a capacity residing in the circuitry between the amygdala and the left prefrontal lobe.[14]

No matter what drives our passion to do our best work—whether it be the pure excitement it brings, the satisfaction of learning to do something better, or the joy of collaborating with highly talented colleagues (or simply the money we earn)—all the motivators share a common neural pathway. Passion for work, at the brain level, means that circuits linked to the left prefrontal cortex pump out a fairly steady stream of good feeling as we do our work.

At the same time, left prefrontal–based brain circuits perform another motivational favor: They quiet the feelings of frustration or worry that might discourage us from continuing. This means we can take in stride the inevitable setbacks, frustrations, and failures that any worthy goal brings us. We can see the hidden opportunity or the useful lesson in a reversal and keep going.

How well those prefrontal circuits prime motivating feelings and control the discouraging ones makes the difference between a pessimist, who dwells too much on what's wrong and so loses hope, and an optimist, who keeps going despite difficulties by holding in mind the satisfaction to come when the goal is met.

How does all of this apply to leaders and organizations? Motivation on the job too often is taken for granted; we assume people care about what they do. But the truth is more nuanced: Wherever people gravitate within their work role indicates where their real pleasure lies—and that pleasure is itself motivating. Although traditional incentives such as bonuses or recognition can prod people to better performance, no external motivators can get people to perform at their absolute best.

### The Smart Guess

Intuition, that essential leadership ability to apply not just technical expertise but also life wisdom in making business decisions, comes naturally to the self-aware leader. Why should an intuitive sense have any place in business today, amid the plethora of hard data available to leaders? Because attuning to our feelings, according to neurological research, helps us find the meaning in data, and so leads to better decisions. Our emotional memory banks thus enable us to judge information efficiently.[15] Emotions, science now tells us, are part of rationality, not opposed to it.

The smart guess matters to leaders now more than ever precisely because they face such a deluge of data—often with no clear map of what it portends for the future. As Richard Fairbank, CEO at Capital One, put it, "Finding a visionary strategy you believe as a leader is a very intuitive thing. There are many things a leader can't predict using data. How do you know what you will need to have in three years? Yet you've got to start development now or you won't have it when you need it. Our company hires brilliant data analysts; we have one of the biggest Oracle databases in the world. But at the end of the day, I find that all the data does is push us out farther on the frontier where it's uncertain all over again."

Today, as leaders are called on to build their companies by

creating the future rather than investing in the past, vision matters more than ever. Vision requires what looks to others like a leap of faith: the ability to go beyond the data and to make a smart guess.

On the other hand, intuition alone sometimes can lead people to make bad decisions. Intuition works best, it seems, when a gut sense can be used to build on other kinds of data. For instance, in a study of sixty entrepreneurs who built—and led—highly successful companies in California, virtually all said that in making business decisions they weighed the relevant information in terms of their intuitive gut feelings.[16] If, for instance, a business plan looked good on the basis of the data but did not "feel right," they'd proceed with great caution—or not at all. Gut feelings, they recognized, are data too.

Even companies at the top of their game today can fail in the future if their leaders make the wrong bets. The challenge is not unlike trying to predict the weather. Indeed, in a simulation of just such complex decision making, scientists had volunteers try to predict the weather based on clues from meteorological data.[17] The relationship between those clues and their effects on the weather was buried in such a complex probabilistic function that even analytic reasoning was useless. As each person made guesses based on these clues, he or she was told whether the guesses were right or not. In other words, they were given a chance to learn what worked and what didn't—just as happens naturally to any leader over the course of a career.

Surprisingly, even though no one could ascertain the specific connections between the clues and the weather, after fifty trials people were guessing right about 70 percent of the time. They had gradually gained a "feel" for what was going on; their brains had quietly picked up the accumulated lessons. Though their logical intellect was still stumped, those people had grasped the essence of the solution intuitively. It just *felt* right—their intuition told them what to do, based on the lessons learned.

This study offers an elegant microcosm of the cumulative learning that any leader acquires simply through ongoing experience of life's trials and errors. The brain constantly registers decision rules about what works and what doesn't: how people respond to this leadership approach or to another, what tactic succeeds in a given situation. With the eagerness of a constant learner, the brain soaks up life's lessons to better prepare us for the next time we face a similar challenge, uncertainty, or decision point.

Because this kind of learning goes on largely in a deep zone of the brain outside the reach of words (in the basal ganglia, a primitive part of the brain atop the spinal cord), leaders need to learn to trust their intuitive sense to access their life wisdom.[18] The circuitry involved in puzzling decisions, in fact, includes not just the basal ganglia, but also the amygdala, where the brain stores the emotions associated with memories.[19] When it comes to drawing on a lifetime of silent learning as we face decision points again and again, it's not the verbal part of the brain that delivers the best course of action—it's the part that wields our feelings.

Every day that a leader spends in a given business or career, his brain automatically extracts the decision rules that underlie one turn of events or another, or the operating cause-and-effect sequences. As the brain continually learns in this tacit mode, a leader accumulates the wisdom from a life's on-the-job experience. This wisdom increases throughout a leader's career, even as the abilities to pick up new technical skills may wane.

Whenever we face a moment in which these decision rules pertain, the brain applies them silently, coming to its wisest conclusion. Accordingly, the brain won't inform us of these judgments with words; instead, the emotional brain activates circuitry that runs from the limbic centers into the gut, giving us the compelling sense that *this feels right.* The amygdala, then, lets us know its conclusions primarily through circuitry extending into the gastrointestinal tract that, literally, creates a gut feeling.[20] Gut feelings offer a guide when facing a complex decision that goes beyond the data at hand. Gut feeling, in fact, has gained new scientific respect because of recent discoveries about implicit learning—that is, the lessons in life we pick up without being aware that we're learning them.

In short, intuition offers EI leaders a direct pipeline to their accumulated life wisdom on a topic. And it takes the inner attunement of self-awareness to sense that message.

## The Leader's Primal Challenge: Self-Management

From self-awareness—understanding one's emotions and being clear about one's purpose—flows self-management, the focused drive that all leaders need to achieve their goals. Without knowing what we're feeling, we're at a loss to manage those feelings. Instead, our emotions control us. That's usually fine, when it comes to positive emotions like enthusiasm and the pleasure of meeting a challenge. But no leader can afford to be controlled by negative emotions, such as frustration and rage or anxiety and panic.

The problem is that such negative emotional surges can be overwhelming; they're the brain's way of making us pay attention to a perceived threat. The result is that those emotions swamp the thinking brain's capacity to focus on the task at hand, whether it's strategic planning or dealing with news of a drop in market share.

A brain scan of someone who is upset or anxious shows high activity in the amygdala and the right side of the prefrontal area in particular, among other areas. This picture depicts an amygdala hijack: The emotional centers are driving or reverberating with the high activity in the prefrontal zone, which makes us fix our attention on, and obsess about, the cause of our distress. But when the scan shows someone in an upbeat mood, the key circuitry runs from the left prefrontal cortex down to the amygdala. The brain circuitry that generates good moods concentrates in the left prefrontal area and inhibits the action of the amygdala and connected areas that drive distress.

The left side of the prefrontal area, researchers believe, is part of a key circuit that inhibits neurons in the amygdala, and so keeps a person from being captured by distress.[21] This circuitry helps a leader to calm rocky emotions and maintain a confident, enthusiastic tone.

Self-management, then—which resembles an ongoing inner conversation—is the component of emotional intelligence that frees us from being a prisoner of our feelings. It's what allows the mental clarity and concentrated energy that leadership demands, and what keeps disruptive emotions from throwing us off track. Leaders with such self-mastery embody an upbeat, optimistic enthusiasm that tunes resonance to the positive range.

All of this is critically important to emotional intelligence. Because emotions are so contagious—especially from leaders to others in the group—leaders' first tasks are the emotional equivalent of good hygiene: getting their own emotions in hand. Quite simply, leaders cannot effectively manage emotions in anyone else without first handling their own. How a leader feels thus becomes more than just a private matter; given the reality of emotional leakage, a leader's emotions have public consequences.

That doesn't mean, of course, that a leader will never reel from life's slings and arrows. A divorce, a struggling child, or the illness of a loved one will inevitably trouble anyone. But the key is whether the urgencies of a leader's private life spill over into relationships on the job.

Leaders who freely vent their anger, catastrophize, or otherwise let their distressing emotions run amok can't also lead the group into a positive register, where the best work gets done. Again, the brain plays a critical role: In a sense, whenever two people have an encounter, there is a dance of amygdalas that creates either resonance or dissonance. In this neural tug-of-war, the person with stronger emotional self-management abilities tends to win. When a person with a pronounced left prefrontal tilt—that is, a person who is perennially upbeat—talks with someone known to be confrontational about issues they disagree on, the unflappable person typically ends up calming the irritable one.

The secret? Typically, disagreeable people provoke irritation in those they encounter, who then start to feel angry in return. In other words, in the open loop, the irritated amygdala draws the other into perturbation. But when the other person does not return aggression in kind—in fact, remains firmly in a positive register—

then the person with the aroused amygdala has a chance to calm down, or at least not become more provoked. Indeed, in one study the irritable person reported afterward that he just couldn't be confrontational because the other person kept responding with positivity.

Similarly, leaders who can stay optimistic and upbeat, even under intense pressure, radiate the positive feelings that create resonance. By staying in control of their feelings and impulses, they craft an environment of trust, comfort, and fairness. And that self-management has a trickle-down effect from the leader. No one wants to be known as a hothead when the boss consistently exudes a calm demeanor.

Not surprisingly, self-management is also important for competitive reasons. In the current ambiguous environment, where companies continually merge and break apart and technology transforms work at a dizzying pace, leaders who have mastered their emotions are better able to roll with the changes and help the organization to adjust.

Self-management also enables transparency, which is not only a leadership virtue but also an organizational strength.[22] Transparency—an authentic openness to others about one's feelings, beliefs, and actions—allows integrity, or the sense that a leader can be trusted. At a primal level, integrity hinges on impulse control, keeping us from acting in ways that we might regret. Integrity also means that a leader lives his values. Such leaders strike others as genuine because they are not making a pretense of being other than they are. Integrity, therefore, boils down to one question: Is what you're doing in keeping with your own values? EI leaders, we find, hold to an integrity that makes them comfortable with the questions transparency poses.

Ultimately, the most meaningful act of responsibility that leaders can do is to control their own state of mind. The original sense of the hipster term *cool* referred to the capacity of African American jazz musicians who could control their rage at the racism of the times, even as they channeled that anger into an extraordinary expression of deep feeling.[23] Effective leadership demands the same sort of capacity for managing one's own turbulent feelings while allowing the full expression of positive emotions.

## Social Awareness and the Limbic Tango

After self-awareness and emotional self-management, resonant leadership requires social awareness or, put another way, empathy. The ability to empathize, in its most basic form, stems from neurons in extended circuitry connected to, and in, the amygdala that read another person's face and voice for emotion and continually attune us to how someone else feels as we speak with them. This circuitry sends out a steady stream of bulletins—*he's getting a bit upset by that last remark . . . looks a little bored now . . . he liked hearing that*—which the prefrontal zone and related areas use to fine-tune what we say or do next.[24]

By keeping us posted on how the other person has just responded, the amygdala and connected circuits keep us in synch as a key relay station in the interpersonal open loop for emotions. This circuitry also attunes our own biology to the dominant range of feelings of the person we are with, so that our emotional states tend to converge. One term scientists use for this neural attunement is *limbic resonance*, "a symphony of mutual exchange and internal adaptation" whereby two people harmonize their emotional state.[25] Any time we have a genuine connection with someone where we've felt "on the same wavelength"—whether a pleasant time or even a good cry together—it signals that we've just experienced such an interlocking of brains. This tacit harmony occurs in any good human connection—between a mother and child, with friends over a cup of coffee, among team members laughing together as they work. It's the resonance that can trigger a sweep of emotion through a group or crowd, whether the feeling is grief, such as at a funeral, or excitement after a successful IPO.

While empathy represents a necessary ingredient of EI leadership, another lies in leaders' ability to express their message in a way that moves others. Resonance flows from a leader who expresses feelings with conviction because those emotions are clearly authentic, rooted in deeply held values.

EI leaders spread emotions in the positive register: They move people by articulating a dream they hold that elicits optimism, or compassion, or a sense of connection—aspirations that point toward a hopeful future. At the brain level, such messages emanate upbeat emotions, a range of feeling centered in the circuitry to and from the left prefrontal area. This zone of the brain also holds the key to motivation; as these positive visions spread, a group catches fire around that common goal.[26] Think, for example, of Martin Luther King Jr. mobilizing the American civil rights movement with his powerful refrain "I have a dream," which envisioned a world where all people would have equal opportunities.

Social awareness—particularly empathy—is crucial for the leader's primal task of driving resonance. By being attuned to how others feel in the moment, a leader can say and do what's appropriate—whether it be to calm fears, assuage anger, or join in good spirits. This attunement also lets a leader sense the shared values and priorities that can guide the group. By the same token, a leader who lacks empathy will unwittingly be off-key, and so speak and act in ways that set off negative reactions. Empathy—which includes listening and taking other people's perspectives—allows leaders to tune into the emotional channels between people that create resonance. And staying attuned lets them fine-tune their message to keep it in synch.

### Empathy: The Business Case

Of all the dimensions of emotional intelligence, social awareness may be the most easily recognized. We have all felt the empathy of a sensitive teacher or friend; we have all been struck by its absence in an unfeeling coach or boss. But when it comes to business, we rarely hear people praised, let alone rewarded, for their empathy. The very word seems unbusinesslike, out of place amid the tough realities of the marketplace.

But empathy—the fundamental competence of social awareness—doesn't mean a kind of "I'm okay, you're okay" mushiness. It doesn't mean that leaders should adopt other people's emotions as their own and try to please everybody. That would be a nightmare—it would make action impossible. Rather, empathy means taking employees' feelings into thoughtful consideration and then making intelligent decisions that work those feelings into the response. And, most crucially, empathy makes resonance possible; lacking empathy, leaders act in ways that create dissonance.

Empathy builds on self-management, but that means expressing emotions as appropriate, not stifling them. EI leaders' ability to empathize sometimes leads them to tear up or cry when their employees have cried, whether because of a personal tragedy or even during a reprimand or firing. Alternatively, while a considered response doesn't necessarily signal a lack of passion, leaders who swallow their emotions can appear emotionally aloof.

When leaders are able to grasp other people's feelings and perspectives, they access a potent emotional guidance system that keeps what they say and do on track. As such, empathy is the sine qua non of all social effectiveness in working life. Empathetic people are superb at recognizing and meeting the needs of clients, customers, or subordinates. They seem approachable, wanting to hear what people have to say. They listen carefully, picking up on what people are truly concerned about, and they respond on the mark. Accordingly, empathy is key to retaining talent. Leaders have always needed empathy to develop and keep good people, but whenever there is a war for talent, the stakes are higher. Of all the factors in a company's control, tuned-out, dissonant leaders are one of the main reasons that talented people leave—and take the company's knowledge with them.

Finally, in the growing global economy, empathy is a critical skill for both getting along with diverse workmates and doing business with people from other cultures. Cross-cultural dialogue can easily lead to miscues and misunderstandings. Empathy is an antidote that attunes people to subtleties in body language, or allows them to hear the emotional message beneath the words.

## Relationship Management

The triad of self-awareness, self-management, and empathy all come together in the final EI ability: relationship management. Here we find the most visible tools of leadership—persuasion, conflict management, and collaboration among them. Managing relationships skillfully boils down to handling other people's emotions. This, in turn, demands that leaders be aware of their own emotions and attuned with empathy to the people they lead.

If a leader acts disingenuously or manipulatively, for instance, the emotional radar of followers will sense a note of falseness and they will instinctively distrust that leader. The art of handling relationships well, then, begins with authenticity: acting from one's genuine feelings. Once leaders have attuned to their own vision and values, steadied in the positive emotional range, and tuned into the emotions of the group, then relationship management skills let them interact in ways that catalyze resonance.

Handling relationships, however, is not as simple as it sounds. It's not just a matter of friendliness, although people with strong social skills are rarely mean-spirited. Rather, relationship management is friendliness with a purpose: moving people in the right direction, whether that's agreement on a marketing strategy or enthusiasm about a new project.

That is why socially skilled leaders tend to have resonance with a wide circle of people—and have a knack for finding common ground and building rapport. That doesn't mean they socialize continually; it means they work under the assumption that nothing important gets done alone. Such leaders have a network in place when the time for action comes. And in an era when more and more work is done long distance—by e-mail or by phone—relationship building, paradoxically, becomes more crucial than ever.

Given the primal task of leadership, the ability to inspire and move people with a compelling vision looms large. Inspirational leaders get people excited about a common mission. They offer a sense of purpose beyond the day-to-day tasks or quarterly goals that so often take the place of a meaningful vision. Such leaders know that what people value most deeply will move them most powerfully in their work. Because they are aware of their own guiding values, they can articulate a vision that has the ring of truth for those they lead. That strong sense of the collective mission also leaves inspirational leaders free to direct and guide with firmness. As one product director put it, "I'm a company of one—I have no team, no power; I share people with other projects. I can't tell people what to do—but I can convince them by appealing to their agenda."[27]

Finally, as the tasks of leadership become more complex and collaborative, relationship skills become increasingly pivotal. For instance, every large organization must distribute its leadership among its division heads, and that creates a de facto team. Beyond that, as organizations realize that the old functional silos—marketing over here, strategy there, compensation here—must be broken down, more leaders routinely work with their peers as part of cross-functional teams. If any group needs to maximize its effectiveness, it's the team at the top. And that means establishing close and smooth relations so that everyone can share information easily and coordinate effectively.

Relationship skills allow leaders to put their emotional intelligence to work. But there's more to it than that. When it comes to getting results, the competencies that distinguish the best leaders operate in well-orchestrated unison, becoming distinctive leadership styles—as we shall see in the next chapter.

### CHAPTER FOUR

# THE LEADERSHIP REPERTOIRE

RESONANCE STEMS NOT JUST from leaders' good moods or ability to say the right thing, but also from whole sets of coordinated activities that comprise particular leadership styles. Typically, the best, most effective leaders act according to one or more of six distinct approaches to leadership and skillfully switch between the various styles depending on the situation.

Four of these styles—visionary, coaching, affiliative, and democratic—create the kind of resonance that boosts performance, while two others—pacesetting and commanding—although useful in some very specific situations, should be applied with caution, as we shall see.

To find out how particular leadership styles affect an organization and its emotional climate, we drew from research on a global database of 3,871 executives in which several key factors that influenced the working environment were assessed.[1]

Analysis went one step further to look at how the climate that resulted from various leadership styles affected financial results, such as return on sales, revenue growth, efficiency, and profitability. Results showed that, all other things being equal, leaders who used styles with a positive emotional impact saw decidedly better financial returns than those who did not. Perhaps most important, leaders with the best results didn't practice just one particular style. Rather, on any given day or week, they used many of the six distinct styles—seamlessly and in different measures—depending on the business situation. Imagine the styles, then, as the array of clubs in a golf pro's bag. Over the course of a match, the pro picks and chooses from his bag based on the demands of the shot. Sometimes he has to ponder his selection, but usually it is automatic. The pro "senses" the challenge ahead, swiftly pulls out the right tool, and elegantly puts it to work. That's how high-impact leaders operate too.

Although these styles of leadership (see the chart) have all been identified previously by different names, what's new about our model of leadership is an understanding of the underlying emotional intelligence capabilities that each approach requires, and—most compelling—each style's causal link with outcomes. The research, in other words, allows us to see how each style actually affects climate, and therefore performance. For executives engaged in the daily battle of getting results, such a connection adds a much-needed dose of science to the critical art of leadership.

We'll look first at those four leadership styles that foster resonance, then at the two that too readily generate dissonance when not used effectively.

## The Visionary Leader

When Shawana Leroy took over as director of a social work agency for impoverished families in a large city, there were clearly problems—most a legacy from her predecessor, a longtime civil

## The Leadership Styles in a Nutshell

VISIONARY
HOW IT BUILDS RESONANCE: Moves people toward shared dreams
IMPACT ON CLIMATE: Most strongly positive
WHEN APPROPRIATE: When changes require a new vision, or when a clear direction is needed

COACHING
HOW IT BUILDS RESONANCE: Connects what a person wants with the organization's goals
IMPACT ON CLIMATE: Highly positive
WHEN APPROPRIATE: To help an employee improve performance by building long-term capabilities

AFFILIATIVE
HOW IT BUILDS RESONANCE: Creates harmony by connecting people to each other
IMPACT ON CLIMATE: Positive
WHEN APPROPRIATE: To heal rifts in a team, motivate during stressful times, or strengthen connections

DEMOCRATIC
HOW IT BUILDS RESONANCE: Values people's input and gets commitment through participation
IMPACT ON CLIMATE: Positive
WHEN APPROPRIATE: To build buy-in or consensus, or to get valuable input from employees

PACESETTING
HOW IT BUILDS RESONANCE: Meets challenging and exciting goals
IMPACT ON CLIMATE: Because too frequently poorly executed, often highly negative
WHEN APPROPRIATE: To get high-quality results from a motivated and competent team

COMMANDING
HOW IT BUILDS RESONANCE: Soothes fears by giving clear direction in an emergency
IMPACT ON CLIMATE: Because so often misused, highly negative
WHEN APPROPRIATE: In a crisis, to kick-start a turnaround, or with problem employees

servant with a penchant for rules and regulations. The agency's mission attracted talented employees and fostered tremendous commitment—at least when they first came on board. Typically, though, that enthusiasm got lost as workers became mired in the byzantine rules established for carrying out their jobs. The mission became hard to find behind the regulations. Despite increasing needs for the agency's services—and complaints from funders—the pace of work was slow and effectiveness abysmal.

As a first step, Leroy talked to employees, one-on-one, to find out what worked and what people were proud of in the agency. People seemed relieved to have a chance to talk about how meaningful their work felt, and about the frustrations they faced trying to get things done. Leroy found she was not alone in feeling a commitment to the mission of helping poor families, and she gambled that this vision would sustain people during the changes to come at the agency.

By starting the conversation on this positive note, Leroy gave people a sense of the dream they wanted to reach for, and why. She got people talking about their hopes for the future, and she tapped into the compassion and dedication they felt. She then articulated this vision whenever the opportunity arose, voicing the shared values that had brought them all there.

As a next step, Leroy called on people to question whether they were really living the mission of helping the poor, and she guided them in looking at how what they did, day to day, affected the agency's ability to meet that goal. That process of inquiry had another payoff: building people's sense of initiative and their belief that they had the answers inside themselves.

Examining the agency's problems got down to specifics, as it must: which management practices were getting in the way, which rules made no sense, and which outdated systems needed to go. Meanwhile, Leroy made sure she modeled the principles of the new organization she wanted to create: one that was transparent and honest; one that focused on rigor and results. Then, as the process moved from talk to action, Leroy and her team tackled some of the most rigid bureaucratic practices and changed them with the support of almost all staff. With her at the helm, the agency's emotional climate changed to reflect her passion and commitment; she set the tone for the entire organization.

## The Visionary Resonates

Shawana Leroy, of course, exemplifies the visionary style, which strongly drives emotional climate upward and transforms the spirit of the organization at many levels. For instance, visionary leaders articulate where a group is going, but not how it will get there—setting people free to innovate, experiment, and take calculated risks. Knowing the big picture and how a given job fits in gives people clarity; they understand what's expected of them. And the sense that everyone is working toward shared goals builds team commitment: People feel pride in belonging to their organization.

Visionary leaders reap another benefit: retaining their most valued employees. To the extent that people resonate with a company's values, goals, and mission, that company becomes their preferred employer. A smart company realizes that it's vision and mission offers its people a unique "brand," a way of distinguishing itself as an employer from other companies in the same industry.

Moreover, by framing the collective task in terms of a grander vision, this approach defines a standard for performance feedback that revolves around that vision. Visionary leaders help people to see how their work fits into the big picture, lending people a clear sense not just that what they do matters, but also why. Such leadership maximizes buy-in for the organization's overall long-term goals and strategy. This is the classic mold of leadership, the one most often described in business school courses.

Consider the example of Bob Pittman, then-CEO of Six Flags Entertainment. Hearing that the janitors at the amusement parks were being surly to customers, Pittman decided to get a grounds-eye view of the problem: He went undercover as a janitor.[2] While sweeping the streets, he began to understand the problem. Although managers were ordering janitors to keep the parks immaculate, customers kept the workers from accomplishing that mission by continually littering in the parks, thus creating headaches for janitors.

Pittman's visionary strategy was to have managers redefine the janitors' main mission: It would now be to keep customers happy. And since a dirty park would make things less enjoyable for customers, the janitors' job was to clean up—but in a friendly spirit. With this reframing, Pittman tied the small part the janitors played into a larger vision.

Of the six leadership styles, our research suggests that overall, this visionary approach is most effective. By continually reminding people of the larger purpose of their work, the visionary leader lends a grand meaning to otherwise workaday, mundane tasks. Workers understand the shared objectives as being in synch with their own best interests. The result: inspired work.

### What Makes a Visionary

Inspirational leadership, of course, is the emotional intelligence competence that most strongly undergirds the visionary style. (For a fuller description of the EI competencies, see Appendix B.) Using inspiration together with the EI triad of self-confidence, self-awareness, and empathy, visionary leaders articulate a purpose that rings true for themselves and attune it to values shared by the people they lead. And because they genuinely believe in that vision, they can guide people toward it with a firm hand. When it comes time to change directions, competencies in self-confidence and in being a change catalyst smooth the transition.

Transparency, another EI competence, is crucial too; to be credible, leaders must truly believe their own visions. If a leader's vision is disingenuous, people sense it. Moreover, transparency means the removal of barriers or smokescreens within the company. It's a movement toward honesty and toward sharing information and knowledge so that people at all levels of the company feel included and able to make the best possible decisions. While some managers might have the misimpression that withholding information gives them power, visionary leaders understand that distributing knowledge is the secret to success; as a result, they share it openly and in large doses.

Of all the EI competencies, however, empathy matters most to visionary leadership. The ability to sense how others feel and to understand their perspectives means that a leader can articulate a truly inspirational vision. A leader who misreads people, on the other hand, simply can't inspire them.

Because of its positive impact, the visionary style works well in many business situations. But it can be particularly effective when a business is adrift—during a turnaround or when it is in dire need of a fresh vision. Not surprisingly, the visionary mode comes naturally to "transformational" leaders—those who seek to radically change an organization.[3]

Powerful as it is, however, the visionary style doesn't work in every situation. It fails, for instance, when a leader is working with a team of experts or peers who are more experienced than he—and who might view a leader expounding a grand vision as pompous or simply out of step with the agenda at hand. This kind of misstep can cause cynicism, which is a breeding ground for poor performance. Another limitation: If a manager trying to be visionary instead becomes overbearing, he can undermine the egalitarian spirit of team-based management.

These caveats aside, any leader would be wise to grab for the visionary "golf club" more often than not. It may not guarantee a hole in one, but it certainly helps with the long drive.

## The Art of the One-on-One: The Coaching Style

She was new at the firm, and eight months pregnant. Staying late one night, she looked up from her work and was startled to see her boss standing outside her door. He asked how she was doing, sat down, and started to talk with her. He wanted to know all about her life. How did she like her job? Where did she want to go in her career? Would she come back to work after she had the baby?

These conversations continued daily over the next month, until the woman had her baby. The boss was David Ogilvy, the legendary advertising executive. The pregnant newcomer was Shelley Lazarus, now CEO of Ogilvy & Mather, the huge ad agency that Ogilvy founded. One of the main reasons Lazarus says she's still there, decades later, is the bonds she forged with her mentor Ogilvy in those first after-hours conversations.[4]

Ogilvy's leadership included a large dose of the coaching style: having a deep conversation with an employee that goes beyond short-term concerns and instead explores the person's life, including dreams, life goals, and career hopes. Despite the commonly held belief that every leader needs to be a good coach, leaders tend to exhibit this style least often. In these high-pressure, tense times, leaders say they "don't have the time" for coaching. By ignoring this style, however, they pass up a powerful tool.

Even though coaching focuses on personal development rather than on accomplishing tasks, the style generally predicts an outstandingly positive emotional response and better results, almost irrespective of the other styles a leader employs. By making sure they have personal conversations with employees, coaching leaders establish rapport and trust. They communicate a genuine interest in their people, rather than seeing them as simply tools to get the job done. Coaching thereby creates an ongoing conversation that allows employees to listen to performance feedback more openly, seeing it as serving their own aspirations, not just the boss's interests.

As Patrick O'Brien, president of Johnson Outdoors, an outdoor recreation company, told us, "Getting to know people individually is more important than ever. If you have that one-hour personal conversation at the start with someone, six months later, on a Friday at 4 P.M., they're jumping with you."

### The Coach in Action

What does able coaching look like in a leader? Coaches help people identify their unique strengths and weaknesses, tying those to their personal and career aspirations. They encourage employees to establish long-term development goals, and help them to conceptualize a plan for reaching those goals, while being explicit about where the leader's responsibility lies and what the employee's role will be. As we discussed earlier, people tend to gravitate toward the aspects of their job they like the most, namely, the aspects that tie in to their dreams, identity, and aspirations. By linking people's daily work to these long-term goals, coaches keep people motivated. Only by getting to know employees on a deeper, personal level can leaders begin to make that link a reality.

Coaches are also good at delegating, giving employees challenging assignments that stretch them, rather than tasks that simply get the job done. (That kind of stretching, by the way, has a particularly positive impact on a person's mood; there's a special sweetness to success that pushes people beyond their abilities.[5]) Further, coaches usually tolerate a short-term failure, understanding that it can further an employee's dreams.

Not surprisingly, coaching works best with employees who show initiative and want more professional development. On the other hand, coaching will fail when the employee lacks motivation or requires excessive personal direction and feedback—or when the leader lacks the expertise or sensitivity needed to help the employee along. When executed poorly, the coaching approach looks more like micromanaging or excessive control of an employee. This kind of misstep can undermine an employee's self-confidence and ultimately create a downward performance spiral. Unfortunately, we've found that many managers are unfamiliar with—or simply inept at—the coaching style, particularly when it comes to giving ongoing performance feedback that builds motivation rather than fear or apathy.

For example, leaders who are also pacesetters—focused exclusively on high performance—often think they're coaching when actually they're micromanaging or simply telling people how to do their jobs. Such leaders often concentrate solely on short-term goals, such as sales figures. That solution-oriented bent keeps them from discovering employees' long-term aspirations—and employees, in turn, can believe that the leader sees them as mere tools for accomplishing a task, which makes them feel underappreciated rather than motivated.

When done well, however, coaching boosts not just employees' capabilities but also their self-confidence, helping them function both more autonomously and at a higher performance level.

### What Makes a Coach

Coaching exemplifies the EI competence of developing others, which lets a leader act as a counselor, exploring employees' goals and values and helping them expand their own repertoire of abilities. It works hand in hand with two other competencies that research shows exemplify the best counselors: emotional self-awareness and empathy.

Emotional self-awareness creates leaders who are authentic, able to give advice that is genuinely in the employee's best interest rather than advice that leaves the person feeling manipulated or even attacked. And empathy means leaders listen first before reacting or giving feedback, which allows the interaction to stay on target. Good coaches, therefore, often ask themselves: Is this about my issue or goal, or theirs?

Coaching's surprisingly positive emotional impact stems largely from the empathy and rapport a leader establishes with employees. A good coach communicates a belief in people's potentials and an expectation that they can do their best. The tacit message is, "I believe in you, I'm investing in you, and I expect your best efforts." As a result, people sense that a leader cares, so they feel motivated to uphold their own high standards for performance, and they feel accountable for how well they do.

Sometimes coaching takes the form of an active mentoring program. And at "built-to-last" companies, which have thrived over decades, the ongoing development of leadership marks a cultural strength as well as a key to continued business success.[6] In a time when more and more companies are finding it difficult to retain the most talented and promising employees, those companies that provide their people nourishing development experiences are more successful in creating loyal employees. In short, the coaching style may not scream "bottom-line results," but, in a surprisingly indirect way, it delivers them.

## Relationship Builders: The Affiliative Style

Joe Torre might be called both the heart and soul of the New York Yankees. As the manager of that venerable baseball team as it won yet another World Series in 1999, Torre was credited with tending ably to the psyches of his players as they went through the emotional pressure cooker of the drive to win the championship. In a job often filled by notorious exemplars of unruly tempers and insensitivity, Torre stands out as an exception, exemplifying the teamwork and collaboration competence in action.

Take the celebration on the field right after the final 1999 game. Torre sought out particular players to embrace, especially Paul O'Neill, whose father had just died at age 79. Though he had barely received the news of his father's death, O'Neill chose to play in the decisive game that night—and burst into tears the moment the game ended. Later, at the victory party in the clubhouse, Torre made a point of acknowledging O'Neill's personal struggle, praising him as "a warrior."

Torre sought out two other players, as well—both of whom also had lost family members during the season. One, Scott Brosius, had repeatedly been praised by Torre over the previous months for willing himself to stay upbeat when at work with the team, even as he worried about his father's terminal illness. Finally, Torre used the spotlight that the victory celebration offered to go to bat for two players whose return the following year was threatened by contract disputes. He singled out both players for praise, to make a point to his own boss, the club's owner, that they were just too valuable to lose.

To be sure, Torre is no softy: He's firm with reprimands when needed. But he's also open about his own feelings with those he leads. The year his brother was near death while awaiting a heart transplant, Torre did little to hide his concern, sharing his worries with his players—as he did about his own treatment for prostate cancer the spring before his team won the pennant.

Such open sharing of emotions is one hallmark of the affiliative leadership style, which Torre exemplifies. These leaders also tend to value people and their feelings—putting less emphasis on accomplishing tasks and goals, and more on employees' emotional needs. They strive to keep people happy, to create harmony, and—as Torre did so well—to build team resonance.

Although limited as a direct driver of performance, the affiliative style has a surprisingly positive impact on a group's climate, behind only the visionary and coaching styles in impelling all measures upward. By recognizing employees as people—for example, offering them emotional support during hard times in their private lives—such leaders build tremendous loyalty and strengthen connectedness.

When does the affiliative style make sense? Its generally positive impact makes it a good all-weather resonance builder, but leaders should apply it in particular when trying to heighten team harmony, increase morale, improve communication, or repair broken trust in an organization.

Many cultures place tremendous value on strong personal ties, making relationship building a sine qua non of doing business. In most Asian cultures—as well as in Latin America and some European countries—establishing a strong relationship is a prerequisite for doing business. This step comes naturally to leaders who exhibit the affiliative style.

### What Makes an Affiliative Leader

The affiliative style represents the collaborative competence in action. Such leaders are most concerned with promoting harmony and fostering friendly interactions, nurturing personal relationships that expand the connective tissue with the people they lead. Accordingly, affiliative leaders value downtime in the organizational cycle, which allows more time to build emotional capital that can be drawn from when the pressure is on.

When leaders are being affiliative, they focus on the emotional needs of employees even over work goals. This focus makes empathy—the ability to sense the feelings, needs, and perspectives of others—another fundamental competence here. Empathy allows a leader to keep people happy by caring for the whole

---

## WHEN BEING "NICE" ISN'T ENOUGH

"WE DON'T KNOW how to be both kind and candid here," a senior vice president at a $6 billion global consumer products company told us. "We're a family-owned, relationship-oriented company. Our leaders focus on valuing and respecting people. If we err, it's in being too concerned about keeping things harmonious. We're overly nice. Since we tend to shy away from confrontation, we don't give the kind of feedback that helps people grow."

There's an obvious flaw when a leader relies solely on the affiliative approach: Work takes second place to feelings. Leaders who overuse this style neglect to offer corrective feedback on performance that could help employees improve. They tend to be overly worried about getting along with people, often at the expense of the task at hand. This "anxious" type of affiliation has been found to drive down the climate rather than raise it.[7] Stewing about whether they're liked or not, such leaders' avoidance of confrontation can derail a group, steering them to failure.

Such leaders can easily become clueless, their overly affiliative stance creating a situation where they're the last to hear bad news. In crises or when people need clear directives to steer through complex challenges, clueless leaders—chummy though they may be—leave followers rudderless.

---

person—not just the work tasks for which someone is responsible. A leader's empathy makes the affiliative approach a booster of morale par excellence, lifting the spirits of employees even as they trudge through mundane or repetitive tasks. Finally, the affiliative style sometimes also relies on the EI competence of conflict management when the challenge includes knitting together diverse or even conflicting individuals into a harmonious working group.

Despite its benefits, the affiliative style should not be used alone. The style's exclusive focus on praise can allow poor performance to go uncorrected, and employees may perceive that mediocrity is tolerated. In addition, because affiliative leaders rarely offer constructive advice on how to improve, employees are left on their own to figure out how to do so.

Perhaps that's why many affiliative leaders—including Joe Torre—use this style in close conjunction with the visionary approach. Visionary leaders state a mission, set standards, and let people know whether their work is furthering the group goals. Ally that with the caring approach of the affiliative leader, and you have a potent combination.

## Let's Talk It Over: The Democratic Style

The private Catholic school, located in an impoverished neighborhood of a large metropolitan area, had been losing money for years. No longer able to afford to keep the school going, the archdiocese ordered Sister Mary, who headed the Catholic school system in the area, to shut it down.

But rather than immediately locking the doors, Sister Mary called a meeting of the teachers and staff and explained the details of the financial crisis that threatened the school. She asked for their ideas on ways to help keep the school open, and how to handle the closing, should it come to that. And then she simply listened. She did the same thing at later meetings for school parents, for the community, and then during a successive series of meetings for teachers and staff.

By the end of a round of meetings that lasted several months, the consensus was clear: The school would have to close. Students who wished to attend a school in the Catholic system would be transferred.

Although the final outcome was no different than if Sister Mary had immediately closed the school herself, the process she used made all the difference. By allowing the school's constituents to reach that decision collectively, Sister Mary received none of the backlash that would have accompanied such a move. People mourned the loss of the school, but understood its inevitability. Virtually no one objected.

Compare Sister Mary's approach with that of a priest who headed another Catholic school, also given the order to close. The priest immediately shut the school down—by fiat. The result: Parents filed lawsuits, teachers and parents picketed, and local newspapers ran editorials attacking his decision. The disputes kept the school open a full year before it could finally close down.

In contrast, Sister Mary's democratic style of getting buy-in from her constituents built feelings of trust and respect—and, in a word, commitment. By spending time one-on-one and in meetings listening to the concerns of employees (or, as with Sister Mary, of stakeholders such as parents), the democratic leader keeps morale high. The resulting impact on climate is positive across the board.

### When to Be Democratic

A democratic approach works best when, like Sister Mary, the leader is uncertain about what direction to take and needs ideas from able employees.

That seems to have been the case with Louis Gerstner Jr., who became chairman of IBM in 1993 when the company was on the brink of death. An outsider to the computer industry, Gerstner had to rely on a democratic style, turning to more seasoned colleagues for advice. In the end, even though he had to cut $9 billion a year in expenses and lay off thousands of employees, Gerstner led a sensationally successful turnaround, charting a new strategic course for the company. Looking back, Gerstner mused that his day-to-day decisions had been based on "getting some good advice from my colleagues who knew a heck of a lot more about IBM and this industry than I would ever know."[8]

Even if a leader has a strong vision, the democratic style works well to surface ideas about how to implement that vision or to generate fresh ideas for executing it. For example, David Morgan, CEO of Westpac Bank in Australia, spends up to twenty days each year meeting with various groups of his top 800 people, 40 at a time. "It's a session where they give me feedback," Morgan told us. "I want to know how it really is. If it was ever true that someone sitting in an isolated corner office could run this business, it's not true today. The greatest risk is being out of touch with what's going on."

For such feedback sessions to be useful, the leader must be open to everything—bad news as well as good. "You have to listen to some pretty tough stuff," Morgan adds. "But the first time I chop someone's head off for telling me the hard truth, that's when they'll stop talking to me. I have to keep it safe for everyone to speak up. There's no problem we can't solve if we can be open about it."

Of course, the democratic style can have its drawbacks. One result when a leader overrelies on this approach is exasperating, endless meetings in which ideas are mulled over, consensus remains elusive, and the only visible outcome is to schedule yet more meetings. A leader who puts off crucial decisions, hoping to thrash out a consensual strategy, risks dithering. The cost can be confusion and lack of direction, with resulting delays or escalating conflicts.

It almost goes without saying, of course, that seeking employees' advice when they're uninformed or incompetent can lead to disaster. Similarly, consensus building is wrong-headed in times of crisis, when urgent events demand on-the-spot decisions. Take the case of a CEO we observed whose computer company was threatened by a changing market, yet he persisted in seeking consensus about what to do. As competitors stole customers—and customers' needs changed—this CEO continued to appoint committees to consider alternative responses. Then, when the market suddenly shifted because of a new technology, the CEO froze in his tracks. Before he could convene yet another task force to consider the situation, the board replaced him.

### What Makes a Democratic Leader

The democratic style builds on a triad of emotional intelligence abilities: teamwork and collaboration, conflict management, and influence. The best communicators are superb listeners—and listening is the key strength of the democratic leader. Such leaders create the sense that they truly want to hear employees' thoughts and concerns and that they're available to listen. They're also true collaborators, working as team members rather than top-down leaders. And they know how to quell conflict and create a sense of harmony—for instance, repairing rifts within the group.

The EI competence of empathy also plays a role in democratic leadership, especially when the group is strongly diverse. Without the ability to attune to a wide range of people, a leader will be more prone to miscues.

The first four leadership styles—visionary, coaching, affiliative, and democratic—are sure-fire resonance builders. Each has its own strong, positive impact on the emotional climate of an organization. The last two styles—pacesetting and commanding—also have their place in a leader's tool kit. But each must be used carefully and with skill if it is to have a positive impact. When pacesetting or commanding leaders go too far, relying on these styles too often or using them recklessly, they build dissonance, not resonance—as we shall see in the next chapter.

### CHAPTER FIVE

# THE DISSONANT STYLES

## Apply with Caution

THE SPECTACULAR RISE of EMC, the data storage systems company, from nonentity to world leader illustrates classic entrepreneurial zeal. For years, the company's top management led its sales force on an intentionally frenzied race to outdo the competition. In fact, CEO Michael Ruettgers said that he selected sales managers based on that drive to win, and he attributes EMC's success to the aggressiveness of its marketing force. As one EMC sales executive told us, "We're like pit bulls— but the difference is pit bulls let go."

That tenacity reaped enormous returns: In 1995, the first year EMC shipped open-storage systems, sales reached $200 million. By 1999, EMC—the company that hadn't been on anyone's radar—was one of only four U.S. companies earning top ratings for shareholder return, sales growth, profit growth, net profit margin, and return on equity.[1]

Ruettgers and his management team embody the pacesetting style in action: leaders who expect excellence and exemplify it. This style can work extremely well, particularly in technical fields, among highly skilled professionals, or—as at EMC—with a hard-driving sales team. Pacesetting makes sense, in particular, during the entrepreneurial phase of a company's life cycle, when growth is all-important. Any time that group members are all highly competent, motivated, and need little direction, the style can yield brilliant results. Given a talented team, the pacesetting leader gets work done on time, or even ahead of deadline.

## Pacesetting: Use Sparingly

Even so, while the pacesetting approach has its place in the leader's tool chest, it should be used sparingly, restricted to settings where it truly works. That advice runs counter to common wisdom. After all, the hallmarks of pacesetting sound admirable: The leader holds and exemplifies high standards for performance. He is obsessive about doing things better and faster, and asks the same of everyone. He quickly pinpoints poor performers, demands more from them, and if they don't rise to the occasion, rescues the situation himself.

But if applied poorly or excessively, or in the wrong setting, the pacesetting approach can leave employees feeling pushed too hard by the leader's relentless demands. And since pacesetters tend to be unclear about guidelines—expecting people to "just know what to do"—followers often have to second-guess what the leader wants. The result is that morale plummets as employees see their leader as driving them too hard—or worse, feel the leader doesn't trust them to get the job done in their own way. What's more, pacesetters can be so focused on their goals that they can appear not to care about the people they rely on to achieve those goals. The net result is dissonance.

Our data show that, more often than not, pacesetting poisons the climate—particularly because of the emotional costs when a leader relies on it too much. Essentially, the pacesetter's dilemma is this: The more pressure put on people for results, the more anxiety it provokes. Although moderate pressure can energize people—the challenge of meeting a deadline, for instance—continued high pressure can be debilitating. As people shift away from pursuing an inspiring vision, pure survival issues take hold. The pressure constricts their talent for innovative thinking. Although pacesetters may get compliance—and therefore a short-term upward blip in results—they don't get true performance that people will sustain.

Take, for example, an executive we'll call Sam. Academically, Sam's career began brilliantly; he graduated at the top of his class. Then, as an R&D biochemist at a large pharmaceutical company, his superb technical expertise made him an early star: He was the one everyone else turned to for technical advice. Driven by high standards of excellence and achievement, he was almost obsessive in his search for better ways to do his job.

When he was appointed to head a team developing a new product, Sam continued to shine, and his teammates were, by and large, as competent and self-motivated as their new head. Sam's métier as team leader became setting the pace, working late, and offering himself as a model of how to do first-class scientific work under tremendous deadline pressure. His team completed its task in record time.

But when Sam was picked to head R&D for his entire division, he began to slip. His tasks had shifted to the larger mission of leadership—articulating a vision, delegating responsibility, and helping to develop people—but Sam didn't trust that his subordinates were as capable as he was. He often refused to delegate real power, becoming a micromanager who was obsessed with details, taking over for others when their performance slackened rather than trusting they could improve with guidance. Finally, at his own boss's suggestion—and to Sam's relief—he returned to his old job as head of a product development team.

Sam's story demonstrates the classic signs of a pacesetter: exceptionally high standards of excellence, impatience with poor performance, an eagerness to roll up his sleeves to get the job done, and a readiness to take over for people when they get into difficulties. This is not to say that the pacesetting approach can't work well. It can—but only in the right situations, namely, when employees are self-motivated, highly competent, and need little direction.

### Effective Pacesetting: The Ingredients

What does it take to be a successful pacesetting leader? The emotional intelligence foundation of this style lies in the drive to achieve by continually finding ways to improve performance— along with a large dose of initiative in seizing opportunities. The achievement competence means pacesetting leaders strive to learn new approaches that will raise their own performance and that of those they lead. It also means these leaders are motivated not by external rewards, such as money or titles, but rather by a strong need to meet their own high standards of excellence. Pacesetting also requires initiative, the go-getter's readiness to seize or create opportunities to do better. But if it arises in the absence of other crucial EI competencies, this drive to achieve can go awry. The absence of empathy, for example, means such leaders can blithely focus on accomplishing tasks while remaining oblivious to the rising distress in those who perform them. Similarly, an absence of self-awareness leaves pacesetters blind to their own failings.

Other competencies such leaders often lack include the abilities to collaborate or communicate effectively (particularly the knack for providing timely and helpful performance feedback). The most glaring lack is emotional self-management, a deficit that manifests as either micromanaging or impatience—or worse.

By and large, pacesetting can work well in tandem with other leadership styles such as the passion of the visionary style and the team building of the affiliative style. The most common problems with pacesetters emerge when a star "techie" gets promoted to management, as happened in our example of Sam, the gifted biochemist who failed as head of research. In fact, Sam exhibited the classic symptoms of the Peter Principle, promoted beyond his competence. He had all the technical skills he needed for his old position, but too narrow a slice of the leadership ones he needed for his new one. So he became a leader who takes over for people when they falter, who can't delegate because he doesn't trust that others can perform as well as he, and who is all too quick to condemn poor performance but stints on praise for work well done. Another sign of Peter Principle pacesetters is that they excel at the technical aspects of the work they manage but disdain the cooperative bent that leadership demands.

When leaders use the pacesetting style exclusively or poorly, they lack not just vision, but also resonance. Too often, such leaders are driven by numbers alone—which aren't always enough to inspire or motivate people.

## Do It Because I Say So: Leading by Command

The computer company was hemorrhaging: Sales and profits were falling, stock was losing value precipitously, and shareholders were in an uproar. The board brought in a new CEO with a reputation as a turnaround artist, and he set to work chopping jobs, selling off divisions, and making the tough, unpopular decisions that should have been executed years before.

In the end, the company was saved—at least in the short term—but at a high price. From the start, the CEO created a reign of terror, most acutely among his direct reports. A modern-day Genghis Khan, he bullied and demeaned his executives, roaring his displeasure at the least misstep. Frightened by his tendency to "murder" the bearer of bad news, his direct reports stopped bringing him any news at all. Soon his top talent defected—and the CEO fired many who remained. Throughout the company, morale was nonexistent, a fact reflected in another downturn in the business after the short-term recovery. Eventually, the CEO was fired by the board of directors.

To be sure, the business world is rife with coercive leaders whose negative impact on those they lead has yet to catch up with them. For instance, when a major hospital system was losing money, the board hired a new president to turn the business around—and the effect was disastrous. As one physician told us, "He cut back staff mercilessly, especially in nursing. The hospital looked more profitable, but it was dangerously understaffed. We just couldn't keep up with patient demand, and everyone felt demoralized."

No surprise, then, that patient-satisfaction ratings plummeted. When the hospital began to lose market share to its competition, the president grudgingly rehired many of the people he'd fired. "But to this day he's never admitted he was too ruthless," the physician reported, "and he continues to manage by threat and intimidation. The nurses are back, but morale is not. Meanwhile, the president complains about patient-satisfaction numbers—but fails to see that he's part of the problem."

### The Commanding Style in Action

What does the commanding approach—sometimes called the *coercive* style—look like in action? With a motto of "Do it because I say so," such leaders demand immediate compliance with orders, but don't bother explaining the reasons behind them. If subordinates fail to follow their orders unquestioningly, these leaders resort to threats. And, rather than delegate authority, they seek tight control of any situation and monitor it studiously. Accordingly, performance feedback—if given at all—invariably focuses on what people did wrong rather than what they did well. In short, it's a classic recipe for dissonance.

Not surprisingly, of all the leadership styles, the commanding approach is the least effective in most situations, according to our data. Consider what the style does to an organization's climate. Given that emotional contagion spreads most readily from the top down, an intimidating, cold leader contaminates everyone's mood, and the quality of the overall climate spirals down. And although someone like the coercive hospital CEO might not perceive a connection between his leadership style and the downward direction of patient satisfaction, the links are there. His interactions with nurses and doctors spoil their moods, and they in turn are less able to exhibit the cheery playfulness that lifts the moods of patients and makes all the difference in how patients experience their medical care.

By rarely using praise and freely criticizing employees, the commanding leader erodes people's spirits and the pride and satisfaction they take in their work—the very things that motivate most high-performing workers. Accordingly, the style undermines a critical tool that all leaders need: the ability to give people the sense that their job fits into a grand, shared mission. Instead, people are left feeling less committed, even alienated from their own jobs, and wondering, How does any of this matter?

In spite of its many negative effects, however, coercive leaders thrive the world over in surprisingly large numbers, a legacy of the old command-and-control hierarchies that typified twentieth-century businesses. Such organizations adopted a military model of leadership (top down, "I order you") that really was most appropriate to the battlefield. Yet even in today's more modernized military organizations, the commanding style is balanced by other styles in the interests of building commitment, *esprit de corps*, and teamwork.

The medical community offers another example. In America today many medical organizations face a crisis of leadership in part because the culture of medicine has favored pacesetting and commanding styles. These styles are, of course, appropriate in, say, the operating or the emergency rooms. But their predominance means that many medical people who rise to positions of leadership have had too few chances to learn a fuller repertoire of styles.

In most modern organizations, then, the "do-it-because-I-say-so" boss has become a dinosaur. As one CEO of a technology company put it, "You can beat people into the ground and make money, but is that company going to last?"

## When Commanding Works

Despite its negative inclinations, the command-and-control style can hold an important place in the EI leader's repertoire when used judiciously. For example, leaders managing a business crisis such as an urgent turnaround can find the commanding style particularly effective—especially at first—to unfreeze useless business habits and shock people into new ways of doing things. Similarly, during a genuine emergency, such as a fire in the building or an approaching hurricane—or when facing a hostile takeover—leaders with a take-control style can help everyone through the tumult. Moreover, when all else has failed, the style sometimes works when dealing with problem employees.

One executive in our research used the commanding style artfully when he was brought in as division president to change the direction of a money-losing food company. He began by acting forcefully in his first weeks to signal the changes he meant to engineer.

For example, the top management team met regularly in a very formal, rather intimidating conference room and sat in gigantic chairs around a marble-covered table that "looked like the deck of the Starship Enterprise" from the television show *Star Trek*, as the new division president put it. The distances between people stifled spontaneous talk, and the meetings themselves were stilted—no one daring to ever rock the boat. In short, the conference room symbolized the lack of dialogue and true collaboration among the senior management team. To signal a shift toward openness, the new president had the room demolished—a clear command-style move—with positive effects. From that moment on, the management team met in an ordinary conference room, "where people can actually talk to each other," as the new president put it.

He used the same approach regarding a set of very detailed decision-making manuals that specified who had to concur before a management decision was made. The new caveat: no more manuals and endless paper passing. "I want people to talk to each other," the president explained to us. "Anyone who needs to can come to the executive committee meeting to tell us, 'here's what

I'm working on—I need your help and ideas.' I want us to be more of a resource to people than merely a rubber stamp.'

In sending these messages, the new president was forceful and strong. But his strong tactics worked because he attacked the old culture—not the people. In fact, he made it clear that he valued their talents and abilities; it was their way of doing things that he felt needed to change dramatically.

## What It Takes

Such an effective execution of the commanding style draws on three emotional intelligence competencies: influence, achievement, and initiative. And, as with the pacesetting style, self-awareness, emotional self-control, and empathy are crucial to keep the commanding style from going off track. The drive to achieve means a leader exerts forceful direction in the service of getting better results. Initiative, in the commanding style, often takes the form not just of seizing opportunities, but also of employing an unhesitating "command" tone, issuing orders on the spot rather than pausing to ponder a course of action. The commanding leader's initiative also shows up as not waiting for situations to drive him, but taking forceful steps to get things done.

Perhaps most important in the skillful execution of this style is emotional self-control. This allows the leader to keep his anger and impatience in check—or even to use his anger in an artfully channeled outburst designed to get instant attention and mobilize people to change or get results. When a leader lacks the self-awareness that would enable the required emotional self-control—perhaps the most common failing in leaders who employ this style poorly—the dangers of the commanding style are greatest. Coercive leaders who display not just anger but also disgust or contempt can have a devastating emotional impact on their people.

Even worse, if a leader's out-of-control outbursts go hand in hand with a lack of empathy—an emotional tone deafness—the style runs amok: The dictatorial leader barks orders, oblivious to the reactions of people on the receiving end. Executing the commanding style effectively, therefore, requires the leader "to be angry with the right person, in the right way, at the right time, and for the right reason," as Aristotle put it.

That said, the commanding style should be used only with extreme caution, targeted at situations in which it is absolutely imperative, such as a turnaround or impending hostile takeover. If a leader knows when conditions demand a strong hand at the top—and when to drop it—then that skillful firmness can be tonic. But if the only tool in a leader's kit is a chainsaw, he'll leave an organization in shambles.

## The SOB Paradox

Despite the evidence that unduly commanding (or pacesetting) bosses create a disastrous dissonance, everyone can name a rude, hard-hitting CEO who, by all appearances, epitomizes the antithesis of resonance yet seems to reap great business results. If emotional intelligence matters so much, how do we explain those meanspirited SOBs?

First, let's take a closer look at those SOBs. Just because a particular executive is the most visible, is he the person who actually leads the company? A CEO who heads a conglomerate may have no followers to speak of; rather, it's the division heads who actively lead people and affect profitability most. It's been said that Bill Gates and his company, Microsoft, run in this kind of fashion. He can be an effective pacesetter because his direct reports are technically brilliant, self-motivated, and driven. In turn, his direct reports tend to employ resonant leadership styles within their own divisions, where such a repertoire is a must to foster the teamwork the company depends on for results.

Then there are leaders whose success rests on an illusion, such as a high market capitalization or too-drastic restructuring, that hides a ruinous turnover of key people that will cost the company severely in the future. Often, those executives turn out to be egodriven narcissists who are actually terrible leaders.

Take, for example, Al Dunlap, who boasted in his autobiography,

*Mean Business*, that his leadership as CEO of Scott Paper would "go down in the annals of American business history as one of the most successful turnarounds ever." Although Dunlap exalted toughness, even meanness, as a tool of leadership while he fired thousands of employees, later analyses saw his cutbacks as too excessive, damaging the company's ability to do business. And his apparent short-term successes, at least in his subsequent position at Sunbeam, seem due to other tactics: Within two years after being fired as CEO of Sunbeam, Dunlap and other executives were indicted by the Securities and Exchange Commission on a charge of "orchestrating a fraudulent scheme to create the illusion of a successful restructuring of Sunbeam and facilitate the sale of the company at an inflated price."[2]

Leaders with such gargantuan egos typically have a blinder-like fixation on immediate financial goals, without any regard for the long-term human or organizational costs of how they achieve those goals.[3] And too often, as with Al Dunlap, the companies they leave behind may show all the signs of steroid abuse: pumped up for an intense period to show high profitability, but at the expense of the long-term human and economic resources essential to sustain those profits.[4]

Finally, the boss in question might have one or two highly noticeable weaknesses in EI abilities, while still having enough counterbalancing strengths to be effective. In other words, no leader is perfect, nor does he need to be. Our idealizations of leaders can lead us to set unreasonable standards, wanting them to be paragons of every virtue.

When examining the SOB question, we need to consider as well whether the leader has important strengths that counterbalance the caustic behavior but that might not get as much attention in the business press. In his early days at GE, Jack Welch exhibited a strong hand at the helm as he undertook a radical company turnaround. At that time and in that situation, his firm, top-down style was appropriate. What got less press was how Welch in subsequent years settled into a more clearly EI leadership style, especially in articulating a new vision for the company and mobilizing people to follow it.

*Clearing Away the Smoke*

In short, it's all too easy for a skeptic to make a specious argument against the utility of EI by telling an anecdote about a "rough and tough" leader whose business results seem good despite his abrasiveness. Such a naïve argument—that great leaders succeed by being mean-spirited and ruthless (or in spite of it)—can be made only in the absence of hard data about what kinds of leadership truly gets results.

A scientific study of leaders begins by clearing away the smoke, leveling the playing field to make systematic comparisons. Such objective methods control for the false or transient successes a mean-spirited leader may seem to be able to claim credit for but which are actually due, say, to the luck of an entire industry's high-growth period or to such short-term maneuvers as cutbacks or fiddling with accounting methods.

In a rare spirit of open inquiry, for instance, a trade association of U.S. insurance companies commissioned a study of the leadership qualities of CEOs and the business performance of the companies they led. A research team tracked the financial results achieved by nineteen CEOs of major insurance companies and split them into two groups—"outstanding" and "good"—on the basis of measures such as their company's profit and growth.[5] Then the team conducted intensive interviews to assess the capabilities that distinguished the outstanding CEOs from those who merely did a good enough job. The team evaluated each CEO, and also sought candid (and confidential) evaluations from their direct reports.

The singular talent that set the most successful CEOs apart from others turned out to be a critical mass of emotional intelligence competencies. The most successful CEOs spent more time coaching their senior executives, developing them as collaborators, and cultivating personal relationships with them. Of the abilities conspicuously *absent* in the SOB-style leader, of course, high on the list are empathy, artful collaboration, and caring about developing the best in people. Moreover, when the company's

CEO exhibited EI strengths, profits and sustained growth were highest—significantly higher than for companies where CEOs lacked those strengths.

### Who Wants to Work for an SOB?

Another little secret about those SOBs: They drive away talent. The best people in any field—the talented few who contribute greatest business value—simply don't have to put up with the misery perpetuated by a bad boss. And, increasingly, they leave for other jobs. The number one reason that people cite for quitting is dissatisfaction with the boss. In a tight labor market, when people have the ability to get an equivalent job easily, those with bad bosses are four times more likely to leave than are those who appreciate the leader they work for.[6]

Indeed, interviews with 2 million employees at 700 American companies found that what determines how long employees stay—and how productive they are—is the quality of their relationship with their immediate boss. "People join companies and leave managers," observes Marcus Buckingham of the Gallup Organization, who analyzed the data.

The conclusion from the data seems all too clear: The SOB leader must reform or go.

## The Business Impact of Flexible Styles

By expanding their repertoire of leadership abilities, dissonant leaders can indeed reform. Remember that Harvard professor David McClelland found that leaders with strengths in a critical mass of six or more EI leadership abilities were far more effective than peers who lacked such strengths.[7] He also found that various kinds of star leaders fostered resonance from uniquely different sets of leadership competencies. For example, one leader might excel through self-confidence, flexibility, initiative, the drive to achieve, empathy, and a knack for developing the talents of others, whereas another leader's strengths might be in self-awareness, integrity, staying calm under pressure, organizational awareness, influence, and collaboration.

Having a larger repertoire of emotional intelligence strengths can make a leader more effective because it means that leader is flexible enough to handle the wide-ranging demands of running an organization. Each style draws on different emotional intelligence abilities; the best leaders are able to use the right approach in the right moment, and flip from one to another as needed. People who lack the underlying abilities have a narrowed leadership repertoire, and so are too often stuck relying on a style that's ill matched to the challenge of the moment. Consider again that study of nineteen CEOs in the American insurance industry. The research, as we saw, found that the most successful companies were led by CEOs with a critical mass of emotional intelligence capabilities—such as the drive to improve, an ability to catalyze change, the capacity for empathy, and a talent for developing other leaders. But that research went one step further: The research team asked key employees what it was like to work at the companies these nineteen CEOs led, focusing on areas that directly affected people's ability to do their jobs well—not just how "satisfied" they were.

There was a marked difference between the feel of organizations led by those CEOs whose business results were outstanding and those who had less sterling results. The organizations led by the outstanding CEOs did better on every measure of climate, from clarity in communicating standards to making people feel flexible and free to innovate in getting their jobs done. The high-performing CEOs encouraged workers to feel ownership and responsibility for their work, they set higher performance standards, and they mobilized people to meet more demanding "stretch" goals. In short, these CEOs created a climate where people felt energized and focused, had pride in their work, loved what they did—and stuck around.

Leadership drives performance in organizations of every kind—not just businesses. In the United Kingdom, the government commissioned a study that analyzed leadership styles in forty-two schools and discovered the styles that drove students' academic achievement.[8] In 69 percent of the high-performing schools, the school's headmaster exhibited four or more resonance-building leadership styles as needed. But in two-thirds of the low-performing schools, the head relied on just one or two leadership styles—typically dissonant ones. The hidden link was climate: When school leaders were flexible in their style repertoire—able to take a teacher aside for a one-on-one, or to articulate inspiring goals for the whole group, or to just listen, as needed—the climate among teachers was most positive. When the leader's style was rigid—stuck in the command-and-control mode—teachers were most demoralized.

The more of the six styles a leader can deploy, then, the better. Leaders who have mastered four or more, our data suggest—especially the resonance-building styles—foster the very best climate and business performance. Moreover, style switching was used both by seasoned veterans, who could explain exactly how and why they led, and by entrepreneurs who claimed they led by "gut" alone.

Consider how such fluid leadership looks in action.

## *Leading with Style—The Right One at the Right Time*

Joan, the general manager of a major division at a global food and beverage company, was appointed to her job while the division was in deep crisis. It hadn't made its profit targets for six years, most recently missing by $50 million. Morale among top management was miserable; mistrust and resentments were rampant. Joan's directive from above was clear: Turn the division around.

Joan did so with a nimbleness in switching among styles that we find marks the performance of star leaders. From the start, she realized she had a small window to demonstrate effective leadership and to establish rapport and trust—and that she urgently needed to learn about what wasn't working. During her first week on the job, therefore, she had lunch and dinner meetings one by one with each member of the management team. Joan sought each person's understanding of the current situation from a business and organizational standpoint. But her focus was not so much on how a given manager diagnosed the problems as on getting to know each as a person. Employing the affiliative style, she explored their lives, their dreams, and aspirations.

She also stepped into the coaching role, looking for ways she could help each get what they sought for his or her career. For instance, one manager who often received feedback that he was a poor team player confided his worries to her. He felt he was actually a good team member, but was plagued by persistent complaints that he knew he had to dispel if he were to succeed at the company. Recognizing that this was a talented executive and a valuable asset to the company, Joan made an agreement with him to point out ways he undermined his team abilities. She sensed that he could sometimes be abrasive, inadvertently saying something that would anger someone—and she promised she would take him aside after a meeting where she saw this happen, to help him get better at recognizing the behavior himself.

Joan then followed up these one-on-one meetings with a three-day offsite meeting for the management team. Her goal was team building, so that everyone would own whatever solution emerged for the business problems. Using an initial stance of the democratic leader, she encouraged everybody to express their frustrations and complaints freely in, as she put it, a "kind of cleansing of everything that's wrong."

The next day, Joan felt the group was ready to focus on solutions, and she asked each person to propose three specific ideas about what should be done. As Joan clustered the suggestions, a natural consensus emerged about priorities for the business, such as cutting costs. As the group came up with specific action plans for each priority, Joan got the commitment and buy-in she sought.

With that vision for the future in place, Joan shifted into the visionary style, assigning accountability for each follow-up step to specific executives and holding them responsible for their accomplishment. For example, the division had been dropping prices on products but getting no increase in volume; one obvious solution was to raise prices a bit. The previous vice president for sales had dithered, letting the problem fester; the new sales vice president now had specific responsibility to adjust the price points to fix the problem.

Over the following months, Joan continued to lead mainly with the visionary style, continually articulating the group's new mission in a way that reminded each person of how crucial he or she was to achieving it. Still, especially during the first few weeks when the plan was put in place, Joan felt that the urgency of the business crisis justified an occasional shift into the commanding style should someone fail to meet his or her responsibility. As she put it, "I had to be brutal about this follow-up on what we had to do. It was going to take discipline and focus."

Seven months later, when our research team interviewed Joan, the division was $5 million dollars ahead of its yearly profit target—up from lagging $50 million the year before Joan stepped in. It was the first time the division had met its target in five years.

## The Right Tools for the Job

How do you know when to apply which leadership style?

The most resonant leaders go beyond a mechanical process of matching their styles to fit a checklist of situations; they are far more fluid. They scan people individually and in groups, reading cues in the moment that tip them to the right leadership need, and they adjust their style on a dime. This means they can apply not just the four sure-fire resonance-building styles, but also be pace-setters or even exhibit the positive side of the commanding style—with strong, urgent direction—as appropriate. But when they lead through these more risky styles, they do so with the requisite dose of self-discipline so that they avoid creating dissonance by acting with anger or impatience or by giving in to the impulse to attack character. As a result, these leaders not only get performance results, but also build commitment and enthusiasm in those they lead.

Given the crucial importance for effective leadership of a wide repertoire of leadership styles, one immediate lesson applies to hiring, promotions, and succession planning. Simply put, when it comes to filling a leadership position, it pays to find someone who has the flexible repertoire of four or more styles that marks the most outstanding leader. Failing that, ask whether the person you're considering for a given leadership slot at least has mastered the specific style or styles that are most obviously salient to your business reality.

For example, a leader required for a turnaround needs the skills of a visionary—the ability to articulate a new vision that will drive change. If the position demands emergency steps, such as quick and radical surgery of incompetent people, the person will need to step into the commanding style for the time being— and then step out again. When the business need requires getting consensus from employees, building commitment, or just generating new ideas, the person will need to lead democratically. If what's required is simply guiding a highly competent and self-motivated team—say of lawyers or research pharmacologists— the leader's repertoire should include judicious use of the pacesetting style.

Whatever a leader's repertoire of styles today, it can grow wider tomorrow. The key lies in strengthening the underlying emotional intelligence abilities that drive a given style. Leadership *is* learnable—as we shall see in the next part of this book. The process is not easy. It takes time and, most of all, commitment. But the benefits that flow from leadership with a well-developed emotional intelligence, both for the individual and the organization, make it not only worthwhile but invigorating.

# PART TWO

# MAKING LEADERS

### CHAPTER SIX

# BECOMING A RESONANT LEADER

## The Five Discoveries

THE ENTIRE TOP TEAM of the retail chain was in flux—moving up, down, or out as the company struggled to reinvent itself. Not surprisingly, there was more than the usual amount of intrigue, political jostling, and even subterfuge. And Bill, the human resources manager, was smack in the middle of it, involving himself in every conversation and debate. He made sure he let everyone know what he thought—and thought that he knew—setting himself up as "the guy in the know."

Some of the top team went along with Bill's highly developed sense of self-importance, humoring him because it served their own purposes. Others just avoided him. Then, at one point in the middle of the transition debacle, the board asked a prominent, but coercive, executive committee member to step down—an upsetting event for the whole team. Bill responded by analyzing the situation ad nauseum with anyone who would listen. He cast aspersions and spread rumors. When his boss got wind of one of these conversations, he was heard to say ruefully, "Bill is ignorance on fire."

Yet neither that boss nor any other member of top management had ever taken Bill aside and offered him an honest assessment of his behavior—something that would have helped him begin to improve. Meanwhile, Bill saw himself as the "go-to guy" and a respected member of the team. Not knowing how to read his complex environment, let alone manage himself in it, Bill's lack of self-awareness was matched only by his spectacular deficit in political awareness and empathy.

How can a high-level leader like Bill be so out of touch with the truth about himself? It's more common than you would imagine. In fact, the higher up the ladder a leader climbs, the less accurate his self-assessment is likely to be. The problem is an acute lack of feedback, as was the case with Bill. Leaders have more trouble than anybody else when it comes to receiving candid feedback, particularly about how they're doing *as leaders*. More specifically—given the clear contribution of emotional intelligence to outstanding leadership—leaders need to know where they can improve on the EI competencies. Bill's spreading of rumors generated tension in the organization, while his excessive analysis was boring. A result was that people did not take him seriously.

The paradox, of course, is that the higher a leader's position in an organization, the more critically the leader needs that very kind of feedback.

## CEO Disease

"I so often feel I'm not getting the truth," the CEO of a European company told us. "I can never put my finger on it, because no one is actually lying to me. But I can sense that people are hiding information, or camouflaging key facts so I won't notice. They aren't lying, but neither are they telling me everything I need to know. I'm always second guessing."

This is a clear case of *CEO disease*: the information vacuum around a leader created when people withhold important (and usually unpleasant) information.[1] Why are leaders denied accurate information about vital matters? Sometimes the people who should provide the facts fear the leader's wrath—particularly when the leader's main style is commanding or pacesetting. Anyone delivering bad news to such a leader could be symbolically executed for being the messenger. Some offer the leader only positive information as a way of being a "good citizen" or team player—or for fear of seeming a blasphemous heretic if they spoke against the party line. Or they may just want to be seen as upbeat, and so they suppress negative facts.

Whatever the motives, the result is a leader who has only partial information about what's going on around him. This disease can be epidemic in an organization—not just among CEOs, but also for most high-level leaders. It is fed by the natural instinct to please the boss, resulting in a widespread tendency to give positive feedback and withhold the negative whenever information flows upward.

When it comes to leaders receiving helpful feedback specifically about their *own* performance, the problem worsens. It may take a small act of courage to confront the boss with bad news about the company, but you have to be even braver to let the boss know he's out of touch with how people are feeling, or that his "inspiring" talks fall flat.

Of course, many people—not just leaders—complain that they get too little useful performance feedback. But top executives typically get the least reliable information about how they are doing. For instance, an analysis of 177 separate studies that assessed more than 28,000 managers found that feedback on performance became less consistent the higher the manager's position or the more complex the manager's role.[2] The problem is compounded for leaders who are women or belong to a minority.[3] Women, in general, get even less useful feedback on their performance in any position—as a leader or otherwise—than do men. The same is true for members of visible minority groups, whether they be Chinese managers in Malaysia or Sikh executives in London.

People deprive their co-workers—whether bosses or subordinates—of honest performance feedback for several reasons, chief of which is that it can be uncomfortable to give such feedback. We're afraid of hurting others' feelings or otherwise upsetting them. Yet, while we tend to keep the truth about how others are actually doing to ourselves (oddly, not just the negatives, but also the positives), all of us generally crave that kind of appraisal. Candid evaluations matter deeply, in a way that other information does not.

### Can Everyone Be Better Than Average?

But what about the role of *self*-assessment in the CEO disease? Without a doubt, a leader's self-awareness and ability to accurately perceive his performance is as important as the feedback he receives from others. Yet therein lies perhaps the most pernicious strain of the illness: While most people tend to overestimate their own abilities to some extent, it's the very poorest performers who exaggerate their abilities the most.[4] This all-too-human foible can have great consequences, not just for leaders, but also for the companies they lead.

For instance, a study of CEOs of health services companies by Eric Harter, CEO of Health Care Partners in Lexington, Kentucky, found that self-awareness of leadership abilities was greatest for CEOs of the best-performing companies and poorest for CEOs of the worst performers.[5] Harter, a CEO with a scholarly bent, went to graduate school to research the qualities that separate the most effective executives in top positions from the least effective. He studied CEOs of health services companies that showed ten years of positive financial performance (measured by balance sheet results and return on equity) and compared them with their peers at companies with negative financial performance for many of the same ten years.

Focusing on levels of self-awareness, he compared the CEOs' own assessments of their performance on ten leadership abilities with assessments their subordinates made of the leaders on those same abilities (including, for example, self-confidence and empathy). Tellingly, the CEOs from the poorest-performing companies gave themselves the highest ratings on seven of the ten leadership abilities. But the pattern *reversed* when it came to how their subordinates rated them: They gave these CEOs low ratings on the very same abilities. On the other hand, subordinates saw the CEOs of the best-performing companies as demonstrating all ten of these leadership abilities most often.

Harter's data fit our own findings on 787 people, in positions ranging from low to high levels, in a wide variety of organizations.[6] When we analyzed the data by organizational level, a striking effect emerged: High-level executives and managers, compared with those in the lower rungs, were more likely to rate themselves more generously on twenty EI competencies than others rated those leaders on the same competencies. The higher leaders were in an organization, the greater the inflation rate— that is, the number of times they saw themselves as doing better on a competence than did those around them. A result of this misperception was that the gap between how the executives and managers saw themselves and how others saw them was greater for those higher in the organization. Those at the highest levels had the least accurate view of how they acted with others.

Clearly, then, seeking honest information on leadership capabilities can be vital to a leader's self-awareness and, therefore, his growth and effectiveness. So why don't more top leaders solicit and encourage accurate feedback? It isn't because they're monumentally vain or think they're infallible. Our conversations with leaders lead us to believe that it's often because they truly believe that they can't change. So even if they did receive good feedback about how their leadership styles affected the team or organization, and even if they saw the truth of that feedback, in their hearts they wouldn't believe that they could alter the way they've done things for so many years—in many cases for most of their lives. The parallel often appears with the people around the leader: If they believe the leader cannot truly change, then why go through the trouble of offering distasteful and awkward negative feedback? Yet we have seen evidence that points emphatically to the contrary: Old leaders *can* learn new tricks. Leaders can and do make significant, in some cases life-altering, changes in their styles that ripple into their teams and trigger important changes throughout the entire organization.

## Nurture over Nature

Nick Mimken had been the star at his insurance agency, consistently winning awards for his salesmanship. But when he was made the head of an agency in a new city, with twenty-five salespeople as direct reports, he wouldn't have won any awards for his leadership abilities. He could see that himself early on—and he knew he couldn't afford to make a mistake: His new agency was ranked in the bottom quartile of sales performance among his company's offices across the United States.

When leadership consultants McBer & Company, now the Hay Group, began working with him within a few months of starting his job, feedback from his subordinates revealed that Mimken's success as a salesman had translated into a pacesetting leadership style. He was relying on the same high-pressure drive to improve results that made him so good at sales. But in his new office, it was demotivating his salespeople. Worse yet, when stress increased and deadlines loomed, Mimken slipped into using a commanding style, telling people the sales targets they *should* have instead of setting realistic targets together. Meanwhile, the agency's atmosphere was growing increasingly tense.

As a first step, Mimken was encouraged to focus on his salespeople's performance, rather than on his own. That meant finding ways to help each of his reports develop themselves—in short, to use the coaching and visionary leadership styles. Fortunately, those styles draw on many of the abilities that Mimken already possessed—the same ones that had made him so effective as a salesman—such as empathy, self-management, and inspirational leadership. Now he needed to learn to use them to lead his staff.

Over time, he began to seize opportunities for one-on-one coaching sessions with his salespeople, which included ongoing dialogue about goals and performance. He worked at managing his impulse to jump in and take over when he got impatient with a salesperson's work, and he made sure that he balanced criticism with positive reinforcement. Accordingly, he found ways to couch the agency's goals in terms of values and a vision shared by all.

Eighteen months later, there were clear signs of progress. Evaluations from Mimken's subordinates showed that he had shifted his dominant styles from pacesetting and commanding to a coaching style, and he was beginning to develop the visionary style. Moreover, a survey showed that these shifts were paying off: Salespeople reported a dramatic increase in their feelings that rewards were fair and that work was motivating. They also had greater clarity about their priorities, thanks to Mimken's guidance.

Within three years, as Mimken continued to develop leadership strengths, his agency won the first of two consecutive national awards for growth, one of just eight awarded among the 100 agencies nationwide. Mimken was one of the youngest recipients of the award in the company's history. Within five years from the day that he walked into the office as the new manager, the agency had moved from the bottom to the top quartile in productivity.

We've seen stories such as Mimken's again and again (see the box "Leaders Are Made, Not Born"). They demonstrate not only that leaders *can* be made, but also that emotional intelligence can be learned—just as Mimken was able to learn and apply more resonant leadership styles.

Still, the question remains: Are some people simply born with certain levels of empathy or do they learn it? The answer is both. There is a genetic component to emotional intelligence, to be sure, but nurture plays a major role as well. Although people may differ in the initial level of their natural abilities, everyone can learn to improve, no matter where he or she starts out.

Sometimes it's just a question of building on skills one already has. For instance, where Mimken-the-salesman had been using empathy with his clients for years, Mimken-the-boss had the pacesetter's weakness for fixating on what his subordinates did wrong rather than on what they needed to do better. With practice, he dramatically increased his empathy with his salespeople so that they came to feel that he understood their needs. Mimken also mastered tools that buttressed the leadership styles he was developing. For instance, he became adept at constructing performance plans, and as he coached his salespeople to achieve them, they began to believe in his ability to help them succeed. What's more, Mimken's changes in the office carried over to his home life. His wife reported that he had become much more attuned to her and his family's needs.

Mimken's story illustrates another critical point: Not only can emotional intelligence be learned, but it also can be retained over the long term. Our research has shown that there are very specific steps for leaders to take to ensure such learning will last. We have tracked these leadership gains up to seven years beyond their initial development—past what is sometimes called the honeymoon effect.

### Beyond the Honeymoon Effect

We continually see the kind of learning that lasts—and its impact on business performance—that Mimken's story demonstrates. These are dramatic results compared with the all-too-familiar honeymoon effect of most training, where an immediate improvement fades almost entirely within three to six months. The familiar cycle goes something like this: A person leaves the program enthusiastic and committed to improving. But, back in the office, dozens of e-mails, letters, and calls await him. The boss and a subordinate have each called with an emergency, and he is sucked into the swamp of demands. All of the new learning slips away as old, knee-jerk responses take over. Soon he is acting the way he always has—not the new way committed to at the end of the training. The honeymoon has come to an abrupt end.

Human resource professionals have been frustrated by this phenomenon for decades. They've watched again and again how people emerge from training enthusiastic, only to have their good intentions atrophy over time. Although studies have shown that real change can result from training, most of the time the change doesn't seem to be sustained, which is why it is often called the honeymoon effect.[7] Considering the more than $60 billion dollars spent in North America alone on training, this is a sobering observation.

Possibly because of this widespread belief that the effects of training don't last, there have been relatively few studies of the impact of training on people's behavior.[8] Of the few studies examining the improvement in the way people act, even fewer have tested people before and after the training or compared these effects with the behavior of people not going through the training.[9]

There are exceptions. It has been shown that we can create improvements in a person's presentation and communication skills. One study of sales branch managers showed a 37 percent improvement in effective communication skills one week following training.[10] But we cannot infer sustainable change from one week.

When a broader array of self-management and relationship management skills that represent the emotional intelligence competencies discussed in this book are examined, training programs typically have a less dramatic impact.[11] Studies of this broad array of EI skills find about a 10 percent improvement measured between three months and a year and a half after training.[12] With so much money and effort invested, why are the results so meager?

When it comes to building leadership skills that last, motivation and how a person feels about learning matters immensely. People learn what they want to learn. If learning is forced on us, even if we master it temporarily (for instance, by studying for a test), it is soon forgotten. That may be why one study found that the half-life of knowledge learned in an MBA course was about six weeks.[13] So when a company requires people to go through a one-size-fits-all leadership development program, participants may simply go through the motions—unless they truly want to learn.

## LEADERS ARE MADE, NOT BORN

➤ *He had just come to America, and, as a 13-year-old in a new school, was eager to fit in and be liked. So he joined the lacrosse team. A fair—but not great—lacrosse player, he decided that, rather than play on the team himself, he'd coach the new players in learning the game. That was the first time he became aware of what's involved in helping others develop their abilities. Then, at 24, in his first job after college, he was made head of a sales team. He had to learn the ropes himself—no one showed him how to make a sales call. But once he got the hang of it, he started taking his team members on demo calls to help hone their abilities. Later, when he joined a pharmaceutical firm, he was so good at teaching that he was asked to make a video to be used for sales training. By the time he became a manager, he'd become a master at developing people.*

➤ *In college, as a member of an international business club, the young woman saw that many members' objectives were at odds with those of the club—and she found a way to get everyone to buy into a common goal. Later, in her first job after college as a lone sales rep, she had to create a virtual team with other reps by phone and e-mail—and so learned how to motivate people to cooperate. Then, when she became a team leader, she learned about building team spirit from a direct report who had a knack for finding ways to recognize members' contributions. Finally, as part of a cross-functional top leadership team, her mastery at paving the way for smooth consensus was apparent in the way she would seek out and talk to key stakeholders before major decisions were to be made.*

IN BROAD STROKES, these two tales illustrate how many top-performing leaders naturally master the EI competencies that make them so effective. The sales manager and the team leader were two of nine outstanding executives studied by a research team at Johnson & Johnson, led by Matthew Mangino and Christine

Dreyfus, to find out how people become masters of the building blocks of leadership.[14] The same pattern emerged over and over: Leaders' first awareness of a competence came in late childhood or adolescence; then, in their first jobs, or when some other radical transition made it crucial for survival, they used the competence more purposefully. As the years went by, and as they continued to practice the skill, they became increasingly better at it; there were distinct moments when they first used these competencies and used them regularly. The progression from a person's first awareness of a competence to the point of mastery—in other words, being able to use the competence regularly and effectively—offers a fine-grained look at how leadership excellence develops in life. Although it may seem that the leaders in our examples were "born" because they acquired leadership strengths tacitly and mostly invisibly, neither was born knowing how to lead a team or develop strengths in others. They learned how. Great leaders, the research shows, are *made* as they gradually acquire, in the course of their lives and careers, the competencies that make them so effective. The competencies can be learned by any leader, at any point.

The challenge of mastering leadership is a skill like any other, such as improving your golf game or learning to play slide guitar. Anyone who has the will and motivation can get better at leading, once he understands the steps.

Indeed, in analysis of data from the ECI, we find that over the course of a career, people tend naturally to develop more strength in EI competencies—they get better with age.[15] This shows up not just in better self-evaluations as people get older, but—more convincingly—in others' evaluations of them, which also improve over time.

But beware: That general trend toward improvement by no means guarantees that all leaders will naturally develop the EI competencies to the levels they need, when they need them. That's why a solid diagnosis of a given leader's strengths and weaknesses—and a plan for development—remains crucial.

In fact, a well-established principle of behavior change tells us that when a person has been forced to change, the change will vanish once the browbeating ends.[16]

The good news is that, even though many leadership programs lose their impact over time, if leadership building follows the right basic principles, improvements can last. Pacesetters can reform themselves, cultivating abilities as coaches and visionary leaders. Greater empathy can be built—and remain. What this requires is intentional effort, motivation, and an emotional commitment from participants.

What's more, we even know how that kind of learning occurs in the brain.

### How the Brain Matters

Emotional intelligence, as we saw in chapters 2 and 3, involves circuitry that runs between the brain's executive centers in the prefrontal lobes and the brain's limbic system, which governs feelings, impulses, and drives. Skills based in the limbic areas, research shows, are best learned through motivation, extended practice, and feedback.[17] Compare that kind of learning with what goes on in the neocortex, which governs analytical and technical ability. The neocortex grasps concepts quickly, placing them within an expanding network of associations and comprehension. This part of the brain, for instance, can figure out from reading a book how to use a computer program, or the basics of making a sales call. When learning technical or analytic skills, the neocortex operates with magnificent efficiency.

The problem is that most training programs for enhancing emotional intelligence abilities, such as leadership, target the neocortex rather than the limbic brain. Thus, learning is limited and sometimes can even have a negative impact. Under a microscope, the limbic areas—the emotional brain—have a more primitive organization of brain cells than do those in the neocortex, the thinking brain. The design of the neocortex makes it a highly efficient learning machine, expanding our understanding by linking new ideas or facts to an extensive cognitive network. This associative mode of learning takes place with extraordinary rapidity: The thinking brain can comprehend something after a single hearing or reading.

The limbic brain, on the other hand, is a much slower learner —particularly when the challenge is to relearn deeply ingrained habits. This difference matters immensely when trying to improve leadership skills: At their most basic level, those skills come down to habits learned early in life. If those habits are no longer sufficient, or hold a person back, learning takes longer. Reeducating the emotional brain for leadership learning, therefore, requires a different model from what works for the thinking brain: It needs lots of practice and repetition.

If the right model is used, training can actually alter the brain centers that regulate negative and positive emotions—the links between the amygdala and the prefrontal lobes. For example, researchers at the University of Wisconsin taught "mindfulness" to R&D scientists at a biotech firm who were complaining about the stressful pace of their jobs.[18] Mindfulness is a skill that helps people keenly focus on the present moment and drop distracting thoughts (such as worries) rather than getting lost in them, thus producing a calming effect. After just eight weeks, the R&D people reported noticeably less stress, and they felt more creative and enthusiastic about their work. But most remarkably, their brains had shifted toward less activity in the right prefrontal areas (which generate distressing emotions) and move in the left—the brain's center for upbeat, optimistic feelings.

These findings—and many more like them—belie the popular belief that starting early in adulthood, neural connections inevitably atrophy and cannot be replaced (and the corollary belief that as adults, it's too late to change our fundamental personal skills). Neurological research has shown quite the opposite. Human brains *can* create new neural tissue as well as new neural connections and pathways throughout adulthood. For example, researchers have found that London taxi drivers, famous for their navigational feats in a maze of one-way streets and clock-stopping traffic, show brain plasticity as they learn their trade. Over their years of driving through London, the part of the brain that handles spatial relationships (i.e., how to navigate) grows in size and strength of activity.[19] At any point in life, neural connections used over and over become stronger, while those not used weaken.[20]

Clearly, then, the act of learning is the key to stimulating new neural connections.[21] When it comes to developing leadership, it takes an emotionally intelligent approach to create these neural changes: one that works directly on the emotional centers. As scientists have concluded, "When a limbic connection has established a neural pattern, it takes a limbic connection to revise it."[22]

The original window of opportunity for learning effective leadership abilities extends through adolescence into the early twenties. During this period, the brain—the last organ of the body to develop anatomically—continues to lay down the original circuitry for emotional habits. Young people who work at mastering a discipline of any kind or who are members of teams or who have the chance to hone public speaking skills are laying down a neuronal scaffold that, later in life, will offer crucial support for leadership. This early learning will support competencies such as self-control and the drive to achieve, collaboration, and persuasion.

If people lack the previous experiences that allow them to master a given leadership competence, however, it is still not too late—but it requires motivation. The brain's ability to sprout fresh connections continues throughout life. It just takes more effort and energy to learn in adulthood lessons that would have come more readily in our early years, because these new lessons fight an uphill battle against the ingrained patterns the brain already has in place. The task is doubled—we have to undo habits that do not work for us, and replace them with new ones that do. That's why motivation becomes crucial for leadership development: We have to work harder and longer to change a habit than when we learned it in the first place. Building emotional intelligence happens only with sincere desire and concerted effort. A brief seminar won't help, and it can't be learned through a how-to manual. Because the limbic brain learns more slowly—and requires much more practice—than the neocortex, it takes more effort to strengthen an ability such as empathy than, say, to become adept at risk analysis. But it can be done.

### Sustainable Learning: The Evidence

Because the kind of limbic-brain learning we've just described takes more time and practice, it's also much more likely to be retained. So people not only *can* improve on the emotional intelligence competencies, but also can sustain those gains for years, as data from a unique series of longitudinal studies still under way at the Weatherhead School of Management at Case Western Reserve University have already shown. The studies, conducted with students since 1990 as part of a required course on competence building,[23] allow students to assess their emotional intelligence competencies (as well as some cognitive ones), choose which competencies they wish to strengthen, and be guided by an individualized learning plan to strengthen the targeted skills. Objective assessments of students at the beginning of the course, again at graduation, and again years later in their jobs have allowed a unique opportunity to gauge the long-term power of this approach to leadership development.[24]

The results have been impressive. In contrast to the honeymoon effect of most leadership development programs, the gains lasted years for these MBA students. Up to two years after going through the change process, they still showed 47 percent improvement on self-awareness competencies such as self-confidence, and on self-management competencies such as adaptability and the drive to achieve. When it came to social awareness and relationship management skills, improvements were even greater: 75 percent for competencies such as empathy and team leadership.

These gains are also in stark contrast to results from standard MBA programs, where there is little to no attempt to enhance emotional intelligence abilities. The best data here come from a research committee of the American Assembly of Collegiate Schools of Business.[25] In its study of two highly ranked business schools, it found that, compared with when they began their MBA programs, graduating students showed improvements of only 2 percent in emotional intelligence skills. In fact, when students from four other high-ranking MBA programs were assessed on a more thorough range of tests, they showed a gain of 4 percent in self-awareness and self-management abilities but a *decrease* of 3 percent in social awareness and relationship management (see the figure).[26]

Looking again at the Weatherhead study, gains in emotional intelligence were also found in part-time MBA students, who typically take three to five years to graduate. By the end of their program, these groups showed 67 percent improvement in self-awareness and self-management competencies and 40 percent improvement in social awareness and relationship management competencies. But even two years after these part-timers had graduated (which was between five and seven years since they had taken the courses), Jane Wheeler, a professor at Bowling Green State University, found that the gains continued: 63 percent showed improvement on the self-awareness and self-management competencies, and 45 percent had improved on the social awareness and relationship management competencies.

Among full-time MBA students, the improvements documented in these studies showed up across the spectrum of all fourteen emotional intelligence competencies assessed. There was not a single competence in which students were not able to improve, provided they targeted it in their learning plans.[27]

These remarkable results are the first to demonstrate gains sustained over many years in the emotional intelligence building blocks of resonant leadership. They are hopeful in light of the 10 percent improvements shown from training programs over the one to two years in which the results were tracked, or the 2 percent improvement in emotional intelligence competencies shown from typical MBA programs. But there was yet another, unexpected, bonus that Jane Wheeler found in her data: Five to seven years after the original course, people were showing improvements on *additional* competencies, not just those on which they'd already

## Percentage Improvement of Emotional Intelligence

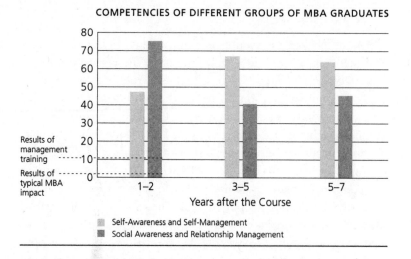

COMPETENCIES OF DIFFERENT GROUPS OF MBA GRADUATES

Results of management training

Results of typical MBA impact

Years after the Course

■ Self-Awareness and Self-Management
■ Social Awareness and Relationship Management

improved after three to five years. In other words, once they'd learned *how* to improve the emotional intelligence abilities that make leaders great, they continued developing new strengths on their own. That finding provides solid evidence that these competencies can continue to be acquired throughout life.

More evidence of this kind of lifelong learning comes from a study done with senior executives in the Professional Fellows Program at Case Western Weatherhead School of Management. The program, designed for experienced executives and advanced professionals (with an average entering age of 48, versus 27 for MBA students), attracts top executives, lawyers, and physicians who want to hone their business and leadership skills. In longitudinal studies of these senior executives up to three years after the program, improvement was found on two-thirds of emotional intelligence competencies.[28]

Clearly, then, leaders can be made more effective—if they are offered the right tools for learning. Such deep learning, however, goes even beyond using the right tools. It is a process that isn't necessarily linear and smooth; rather, it is a journey full of surprises and moments of epiphany.

## A Wake-up Call

As he clicked his mouse on Send, Nolan Taylor realized he had just sent a scathing e-mail criticizing the company's recent announcement of layoffs—and his boss's role in it—not to his friend in another division, as he'd intended, but *to his boss*. Yet even as he was trying to think of ways he could somehow retrieve the message before his boss read it, the larger issue that this e-mail represented struck him. It was a shocking moment of awakening: He realized that he was not acting like the person he wanted to be.

For years, Nolan Taylor had vowed to control his outbursts and find ways to increase his self-control. The shock of such a glaring misstep, and its possible consequences, resulted in a different, much stronger commitment to his goal. He wanted to increase his optimism and to see the positive possibilities in daunting situations without resorting immediately to cynicism and criticism of others. With that sent e-mail, he had to confront a *discontinuity*—the glaring gap between his ideal self and the reality. And in that moment he committed himself to changing.

Such discontinuities can lead to powerful change, even in the natural world. Complexity, or chaos, theory states that many processes are better described as abrupt changes rather than as smooth transitions. An earthquake, for example, occurs as a sudden fracture of the earth, even though the pressure beneath the earth's surface may have built over time.

Likewise, in building leadership, sudden, shocking discoveries about our lives may shake us into action, "wowing" us with a stark truth about ourselves and offering new clarity about our lives. Such startling discontinuities can be frightening or enlightening. Some people react by running from them. Some simply deny their power and shrug them off. Others hear the wake-up call, sharpen their resolve, and start to transform self-defeating habits into new strengths. But how do they actually make those changes?

# Self-Directed Learning

The crux of leadership development that works is *self-directed learning*: intentionally developing or strengthening an aspect of who you are or who you want to be, or both. This requires first getting a strong image of your *ideal self*, as well as an accurate picture of your *real self*—who you are now. Such self-directed learning is most effective and sustainable when you understand the process of change—and the steps to achieve it—as you go through it.

This model of learning was developed by Richard Boyatzis during three decades of work in leadership development, both as a consultant to organizations and as an academic researcher.[29] The figure below outlines the process of self-directed learning.[30]

## *The Five Discoveries*

Self-directed learning involves five discoveries, each representing a discontinuity. The goal, of course, is to use each discovery as a tool for making the changes needed to become an emotionally intelligent leader on the eighteen EI leadership competencies reviewed earlier in this book (see the chart in chapter 3).

This kind of learning is recursive: The steps do not unfold in a smooth, orderly way, but rather follow a sequence, with each step demanding different amounts of time and effort. The results of practicing new habits over time are that they become part of your new real self. Often, with changes in your habits, EI, and leadership styles, come changes in your aspirations and dreams, your ideal self. And so the cycle continues—a lifelong process of growth and adaptation.

When you go through the discovery of uncovering an ideal vision of yourself, you feel motivated to develop your leadership abilities. That is, you see the person you want to be. Whether this vision actually comes to you in a dream, through getting in touch with the values and commitments that guide your life, or through

Boyatzis's Theory of Self-Directed Learning

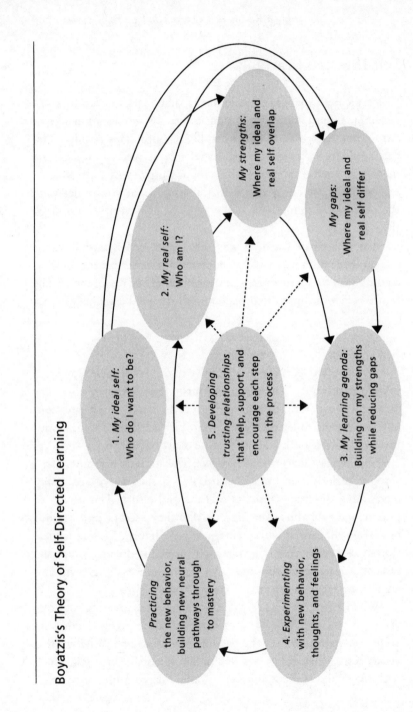

simple reflection, the image is powerful enough to evoke your passion and hope. It becomes the fuel that maintains the drive you need to work at the difficult and often frustrating process of change.

The second discovery is akin to looking into a mirror to discover who you actually are now—how you act, how others view you, and what your deep beliefs comprise. Some of these observations will be consistent with your ideal self, and can be considered strengths; others will represent gaps between who you are and who you want to be. This realization of your strengths and gaps prepares the way for changing your leadership style. This is the antidote to the CEO disease we described earlier.

But for that change to succeed, you'll need to develop an agenda for improving your abilities, which is the third discovery. A plan of action needs to be constructed that provides detailed guidance on what new things to try each day, building on your strengths and moving you closer to your ideal. The plan should feel intrinsically satisfying, fitting your learning preferences as well as the realities of your life and work.

The fourth discovery comes in practicing new leadership skills.

The fifth discovery may occur at any point in the process. It is that *you need others* to identify your ideal self or find your real self, to discover your strengths and gaps, to develop an agenda for the future, and to experiment and practice. Leadership development can only occur in the tumult and possibilities of our relationships. Others help us see things we are missing, affirm whatever progress we have made, test our perceptions, and let us know how we are doing. They provide the context for experimentation and practice. Although the model is called a self-directed learning process, it actually cannot be done alone. Without others' involvement, lasting change can't occur.

To summarize the process, people who successfully change in sustainable ways cycle through the following stages:

- *The first discovery:* My ideal self—Who do I want to be?
- *The second discovery:* My real self—Who am I? What are my strengths and gaps?

- *The third discovery:* My learning agenda—How can I build on my strengths while reducing my gaps?
- *The fourth discovery:* Experimenting with and practicing new behaviors, thoughts, and feelings to the point of mastery.
- *The fifth discovery:* Developing supportive and trusting relationships that make change possible.

Ideally, the progression occurs through a discontinuity—a moment of discovery—that provokes not just awareness, but also a sense of urgency. The following chapters explore each of these discoveries and their corollary processes that enable leadership mastery.

### CHAPTER SEVEN

# THE MOTIVATION TO CHANGE

A BDINASIR ALI was about to discover his dream. A hydrogeologist for the last eight years at an integrated-energy multinational in the United States, Ali appeared on the surface to be a mild-mannered employee and a steady provider for his family. But Ali was a man with a plan—although it was one he'd always intended to defer until retirement.

Raised as one of twenty-five siblings in Mandera, northern Kenya, Ali had come to the United States so that he could raise his children with the benefits of better education and medical care. But once the children were grown and he had retired, he hoped to return to Kenya with his wife to educate people about water management and to help drill water wells in his village—something that his country seriously needed.

It was a hope that had developed when, as a child, Ali witnessed long periods of drought in his native village, located in an arid region near the border of Ethiopia and Somalia. During one especially severe drought, he remembers seeing hundreds of cattle, goats, and camels die; his family, accustomed to a diet of meat and milk, had to survive on grain. In more recent years, the lack of water had also severely affected Mandera's irrigation projects and the flow of electricity from Kenya's hydroelectric dams.

Now, at 40, Ali's dream to help his native village in Kenya was still at least two decades away. And although he valued his job and the benefits he received working for a large multinational, he was feeling restless. One conversation was about to change all of that.

"Why wait, Ali?" asked his executive coach.

When Ali answered that he wasn't prepared to give up the benefits he enjoyed working for a multinational, his coach asked: "Do any multinationals have water-management operations in Kenya or East Africa?" When Ali replied that none did, he was pressed further: Had he considered asking his company—or another one—to organize a subsidiary to develop water-resource management in Eastern Africa? Ali said that it was such an expensive proposition, he'd never dare ask.

"Suppose," said the coach, "that you framed it as a way for the company to give back to the community and region."

At that suggestion, Ali fell silent. Slowly, a wave of recognition spread across his face, as if a light had just been turned on in a dark room. He nodded his head, leaned back in his chair, and smiled. And he began to articulate, fluidly and in minute detail, the strategic advantages that a project in water-resource management would present his company. He realized that he could tap into his company's existing Global Social Initiative project to realize his dream. He spoke with such passion, it was as if he were giving a speech before an enthralled audience. Ali had connected with his dream, and in that instant it became a larger dream than he had ever considered.

That was a first critical discovery for Ali: the moment when change began. He had gotten in touch with his passion, and he suddenly felt motivated to pursue his dream as he never had before. Where once Ali could see only a single path to his vision—which was to work hard until he saved enough money to retire—he now saw many paths, with many possibilities.

In the ensuing discussion, Ali saw how his emotional intelligence capabilities could help make his vision happen—particularly his strengths in social awareness and relationship management. He'd always worked well with others and enjoyed collaboration. As a former engineer, he'd developed many of the self-management competencies, although he had some difficulty with self-confidence and adaptability.

To bring his dream to life, Ali knew he would have to act as a change catalyst, a visionary who could drive home to company executives the advantages of a water-resource management operation in his company. That meant working on his self-confidence. And to promote a new strategy among his fellow managers and arouse their innovative spirit, he would have to become more flexible himself. As Ali's dream became more specific, it also expanded in a way that his confidence level hadn't previously allowed: Instead of helping only his village, he could have an impact on Kenya and that entire region of East Africa.

It had taken only a few moments for Ali to reenvision his life's work. His excitement and hope about the future were palpable— he'd found a new sense of his ideal self, of what he could become. Within a week, Ali reported that he'd made headway at his company with his new idea, and more quickly than he'd ever thought possible. While this new role would certainly require him to acquire new EI competencies, he had made the all-important first step of envisioning his ideal self.

## The First Discovery: The Ideal Self—Where Change Begins

Connecting with one's dreams releases one's passion, energy, and excitement about life. In leaders, such passion can arouse enthusiasm in those they lead. The key is uncovering your ideal self—the person you would *like* to be, including what you want in your life and work. That is the "first discovery" of the self-directed learning process mentioned in the last chapter. Developing that ideal image requires a reach deep inside to one's gut level. You know you have touched it when, like Ali, you feel suddenly passionate about the possibilities your life holds.

To begin—or sustain—real development in emotional intelligence, you must first engage that power of your ideal self. There's a simple reason: Changing habits is hard work. One need only think back to one's successes or failures with New Year's resolutions to find ample evidence of this. Whenever people try to change habits of how they think and act, they must reverse decades of learning that resides in heavily traveled, highly reinforced neural circuitry, built up over years of repeating that habit. That's why making lasting change requires a strong commitment to a future vision of oneself—especially during stressful times or amid growing responsibilities.

## YOU, FIFTEEN YEARS FROM NOW

THINK ABOUT where you would be sitting and reading this book if it were fifteen years from now and you were living your *ideal* life. What kinds of people would be around you? What does your environment look and feel like? What might you be doing during a typical day or week? Don't worry about the feasibility of creating this kind of ideal life. Just let the image develop, and place yourself in the picture.

Try doing some "free writing" around this vision of yourself fifteen years from now, or else speak your vision into a tape recorder or talk about it with a trusted friend. When doing this exercise, many people report that they experience a release of energy, feeling more optimistic than they had even moments earlier. This kind of envisioning of an ideal future can be a powerful way to connect with the real possibilities for change in our lives.

In fact, the very act of contemplating change can fill people with worries about perceived obstacles. Sometimes after people have experienced that initial feeling of excitement about their ideal futures, they immediately lose it again, frustrated because they aren't already living that dream today. That's when remembering the brain's role in feelings can help. As discussed in chapter 2, it's the activation of the left prefrontal cortex that gives us a motivating hope, by letting us imagine how great we'll feel the day we reach the goal of our ideal. That's what spurs us on, despite obstacles.

Conversely, if we fixate on what's in our way—rather than on the powerful image of our ideal life—we presumably activate the right prefrontal area and are plunged into a pessimistic view that demotivates us and can actually hinder our success.

## The "Ought" versus the Ideal

In *The Hungry Spirit: Beyond Capitalism, A Quest for Purpose in the Modern World*, Charles Handy describes the difficulty of connecting with his ideal self:

> *I spent the early part of my life trying hard to be someone else. At school I wanted to be a great athlete, at university an admired socialite, afterwards a businessman and, later, the head of a great institution. It did not take me long to discover that I was not destined to be successful in any of these guises, but that did not prevent me from trying, and being perpetually disappointed with myself.*
>
> *The problem was that in trying to be someone else, I neglected to concentrate on the person I could be. That idea was too frightening to contemplate at the time. I was happier going along with the conventions of the time, measuring success in terms of money and position, climbing ladders which others placed in my way, collecting things and contacts rather than giving expression to my own beliefs and personality.[1]*

That illuminating confession comes from a person who was quite successful as an executive in industry, a leader in the London Business School, Chairman of the Royal Society of the Arts, and influential worldwide as an author and professor. But like Charles Handy, over the course of a busy life many people become seduced by the idea of power or fame, or succumb to the expectations of others.

When a parent, spouse, boss, or teacher tells us what we should be, they're giving us *their* version of our ideal self, an image that contributes to our *ought self*—the person we think we should become. When we accept that ought self, it becomes a box within which we are trapped—what sociologist Max Weber called our "iron cage"—moving around like a mime pressing against invisible walls. The same effect occurs when, in organizations, the assumption is that people want to get ahead by moving "up" a career ladder at work, rather than acknowledging that individuals might have their own dreams and definitions of success. Those kinds of assumptions can easily become elements of the work *ought self*.

Over time, people may become anesthetized to their ideal selves; their vision becomes fuzzy, and they lose sight of their dreams. Pressure from responsibilities of a mortgage, paying for the children's college, and the desire to maintain a certain lifestyle can push people ahead on a path, regardless of whether they believe that path will help them reach their dreams. They become numb to their passion, and settle for more of what they currently are doing. The classic example—seen in many professionals who have grown up in highly traditional cultures—is the person who follows a given career simply because his parents said he should. One man we know from India grew up in such a family; he had an intense passion for music, but dutifully followed his family's wishes that he become a dentist, like his father had. Eventually, he ended up leaving his practice in Mumbai, moving to New York, and earning a living—quite happily—as a sitar player.

It can be all too easy to confuse the ought with the ideal self and to act in ways that are not authentic. That's why, in leadership development processes, taking the step to uncover one's ideal self is so important. But many such programs are based on the assumption that an individual simply wants to maximize his performance at work. They skip that vital exploration and neglect to link individuals' learning goals with their dreams and aspirations for the future. When the gap between a person's ideal self and the ideal imposed by the training becomes evident, the result is apathy or rebellion.[2]

## No Vision, No Passion

Sofia, a senior manager at a telecom in northern Europe, knew she needed to develop leadership abilities. She had taken seminars, read books, and worked with mentors. She'd written development plans and set short-term and long-term goals. She knew what she needed to do—but none of those plans ever seemed to guide her development, and after a few weeks were inevitably relegated to the bottom of her desk drawer. "Don't misunderstand," she told us. "I want to succeed in my career. But none of those career plans had much to do with what I really care about. Developing this competency or that one, solely because the job calls for it, isn't enough to keep me motivated."

Sofia's experience is typical of many graduates of leadership development programs. The problem is that many of those programs begin with the wrong assumptions. Real leadership development starts from a much broader place than "career planning": It begins with a holistic vision of one's life, in all its richness. To achieve improved business performance, leaders need to be emotionally engaged in their self-development. And that requires connecting the effort to what really matters to them.

We asked Sofia, therefore, to think about her life at a specific point in the future, to let go and imagine what a typical day would be like: what she would be doing, where she would live, who was there, and how it felt. Then we asked her to pick a date eight to ten years from now—far enough so that life would be different, but close enough to begin to imagine. Sofia chose a date in August of 2007, meaningful to her because her eldest child would be leaving to attend university that year. Sofia then wrote a vision of her life in August, 2007, in the first person, as if it were today. We asked her to consciously consider all of the areas of her life, her values, and her dreams about what she wanted to do and be by that time in her life. Her vision was compelling:

> *I picture myself leading my own company, a tight-knit enterprise staffed by ten colleagues. I'm enjoying a healthy, open relationship with my daughter, and similarly trusting relationships with my friends and co-workers. I see myself as relaxed and happy as a leader and parent, and loving and empowering to all those around me.*

By reflecting on a vision of her life in such a holistic way, Sofia began to see how the various parts of her life intersected, and how crafting a plan to make this dream a reality could be not only motivating but inspiring. As Sofia said at the end of this process: "For years, I've needed to work on how I deal with people when I'm under stress. I can be too much of a pacesetting leader at work. Now, looking at the whole picture, I see that some of my struggles with my daughter stem from the same set of problems." Sofia was then able to begin thinking about how to translate those insights into development goals for dealing with stress using more productive styles.

We find that many young leaders, roughly defined as those under 40, have learning goals that are more holistic—addressing many aspects of their lives rather than just their work—than was the case in previous generations of leaders. In part this shift reflects the fact that, as surveys of Generations X and Y suggest, people in their 20s and 30s have a more balanced view of life and work than was seen in previous generations. Not willing to make some of the sacrifices that they watched their parents make, they are seeking a balanced life along the way. They're not waiting for a heart attack, divorce, or job loss to wake them up to their relationships, spiritual life, community responsibility, and physical health. Many of their older colleagues are coming to the same conclusions, but for them it is part of aging, midlife, and midcareer crises.

*Philosophy: How People Determine Value*

Clearly, values play an important role in uncovering the ideal self. Since values change throughout life, related to events such as marriage, the birth of a child, or being fired, it is one's underlying philosophy that's more enduring.[3] A person's philosophy is the *way* he determines values—and which leadership styles he gravitates toward. A leader who values achieving goals above all else will

---

## MY GUIDING PRINCIPLES

THINK ABOUT the different arenas of your life that are important, such as family, relationships, work, spirituality, physical health. What are your core values in each of those areas? List five or six principles that guide you in your work and life—and think about whether they are values that you truly live by or simply talk about. Now try writing a page or two about what you would like to do with the rest of your life. Or, you might want to number a sheet of paper 1 through 27 and then list all of the things you want to do or experience before you die. Don't worry about priorities or practicality—just write down whatever comes to you.

This exercise is harder than it may seem, because it's human nature to think more in terms of what one *has* to do—by tomorrow, next week, next month. But that short horizon focuses only on what's urgent—not on what's important. When people think in terms of the extended horizon, such as what might be done before dying, they open themselves up to a new range of possibilities. In our work with leaders who do this exercise, we've seen a surprising trend: Most people list a few career goals, but 80 percent or more of their lists have nothing to do with work. When they finish the exercise and begin to study their writing, they see patterns that help them begin to crystallize what their real dreams and aspirations are.

---

naturally be a pacesetter, viewing a more democratic style as a waste of time. Understanding your operating philosophy can help you see how your ideal self reflects your values.

For example, a consultant lists "family" as a dominant value, but still spends five days a week away from his wife and two children, traveling for his job. He says he's enacting his value by providing enough money for his family's needs. By contrast, a manufacturing manager who also lists "family" as his dominant value has turned down promotions so he can have dinner each night with his wife and children.

The difference between those two men might be in how aware they are of their true values, how aligned their actions are with those values, or in the way they *interpret* the value. Accordingly, they reveal deep differences in how they value people, organizations, and activities. Such differences may reflect disparate operating philosophies—the most common of which are pragmatic, intellectual, and humanistic.[4] And although no philosophy is "better" than another, each drives a person's actions, thoughts, and feelings in distinctive ways.

The central theme of a pragmatic philosophy is a belief that *usefulness* determines the worth of an idea, effort, person, or organization.[5] People with this philosophy believe that they are largely responsible for the events of their lives, and often measure things to assess their value. No surprise, then, that among the emotional intelligence competencies, pragmatics rank high in self-management. Unfortunately, their individualistic orientation often —but not always—pulls them into using a pacesetting style over a democratic, coaching, or affiliative style.

Take Larry Ellison, the pacesetting CEO at Oracle Corporation. In his relentless pursuit of market share, he commonly challenges employees to "destroy" and "eliminate" rivals from the marketplace. He also constantly benchmarks the company's progress against competitors, displaying his pragmatic philosophy in the abundance of such comparisons that he cites in his speeches and interviews.[6]

The central theme of an intellectual philosophy is the desire to understand people, things, and the world by constructing an image of how they work, thereby providing some emotional security in predicting the future.[7] People with this philosophy rely on logic in making decisions, and assess the worth of something against an underlying code or set of guidelines that stresses reason. People with this outlook rely heavily on cognitive competencies, sometimes to the exclusion of social competencies. You might hear someone with an intellectual philosophy say, for example, "If you have an elegant solution, others will believe it. No need to try to convince them about its merits." They can use a visionary leadership style, if the vision describes a well-reasoned future.

John Chambers, the CEO of Cisco Systems, reflects an intellectual outlook when he describes a future of living better through technology. He talks, for example, of how integrated electronic systems will adjust the temperature of clothes when people walk from a heated home to a car in winter. Often sounding like a Bible-thumping preacher, he speaks openly of his belief that his company can create this model of the future, thereby allowing everyone to contribute to a better society.[8]

The central theme of a humanistic philosophy is that close, personal relationships give meaning to life.[9] People with this philosophy are committed to human values; family and close friends are seen as more important than other relationships. They assess the worth of an activity in terms of how it affects their close relations. Similarly, loyalty is valued over mastery of a job or skill. Where a pragmatist's philosophy might lead him to "sacrifice the few for the many," a humanistic leader would view each person's life as important, naturally cultivating the social awareness and relationship management competencies. Accordingly, humanistic leaders gravitate toward styles that emphasize interaction with others, such as democratic, affiliative, or coaching.

For example, Narayana Murthy is the inspirational CEO who founded Infosys Technologies Limited, headquartered in Bangalore, India. Part of his vision lies in fully engaging people in their work, using a democratic leadership style. As a result, he's made Infosys one of the most desirable companies in which to work in the customized software development and maintenance field. Indeed, Murthy describes himself as "a capitalist in my mind, but a socialist in my heart."[10]

## The Ever-Changing Ideal

People's dreams and aspirations change as their career unfolds, reshaping what they consider important in life and work; likewise, the ideal self becomes more protean as life goes on. These changes not only determine which of their talents or competencies people are willing to use, but also where they feel most engaged in using them and where they can create resonance. Sometimes people can stray from their calling by just continuing to do the same thing, ignoring changes in their dreams and what is important to them.

That's why one often sees leaders in middle age jump ship to start another career. When leaders reach a point in their career where they feel mastery, having completed most of their career goals, they can lose enthusiasm for what they've been doing. Often at that point such leaders find renewed energy in a new ideal— for example, by giving back to others. Peter Lynch was such a leader. When he was at the peak of his game, head of the dramatically successful Fidelity Magellan Fund, Lynch announced that he was leaving Fidelity—not to take over a company, but to create a philanthropic fund with his wife. He said he wanted to "do good" since he had "done well." And he wanted to do it at a time when he felt energetic and innovative.[11]

Again and again we've seen how the abilities that have made leaders successful in business can find new energy in other settings, as their life focus shifts. John Macomber, former CEO of Celanese, moved on to take a government position as head of the Export-Import Bank.[12] Rex Adams, head of human resources at Mobil, became dean at the Fuqua School at Duke University. Both are examples of how the ideal self can change over the course of a career.

Our ideal self-image engages our passion, emotion, and motivation. A personal vision is the deepest expression of what we want in life, and that image becomes both a guide for our decisions and a barometer of our sense of satisfaction in life.[13]

Still, if you want to lead an organization, having a personal ideal vision is not enough. A leader needs a vision for the organization. It is difficult to spread the contagion of excitement without having a sense of purpose and direction. This is where the individual ideal self-image evolves into a shared vision for the future. To be in tune with others' vision, you have to be open to others' hopes and dreams.

*Leading with Passion*

Jurgen, the head of a Swiss bank, was having a crisis of commitment. The bank was doing well enough, but not all of his top management team were engaged in their work, and a few didn't even belong in their jobs. Jurgen didn't feel he could buck tradition and ask them to leave their positions. Moreover, he didn't have a handle on what was happening elsewhere at the bank. No one ever gave him the right information, as if they were afraid to voice controversial or critical opinions. Feeling ineffective, Jurgen wasn't enjoying his work anymore; his only option, he felt, was to step down.

But in our work with Jurgen over about six months, he was able to craft a vision of his life and his leadership at the bank that he found energizing and inspiring. Equally important, it was inspiring for the people he was leading. Jurgen began by looking inside, reflecting on his own life and personal vision inside and outside of work. He also articulated a clear picture of the reality of the situation at the bank and why it no longer satisfied him. Comparing the real and the ideal gave him much more clarity— and, admittedly, anxiety—about exactly what needed to change. And he asked himself the all-important question: "Is there enough that I love about this company and these people to keep me here through the tough work coming up?"

One summer morning, Jurgen hiked with a friend around an Alpine lake and spoke honestly about his fear that he couldn't bring about the changes that were needed. He looked at the past, present, and future, and he considered the people, some of whom he'd worked with for years. He thought about the problems and about his own commitment—and how good it could be if he just got it right. He reflected on his personal ideal vision, and he focused on what could change if he got back into the bank and really fought. By the end of that walk, he had his answer: "I'm in."

That decision to get back "in" was energizing for Jurgen; somewhere deep inside he'd tapped into his passion for leadership again. And passion breeds courage—enough, Jurgen found, to take on the tough tasks ahead.

Identifying and articulating your ideal self, the path you truly want to follow in life—as Jurgen did—requires self-awareness. But once you clarify your ideal self, you stimulate hope—an antidote to the inertia of habit. As Napoleon observed, "A leader is a dealer in hope."[14] The challenge for every leader lies in reaching inside to the source of hope. There lies the power to evoke and articulate one's personal ideal self-image and the shared ideals that flow from it—and so lead others in that same direction.

That kind of leadership, however, requires not only a vision, but also a clear picture of the realities you are facing.

## The Second Discovery: The Real Self, or Are You a Boiling Frog?

If you drop a frog into boiling water, it will instinctively jump out. But if you place a frog in a pot of cool water and gradually increase the temperature, the frog won't notice that the water's getting hotter. It will sit there until the water boils—and will boil with it. The fate of that poached frog isn't so unlike that of some leaders who settle into routine or let small conveniences solidify into large habits—and allow inertia to set in.

Consider the example of John Lauer. When he took over as

president of BF Goodrich, no one would ever have imagined that such inertia would take hold. A tall, good-looking man with a charming smile, he took on his leadership challenges with vigor, showing particular strengths as a democratic and visionary leader. For instance, during a meeting early in his tenure with top executives of a key division, Lauer listened carefully to their discussion and then articulated a vision for the company that integrated its current strengths but better positioned it for global markets. The nodding heads around the room reflected how his vision had moved them. Over the next few years, as the company restructured, Lauer continued as an effective leader—and as a team player among his top executives.

Then, about six years after taking the helm at BF Goodrich, during a speech he was making to a class of executive MBA students, it was clear that his charisma had dimmed. He talked about business and management issues, but it all sounded routine and even a bit dull. Gone was the excitement that so many had found contagious in his earlier days on the job.

Like a slowly boiling frog, Lauer had gradually adjusted to the disappointment, frustration, and even boredom of the practices and policies of a large corporation. He had lost his excitement for his work. Not surprisingly, within a few months of giving that lackluster speech, Lauer left the company. Seeking a change from corporate life to do something that felt meaningful again, he went to work with his wife, Edie, who was heavily involved in Hungarian relief organizations.

Confronting his loss of energy and interest as a leader, Lauer was beginning a process that would lead him to the second discovery. Further development of emotional intelligence in leaders requires that, once they have at least some vision of their ideal lives, they uncover their real self. It would be a process that would lead him to look deep inside and rediscover the leader within.

Two years after he left BF Goodrich, Lauer took a leadership development seminar as part of the Executive Doctorate in Management program.[15] He still maintained he wanted nothing to do with running companies; that era of his life was past. Pursuit of the doctorate was a door into a new life; he didn't know exactly what he'd be doing, but he was hopeful about the future.

During the leadership seminar, Lauer wrestled with his values, philosophy and aspirations, and his distinctive strengths. In considering the next decade or so of his life and reflecting on his capabilities, he realized how much he'd relished being a leader. He reconnected with the excitement he'd felt at the helm of a company, working with a team of executives and building something important. Then one day he woke up and realized that he'd be open to taking a CEO job again. The right kind of situation could be fun—one where he could apply ideas he'd developed in his doctoral program.

He returned a few headhunters' calls, and within a month Lauer was offered the leadership of Oglebay Norton, a $250 million company in the raw materials business. There he became an exemplar of the democratic style, listening to what employees had to say, and encouraging his leadership team to do the same. And he repeatedly articulated a compelling vision for the company. As one of his executives told us, "John raises our spirits, our confidence, and our passion for excellence."[16] Although the company dealt in unglamorous commodities such as gravel and sand, within the first year Lauer made such improvements that Oglebay Norton was featured in *Fortune*, *Business Week*, and the *Wall Street Journal*.

Lauer had been able to leave BF Goodrich in the first place because he understood that he had a different vision for his life. That was discovery number one—of the ideal self. Then, by confronting the reality of the ruts he'd gotten into and coming to an understanding of his distinctive strengths—discovery number two—he was able to reconnect with his enthusiasm as a leader. And that ultimately led him to get on track again and find fulfillment in a different kind of leadership role.

### The Elusive Real Self

Taking stock of your real self starts with an inventory of your talents and passions—the person you actually are as a leader. This can be more difficult than it might seem. For one thing, it requires a great deal of self-awareness, if only to overcome the inertia of inattention that an accumulation of habits inevitably produces. Because routine creates such gradual changes that take hold over time, the reality of our lives often can be hard to grasp. It's like looking in a clouded mirror: It becomes difficult to see who we really are. And when we finally do begin to get a clear view—

---

## THE "LOGAN TEST"

O N A WEEK-LONG VACATION at his uncle's house, 9-year-old Logan set his alarm so that he would awaken early each morning. Then, the minute he heard his uncle creeping downstairs, no matter what the hour—5:00 A.M., 5:30 A.M.— Logan sprang from bed, not wanting to miss a single second of what the day might hold. This surprised his uncle, who'd thought he might be able to sneak in some work while Logan slept (the child's mother had said that Logan usually awoke around 7:30 to 8:00 A.M.). But Logan was right there each morning, eager to begin the day, when his uncle awoke.

One quick index of whether you've become a boiling frog might be the "Logan Test." Consider a few questions about how you typically act these days, and contrast it with the person you were in the past. Do you awake each morning excited about the day, not wanting to sleep any more than absolutely necessary? Do you laugh as much as you once did? Are you having as much fun in your personal life as you have in the past? Are you having as much fun at work? If you're finding that your work, relationships, and life in general don't make you feel energized and hopeful about the future, that's a good indication that you've probably lost touch with your real self and could use some insight into the person you've become.

often in an epiphanic moment—the reality can be painful. As one manager we worked with, an engineer, put it: "I saw myself being the very person I never wanted to be."

How does such a thing happen to reasonably intelligent people? How does the sense of the person one has become slip away? The boiling frog syndrome—the slow, invisible creep of compromise and complacency—poses perhaps the greatest challenge to an accurate self-image. We no longer quite grasp who we've become—although the people around us usually have a clear view.

Many things conspire to keep people from seeing their real selves. The human psyche itself shields us from information that might undermine our self-perception. These ego-defense mechanisms, as they're called, protect us emotionally so that we can cope more easily with life. But in the process, they hide or discard essential information—such as how others are responding to our behavior. Over time, these self-delusions that the unconscious creates become self-perpetuating myths, persisting despite the difficulties they cause.[17]

Of course, ego-defense mechanisms have their advantages. Most high-functioning people, for instance, are more optimistic about their prospects and possibilities than the average person.[18] Their rose-colored lenses fuel enthusiasm and energy for their undertakings. The problem comes when the defenses go too far, distorting a person's view of his real self—the person he has become—out of all proportion.

The playwright Henrik Ibsen called such self-delusions "vital lies": soothing mistruths people let themselves believe rather than face the more disturbing realities beneath.

### Vital Lies

Self-delusion is a powerful trap indeed, skewing our attempts to assess ourselves. Because of it, we give more weight to what confirms our distorted self-image—and ignore what doesn't. Surprisingly, those distortions aren't always self-serving.

We've often seen, in coaching sessions with leaders, that even very powerful executives don't always see themselves as effective— although their colleagues tell us how great these leaders are. It might appear to be humility that makes such leaders underrate themselves, but usually it's because they hold extremely high standards for their performance. They therefore focus on how they fail to meet their own standards, rather than on the ways they're doing well.

The most obvious way to correct distortions in self-perception, of course, would be to receive corrective feedback from the people around us. It sounds so simple, doesn't it? Given the number of people in our lives who could comment on our behavior, you'd think that we'd all be awash in feedback, and continually able to correct the distortions in our self-perception. So why doesn't that happen?

One reason is the CEO disease that we examined in the previous chapter. That phenomenon makes people deny their leaders important information—not only about their behavior and leadership styles, but also about the state of the organization. The reasons people are silent include fear of the leader's wrath, not wanting to be seen as the bearers of bad news, or wanting to appear as "good citizens" and team players.

But it isn't just CEOs who suffer from this disease: Most leaders are deprived of important feedback. Often the reason is simply that it makes people uncomfortable to give candid feedback on someone else's behavior. Few people want to intentionally hurt another person's feelings—but often they don't know how to deliver feedback in a productive, rather than hurtful, way. They therefore often swing too far in the other direction, making enormous efforts to "be nice." But when people confuse being nice with providing others with accurate observations about their behavior or style, their feedback is rendered useless.

### The Problem with "Being Nice"

The owner and chef of a Paris bistro stood near the door in a white suit and chef's hat. A couple walked in, smiled, and said, "Are you the owner?"

"Yes," the chef replied.

The expectant diners scanned the marvelous ambience, décor, and assortment of dishes on display, then turned back to the chef and said, "Wonderful place—great atmosphere and great food!"

To which the chef replied, "You should wait until after your meal to say that!"

As a business owner, the chef wanted praise, of course, but he wanted it to be genuine, not a solicitous gesture. Likewise, in organizations, people giving feedback to others may confuse attempts to "be nice" with providing accurate observations that are helpful. This applies especially to leaders.

For years, some behavioral scientists advised making performance feedback nonevaluative. It would be devoid of any pro or con, making it more palatable and thus, they argued, more useful: By taking the teeth out of feedback, those receiving it would be more likely to accept it.

But this neutering of feedback actually rendered it less useful, according to a study at the Massachusetts Institute of Technology; a noncommittal, cautious neutrality depleted feedback of important emotional messages.[19] The study, conducted as part of an introductory course in organizational behavior, had MBA students identify a change goal on which they would work during the fifteen weeks of the course. Each week during class, students met in groups to receive feedback on their progress. At the end of each class, everyone would identify up to three instances of feedback that they'd found useful that day.

Contrary to the advice prominent at the time, evaluative feedback—in which people were candidly given specifics about what worked or didn't work in their behavior—was seen as more helpful than nonevaluative feedback. These findings make sense. We all know, on some level, that others watch and judge what we do— so most of us would rather have the full story, not the watered-down version. When others try to keep us comfortable by sanitizing feedback, or "being nice," they do us a disservice: We're deprived of crucial information we need to improve.

That's why we've found that the most emotionally intelligent leaders actively seek out negative feedback as well as positive. Those leaders understand that they need a full range of information to perform better—whether or not that information feels good to hear.

## Getting to the Truth

To become more effective, leaders need to break through the information quarantine around them—and the conspiracy to keep them pleased, even if uninformed. Rare are those who dare to tell a commanding leader he is too harsh, or to let a leader know he could be more visionary, or more democratic. That's why emotionally intelligent leaders need to seek the truth themselves.

How do effective leaders discover that truth? A study of almost 400 executives showed that, for one thing, they use their self-awareness and empathy, both to monitor their own actions and to watch how others react to them. They are open to critiques, whether of their ideas or their leadership. They actively seek out negative feedback, valuing the voice of a devil's advocate. By contrast, less effective leaders most often solicit confirming feedback. Not surprisingly, those leaders held far less accurate views of how well they performed as leaders. The most effective leaders assessed themselves very closely to how others rated them as leaders.[20]

Likewise, information from several thousand questionnaires, using a 360-degree format from bosses, peers, and subordinates, found that seeking out *negative* feedback—not just positive remarks—predicted the accuracy of people's self-awareness and their overall effectiveness. If a leader knows what he needs to improve, he knows where to focus his attention. On the other hand, people who mainly sought positive feedback understandably had poor self-assessment—and lower effectiveness.[21]

Clearly, then, soliciting negative information may be vital to a person's continued growth and effectiveness. But to whom do you turn for advice—and for feedback that might not necessarily affirm how you view yourself? How, in short, does a leader test reality?[22]

### Completing the Second Discovery

As we've seen, the first discovery that promotes self-directed learning is identifying your ideal self-image. The second discovery begins with uncovering the reality: how you see yourself, and how others see you. To complete that discovery, however, you need to develop an understanding of your leadership strengths and gaps—the differences or similarities between the ideal and the real.[23]

This is the real starting point of self-directed learning: taking stock of the parts of yourself that you relish and want to preserve, versus those you'd like to change or adapt to your new circumstances. A person's self-awareness—the realization of this balance between what one wants to keep and what one needs to develop—sparks the readiness to change. You suddenly understand what you value about yourself and therefore want to keep. Likewise, you're able to admit what you need to work on. Each needs to be seen in light of the other—what to keep, what to change.[24] In this sense, sometimes a strength provokes a gap, like using so much initiative that, at times, you do not exert sufficient emotional self-control. Or sometimes a gap actually depends on a strength: A gap in adaptability, for example, may be because you're an inspirational leader who sometimes becomes overzealous and fixates on a particular vision.[25]

Your leadership strengths—what you want to preserve—lie at the intersection of where your real self matches your ideal. Where reality fails to meet your ideal for yourself as a leader, of course, represents your "gaps." Piecing together this image of who you are and who you would like to be is a bit like putting together a jigsaw puzzle. You start by finding the edges, the most obvious pieces, then fill in more pieces, a section at a time. While at first you may not be able to make sense of the image, eventually, when just enough pieces have fallen into place, you see the whole picture clearly.

### An Antidote to Blind Spots

As we saw with the CEO disease, it is not easy for leaders to identify their strengths and gaps on their own. The leader who wants to strengthen his abilities needs to start by seeking out other people's perspectives in order to get an accurate picture of himself. The 360-degree method offers that fuller picture. By collecting information from many people—your boss, your peers, your subordinates—you benefit from multiple perspectives about how you act and how others see it. The 360-degree view offers a consensual image of your profile of competencies. Whether this consensus is an image of the *real you* depends on two givens: (1) that the people who participate in the 360-degree evaluation actually interact with you on a regular basis; and (2) that you reveal yourself to them.[26]

There's a good reason for seeking out many different people to ask for 360-degree feedback: Multiple views render a more complete image. In a very real sense, you are a different person with different kinds of people and in different settings—be they your spouse or partner, your boss, or your subordinates. Indeed, the research on different sources of feedback confirms what seems common sense—bosses, subordinates, and peers each see different aspects of a person's behavioral repertoire. That's why the same leader can look so different when evaluated from each of these perspectives.

For instance, research done at a trucking company by Professors Gene Harris and Joyce Hogan from the University of Tulsa found that on a 360-degree evaluation, subordinates rated their managers as highest in conscientiousness, while bosses rated the same managers as highest in emotional stability.[27] The managers saw themselves as highest in interpersonal maturity—which their subordinates, and even their bosses, rated close to the bottom of the list. Tellingly, there was one characteristic that both sources rated the same: They saw the managers as weakest in providing feedback. These managers needed the multiple perspectives as an antidote to both their own blind spots and the limited view of any one source of feedback.

In other research, Fred Luthans and some of his colleagues from the University of Nebraska looked at leaders in terms of whether "success" and "effectiveness" were the same.[28] They saw success as indicated by promotions, salary increases, and total compensation.

But they defined effectiveness in terms of a consensus view from stakeholders, especially subordinates, who they believed would take a longer-term view. They also collected others' views of the leaders' behavior. Not surprisingly, they found that bosses tended to see building bonds, communications, and influence as key abilities of the managers: Those are the competencies these leaders used in managing upward. On the other hand, their subordinates saw these managers as particularly strong in developing others, in teamwork and collaboration, and in empathy—competencies used in leading these followers.

That difference between how bosses and subordinates see a leader's strengths makes a strong argument for using a 360-degree assessment in leadership development. The best leaders use the competencies selectively, displaying some to one group, others to another. Any given group—subordinates, peers, bosses, clients, or family and friends—will see only a given part of that leader's repertoire.

Of all these perspectives, the views of subordinates and peers— rather than that of bosses themselves—appear to have the most predictive validity of a leader's actual effectiveness.[29] For instance, in a longitudinal study of the effectiveness of leaders in a government agency, how subordinates assessed the leader proved most predictive of the leader's success and effectiveness, both at two and four years following the assessment. Even after seven years, the subordinates' assessments were predicting the leader's success— and with far more accuracy than the boss's own assessments. The subordinates' views were every bit as accurate a predictor as were much more elaborate ratings based on performance simulations done in assessment centers.[30]

### The Tyranny of Gaps

Once you are certain that you're getting a full picture of yourself from feedback, you're ready to look at your strengths and gaps. As most people know, it's all too easy to fixate immediately and exclusively on gaps. After all, they're talked about all the time in organizations, especially when it comes to leadership development.

A work culture may foster this concentration on performance gaps, particularly when the leader's style is one that focuses on what's wrong in the organization rather than on what's right. Often these are leaders who have the pragmatic underlying philosophy that we discussed earlier, which is marked by an extremely strong drive to achieve.

On the other hand, sometimes people look more closely at gaps because they have low self-confidence; they assume they're less capable than they actually are, and therefore tend to distrust or dismiss positive feedback. Typically these leaders, when looking at 360-degree data, exaggerate their gaps while ignoring their strengths.

Emphasis on gaps often arouses the right prefrontal cortex— that is, feelings of anxiety and defensiveness. Once defensiveness sets in, it typically demotivates rather than motivates, thereby interrupting, even stopping, self-directed learning and the likelihood of change.

### The Personal Balance Sheet

Despite the potential downfalls of this approach, many leadership training programs—or managers conducting annual performance reviews—regularly rationalize this error in approach with the adage "leave well enough alone," which means neglecting to recognize people's abilities in favor of giving attention only to the areas that need work.

But that means the capabilities that people value, enjoy, and are most proud of get lost in the process. Focusing on only the gaps is not only depressing and demotivating, but also results in a lopsided balance sheet. Our strengths reveal the important things that we have learned as leaders over the course of our lives and careers. They are the bottom line of our experience, our retained learnings—quite parallel to the retained earnings on a company's balance sheet.

Strengths displayed over the years—sometimes called *signature themes*—typically represent aspects that leaders want to keep, even if those themes are dormant for a period of time.[31] Such signatures offer innate resources to draw on as leaders. For example, Herb Kelleher, the long-time former CEO of Southwest Airlines, always had a strong sense of humor. As a leader, he loved to laugh and make others laugh, and he used that strength to great effect: Playfulness became an organizational strength at Southwest that set it apart from its competitors.

By collecting readings from people in many parts of one's life, not just work, it's easier to recognize these signature capabilities.

We've seen that the first two discoveries—of your ideal and real self, your strengths and gaps—get you motivated to change. But how do you make change happen? For that, you need a road map: a plan for how to build on your strengths, close your gaps, and make your aspirations and dreams become reality.

### CHAPTER EIGHT

# METAMORPHOSIS

## Sustaining Leadership Change

A S A MARKETING EXECUTIVE for the Latin American division of a major integrated energy company, Juan Trebino was charged with growing the company—not only in his home country of Venezuela, but also in the entire region. When, during a leadership seminar, he received 360-degree feedback about his leadership abilities, however, he learned that he wasn't quite equipped to do the job. As a goal-focused former engineer, Trebino needed to develop more of a coaching leadership style; his success at growing new business in his region would turn on his ability to inspire cooperation among those with whom he worked.

Trebino was about to embark upon the third discovery in the self-directed learning process: developing a practical plan that would lead to the new leadership strengths he sought. Such an agenda should focus on improvements about which a person feels passionate, while giving him realistic, manageable steps that will help him realize these possibilities. It should build on his strengths while working on his gaps.

To develop more of a coaching style, Trebino knew he needed to hone his powers of empathy. He decided to commit to actions in many parts of his life that would allow him to practice that skill. As one step in his learning plan, Trebino decided to get to know each of his subordinates; if he understood more about who they were, he could better help them reach toward their own dreams and goals. He made plans with each employee to meet outside of work, in an informal setting, where the employees might be more comfortable revealing where they hoped to go in life.

Trebino also looked for areas outside his job where he could sharpen his empathy and coaching skills—for example, by coaching his daughter's soccer team and volunteering at a local crisis center for families in trouble. Both activities offered an arena to experiment with how well he understood others and to try out new coaching skills.

These new arenas allowed him to stay more attentive, more mindful of his learning goals. It's like getting a new pair of glasses: It gives one a new set of lenses through which to see the world and allows one the chance to become more sensitive to situations where one needs to improve.

In fact, the more parts of our lives that we can identify as relevant to a leadership learning goal, the more chances to practice we give ourselves. A study conducted at the Weatherhead School of Management of Case Western Reserve University by Professor Jane Wheeler found that of people who had developed learning agendas, those who tried out their new skills with many different people and spheres of their lives—not just at work, but also with family, church, and community groups, and so on—improved the most. And those improvements were still apparent up to two or more years later.[1]

Being mindful of learning opportunities when they arise—and spontaneously seizing them as a way to practice new abilities— offers ways to improve more quickly. Life is the laboratory for learning. It's important to bear in mind that plans that tend to simply focus on specific performance goals are less effective that those drawn from comparing your ideal self with your real self.

## The Third Discovery: A Learning Agenda

Too often leadership coaching revolves around a "performance-improvement plan," a phrase that conjures images of a remedial rehabilitation project. But rather than being some rote exercise that will "fix" a person into being a better leader, learning goals should resonate with a person's dreams. Because a "performance agenda" focuses on achieving some measure of success, it becomes something a person has to prove. It can provoke defensiveness. Such agendas don't capture the motivating aspect of how one's personal dreams might coincide with the target (an aspect that can be highly motivating).[2] A learning agenda, however, focuses on the possibility of change that will eventually lead to better performance at work (and probably more contentment in life in general).

Small wonder that improvement plans crafted around learning—rather than performance outcomes—have been found most effective. For instance, in a program to improve communication skills, a learning agenda resulted in dramatically better presentations; a performance agenda tended to make people react defensively—not wanting to "look bad"—while neglecting to give them concrete steps to improve their actual performance.

The best kind of learning agenda helps you focus on what you want to become—your own ideal—rather than on someone else's idea of what you should be. It should lead to setting meaningful standards of performance, rather than taking on an arbitrary, normative standard for success that may or may not fit with personal goals.[3] When crafting specific, manageable learning goals, it works best to tie them in to goals that motivate you and ignite your full range of talents.

On the other hand, being handed a performance goal tends to do the opposite: It undermines motivation by evoking anxiety and doubts about whether or not one *can* improve, and so it does not necessarily increase performance.[4] For example, even in the goal-driven arena of sales, learning goals have been shown to lead to greater improvement than have performance goals.[5] Setting developmental goals that matter takes us from merely contemplating change to making concrete steps that prepare us to change.[6] Our learning goals are a kind of mental rehearsal that pave the way for a change in how we act.

### The Mindful Prefrontal Cortex

As we saw with Juan Trebino, crafting an agenda of specific goals converts life into a learning lab. Spending time with his daughter's soccer team, at a crisis center, and with colleagues from work all became opportunities for Trebino to work on his emotional intelligence. The goals helped him to monitor himself to see how well he was doing; they reminded him to pay attention.[7]

Since the habits he was trying to overcome had become automatic—routines that had taken hold over time, without his realizing it—bringing them into awareness was a crucial step toward changing them.[8] As he paid more attention, the situations that arose—whether while listening to a colleague, coaching soccer, or talking on the phone to someone who was distraught—all became cues that stimulated him to break old habits and try new responses instead.

This cueing for habit change is neural as well as perceptual. Researchers at the University of Pittsburgh and Carnegie Mellon University have shown that as people mentally prepare for a task, they activate the prefrontal cortex—that part of the brain that performs executive functions and moves them into action. Without preparation, the prefrontal cortex does not activate in advance. Thus, the greater the prior activation, the better a person does at the task.[9]

Such mental rehearsal becomes particularly important when we're trying to overcome old leadership habits and replace them with a better way of doing things. As one of the neuroscientists in this study found, the prefrontal cortex becomes particularly active when a person has to prepare to overcome a habitual response. The aroused prefrontal cortex marks the brain's focus on what's about to happen. Without that arousal, a person will act out old, undesirable routines. The executive who just doesn't listen will once again cut off his subordinate; the pacesetter will launch into yet another overly critical attack.

Because leadership skills are part of an unconscious repertoire of habits learned long ago, the old response won't magically disappear. It takes commitment and constant reminders to stay focused on undoing those habits. Over time, the need for reminders will diminish as the new behavior becomes a stronger pathway in the brain.

### Goal Setting: A New Perspective

Setting goals and creating plans to achieve them is nothing new.[10] Benjamin Franklin outlined a step-by-step process for becoming a virtuous person through setting daily and weekly goals to increase admirable behavior. But research has clearly shown that there is a science to this process.

In the 1960s, David McClelland of Harvard University showed that setting specific goals and developing a plan to achieve them made entrepreneurs more successful.[11] David Kolb, a former student of McClelland's, later did a series of studies at MIT that pinpointed which parts of the process of goal setting were essential for improvements to occur.[12]

Managers are all too familiar with goal setting these days. Not only do they have to plan their own days and set agendas for meeting annual performance targets, but they also have to do the same with each of their direct reports. Additionally, they participate in planning at the strategic business unit, division, and corporate level. And they've been inundated with tools with which to make those plans—from daily activity-planning books to electronic Palm Pilots. No wonder managers complain of having to spend too much time planning, with few moments left over to do the actual work.

With all of this planning frenzy, what new information or tools could possibly be of use? Recent studies of people who have improved their emotional intelligence reveal several key points about what works and what doesn't.[13] Although some may seem obvious—even common sense—they are not common practice. The findings include the following:

- Goals should build on one's strengths, not on one's weaknesses.

- Goals must be a person's own—not goals that someone else has imposed.

- Plans should flexibly allow people to prepare for the future in different ways—a single "planning" method imposed by an organization will often prove counterproductive.

- Plans must be feasible, with manageable steps: Plans that don't fit smoothly into a person's life and work will likely be dropped within a few weeks or months.

- Plans that don't suit a person's learning style will prove demotivating and quickly lose his attention.

Let's now look at how each of those points would modify goal setting as we typically know it.

### GOALS SHOULD BUILD ON STRENGTHS

Demetrios, the president of a fast-growing, research-based consulting firm, was an effective, democratic leader. He rated high on his levels of self-awareness and social awareness, and had competencies in building bonds, teamwork, and developing others. Using his talent for drawing out ideas from others, he led the company through a very tough period into one of expanding market share.

But once the company had clearly succeeded, Demetrios faced a leadership dilemma. The firm's partners and staff started wondering where the company was going next. They wanted visionary leadership—and someone ready to make the tough decisions about priorities that would maintain their growth momentum. Demetrios's democratic style felt too laissez faire: It threatened to allow the partners to take parts of the company in any direction they wished—which could tear the company to pieces.

Demetrios's subsequent work with an executive coach offers a good lesson in how learning goals can address a gap while building on strengths. Together, they uncovered telling gaps in Demetrios's style, where he lacked the more assertive, "push" uses of power, such as competencies in influence and conflict management. The coach helped Demetrios see that the inspirational leadership and change-catalyst competencies he often used with clients were left at the door when he came into the office.

To build his visionary leadership strengths inside the company, Demetrios decided on a novel learning goal: to treat his company as if it were his most important client. He would use his strengths in social awareness to understand each challenge that emerged within the company as though it were a client's problem. His action plan included thinking through how this new "client"— his own organization—should approach problems. He even took on the task of writing a consulting memo to himself each day, in which he proposed specific solutions.

His second learning goal dealt with the leadership crisis: He aimed to be inspiring at every company meeting. For example, he made sure he began each small-group meeting with a reminder of why they were in business—their vision, values, and mission. Although at first he felt a bit self-conscious, even awkward, as he persisted in cultivating new habits of the visionary style, it soon felt less gushy and more natural. Here he built on two strengths: his talent at being inspirational with clients, and his teamwork skills. For example, when he would mention the company's mission at the beginning of a meeting, he was then able to go one step further and elicit from the group their collaborative ideas for the company's vision as well.

By calling on his strengths, Demetrios was able to pursue his learning plan with confidence. He knew that he'd already done for clients what he needed to do for his own company. The company more than tripled its revenue in the next six years. In addition to building on strengths to change his leadership style,

Demetrios chose to develop competencies already close to the *tipping point*—the level at which a relatively small improvement or increase in the frequency of a competence will tip someone into outstanding performance.

David McClelland was the first researcher to apply tipping-point analysis to competencies.[14] Prior research had answered the question: *What* competencies are necessary to be outstanding? This new approach answered the question: *How much* of the competencies are sufficient to become outstanding? In Demetrios's case, he had two competency gaps close to the tipping point—the ability to offer inspirational leadership and to be a change catalyst—and two competency gaps distant from the tipping point—skills in influencing people and in conflict management.

If his learning goal had been to develop a vision on his own or with a small group of partners and then to sell it to the staff, he'd have had to really fortify his weaknesses in the influence and conflict-management competencies. But by working on creating new habits closer to his current style, he was more likely to succeed at building an effective visionary leadership style.

### ARE THEY REALLY YOUR GOALS?

When Mark Scott, vice president of public relations at a mortgage bank, reflected on how he'd changed after a leadership development program, he described three improvements. He felt more understanding of people from diverse backgrounds, more able to build effective working relationships with a wide variety of people, and more flexible in new and uncertain situations. These gains reflected the first three learning goals in the agenda he'd developed two years before.

But when asked what happened to the fourth and fifth goals in his plan, he needed to be reminded of what they were. "Oh, those were my boss's goals," he said. "She insisted that a good learning plan should address all of the gaps that appeared in my assessments."

Clearly, someone else's idea of what he should do didn't resonate with Scott. But that kind of misfire happens frequently in goal setting: People agree to development goals because a boss, mentor, coach—or spouse—encourages or pushes them to change. But it's important to remember that the more *personal* the commitment to learning goals, the more likely you are to achieve them.[15] This is where passion and hope—the motivating brain activity inherent in tapping into your dreams—are again so vital to sustainable learning. And the more difficult a goal, the more essential is one's commitment.[16]

### HOW DO YOU THINK ABOUT THE FUTURE?

"I've never set a goal for myself—not for my career or my personal life. But I have always known that whatever I do, it will be in line with what I feel is important." So says an entrepreneur in response to our questions about how he plans for the future. The sole owner of a consulting firm, he's quite successful by anyone's measure—likewise in his personal life.

He "plans" his future based on a very clear sense of what's important to him—his values, his beliefs, the way he wants to live his life. He has charted a path for himself that doesn't have specific mileposts, such as a particular job. It does, however, have guideposts that he uses when making life decisions, and he relies on a high level of self-awareness and a knack for spotting good opportunities.

Contrast that entrepreneur's approach with that of Denise Cesare, CEO of Blue Cross of northeastern Pennsylvania. Since she was young, Cesare has always had clear, specific goals—and a vision of where she would end up. "Public accounting is an up or out profession. So when I entered it, the obvious goal was to become a partner. Then, when I entered health care, I saw myself at the top of a company, someday. I focused on where I wanted to be, kept my sense of humor, stayed clear about my values, and moved toward my goal one step at a time."

And that's exactly what she did. At each juncture, she worked through the path to success for that particular portion of her career, always with an eye on the goal. She's adept at reading her environment, oriented toward achievement, and knows how to manage the ups and downs of change.

At the opposite end of the spectrum are people who don't

consider the future at all, at least not in the way we normally view such planning. They create the future as they go along, almost rebelliously holding on to the right to do what they please. "I don't want to waste my time worrying about what's next," says a leader of a consumer goods company. That doesn't mean that he doesn't achieve success in both his personal and professional life. But he tends to think more about success in terms of the present moment, allowing his understanding of current dynamics to guide his behavior.

There's no "right" way, then, to plan for the future; research has shown that it's a very personal process.[17] When people do try to follow a proscribed model, their learning plans usually get relegated to the bottom drawer. One size does not fit all when it comes to formulating a useful agenda for your future.

That said, we've found that within each of the planning styles that people use are competencies worth learning. Directional or visionary planners, for example, are good at crafting a picture of a meaningful, distant future state—one that's grounded in values, beliefs, and a deep sense of what's important in life.[18] Goal-oriented planners get what they go after; social science research tells us that specific, measurable goals are more likely to be achieved.[19] Knowing how to set such goals can help people focus their energy where and when it's needed.

Action orientation, on the other hand, results in a high level of accomplishment in the short term. Moreover, the freedom inherent in such planning adds an element of serendipity that enhances creativity. Finally, though it is tempting to ignore it, the "shoulds" of reflective planning are a fact of life for most people anyway, so it's best to factor that in to how to think about the future.

### PLANS MUST BE FEASIBLE

Perhaps the greatest mistake that people make when setting goals is committing themselves to activities that are difficult to do in their current lives and work style. Your action plan needs to fit into the structure and rhythm of your life. We saw in previous chapters how improvements last longer when people identify specific emotional intelligence competencies as part of their learning goals, rather than setting a vague target.[20] Even aiming at just one goal for improvement can yield dramatic jumps in effectiveness.

Learning plans that lay out concrete, practical steps yield the most powerful improvement. For instance, people who have tried to improve their ability as speakers—a key to a leader's communications and vital to many competencies—have set some of the following concrete goals for themselves:

- Give at least two formal presentations every month, and have them critiqued by a peer I respect.

- Practice with a friend before giving a presentation.

- Videotape myself giving a speech and critique it with my boss's help.

- Join Toastmasters so I can practice giving more effective talks.

- Talk to people who give oral presentations in a manner that comes across as relaxed and interesting, and find out what they do to prepare—specifically, how they overcome stage fright and relax into the presentation.

Which of these goals will work for a given person depends on the realities of his life. To work on a development goal, it must be squeezed into an already crowded schedule. And since action steps do often take additional time in our lives, the question becomes, What will you say "no" to in order to create the time you need for working on the goal? The alternative is to design your steps so that they're integral to what you do already.

For instance, instead of joining a group in which to practice giving presentations, one midlevel manager we know made a daily staff meeting her microplatform. She gave herself more ways to practice by taking on assignments that arose which offered the opportunity to present reports to the rest of the group. She thereby integrated her learning into each day, using her work setting as a laboratory for strengthening her leadership skills.

KNOW YOUR LEARNING STYLE

Most leaders have a preferred way to learn, a mode that feels most natural. Rather than fighting that learning style, or trying to conform to an imposed style, it makes sense to leverage your preferred style.

Take, for example, two friends—both of whom became CEOs within a few years—who decided to learn to sail one summer. One went out and bought a twelve-foot dinghy, with which he planned to practice during a month on the coast of Maine. At the same time, his friend enrolled in a sailing course in Boston harbor.

On the first day, as the new owner of the dinghy was pushing off the beach in Maine, his friend was sitting in a classroom, learning the principles of sailing. But once he developed a theoretical comfort with sailing, he was able to start sailing large boats right from the beginning. Meanwhile, off the coast of Maine, his friend was out in the water from day one, albeit in a small boat, and discovering on his own things like why a centerboard is useful. In the ensuing years, he practiced his newfound skills in larger and larger boats.

In the end, each friend learned the skill he desired—but in radically different ways from one another. The dinghy owner preferred learning through concrete experience, while his friend learned better by first building his own mental model of sailing. Fortunately for both of these novice sailors, each of them had the ability to also learn, when they had to, from active experimentation.

Research has shown that people actually learn best when they use modes that suit them.[21] The Learning Style Inventory, developed by David Kolb when he was at MIT, has been used for more than thirty years to understand learning in management as well as in fields ranging from medicine to law. Kolb found that people learn most often through one of the following modes:

- *Concrete experience:* Having an experience that allows them to see and feel what it is like

- *Reflection:* Thinking about their own and others' experiences
- *Model building:* Coming up with a theory that makes sense of what they observe
- *Trial-and-error learning:* Trying something out by actively experimenting with a new approach

Learning often happens best through some combination of two or three of these modes.[22] On the other hand, some people rely on styles that can actually hinder their learning—especially if used too early or too much. Such learning styles turn people off to further learning or drain their excitement because they make learning feel boring or irrelevant.

Many leaders, for instance, have had instruction at some point in leading teams more effectively. If they took the course from a college professor, they might have started with a few classes devoted to understanding the theory of group formation and group development. They might have had a class addressing the different philosophical perspectives about groups and teams. Meanwhile, rather than theory, what they might have really needed was a tool to use on Monday morning when they had to quiet down a disruptive team member. So after a few classes, they might have felt the course was irrelevant and stopped paying attention.

Professors organize courses to fit their own preferred learning style, which for academics is typically abstract and reflective. But a leader whose learning style may be more active and concrete needs to begin by learning some practical techniques he can try immediately.

Too often leadership courses and workshops present a fixed, cookie-cutter agenda. To avoid this pitfall in learning, it pays to identify your best learning styles to ensure that your action steps won't be wasted. If you can't identify your styles after a bit of reflection, there are simple tests that can help.[23]

To recap, by entering into the first three discoveries of self-directed learning, it is possible to develop an engaging, but realistic, agenda that can help you reach your leadership goals. You have compared your ideal vision with the reality of your style and behavior, and you've used that to identify your strengths and gaps. Then, with that profile in mind, you've targeted specific leadership abilities in a learning plan, setting a practical course to strengthen them.

You begin the process of the final two discoveries when your agenda, and the steps leading up to it, has prepared and focused your attention on what to do. Now you try it and discover how to make this kind of learning a continuous part of your life as a leader.

## The Fourth Discovery: Reconfiguring the Brain

Jack was head of marketing for a division of a global food company. High-energy and driven to improve results, Jack was a classic pacesetter. He was always striving to find better ways to do things—and too eager to step in to take over when someone seemed about to miss a deadline. Worse, Jack was prone to pounce on anyone who didn't appear to meet his standards, flying into a rage whenever someone deviated from Jack's way of doing things. As his direct reports complained—behind his back—Jack was "a control freak."

In our survey of his direct reports, we found the usual disastrous impact on climate. People were clear about the vision—where they needed to go—but not on how to get there. Jack knew what he wanted people to do, but failed to let them know when they were doing it right, giving no positive performance feedback. One result was a paralysis: People felt they had no flexibility to do their jobs in the way that made sense to them, but rather had to guess how Jack wanted them to do it. No surprise that in the two years since Jack had taken over the division, its business results had stalled. On the suggestion of his boss, Jack sought out a coach.

The first step was to get an accurate diagnosis of Jack's strengths and limitations through a 360-degree evaluation on the emotional intelligence competencies. He knew his strengths: self-confidence, high energy, achievement orientation, initiative, and conscientiousness. For Jack, the most revealing data were the large gaps between his self-evaluation and how his direct reports rated him on two leadership competencies: self-control and empathy.

To assist Jack in crafting a learning plan that could develop his skills in those two areas, Jack's coach spent a good deal of time, at first, simply helping him to digest the feedback data. The coach tied the reports of weak self-control and empathy to two of Jack's particular strengths: his ability to quickly see alternative solutions and his passionate desire to fix things immediately. Because Jack overused those strengths, he consequently underused more positive leadership styles, such as visionary and coaching styles, which rely on self-control and empathy.

Once Jack saw how his weaknesses were keeping him back from his ideal vision of himself as an effective leader, he was able to zero in on what he needed to improve. He then committed himself to shifting the balance between his strengths and gaps, and his coach helped him work up a learning plan. The plan emphasized specific ways to use on-the-job, day-to-day events as the laboratory for learning.

For example, Jack saw that he had no problem empathizing with people when things were calm, but once he began to feel stress, he'd tune out other people completely. That lack of self-control sabotaged his ability to listen to what people were telling him in the very moments he most needed to do so. Jack's learning plan, therefore, focused on handling emotions effectively. His coach showed Jack a method to tune in to the sensations in his body so he could monitor himself for early warning signs that he was about to fly off the handle again. Whenever he started to feel upset, he had four specific steps to take:

1. Step back—listen, don't jump in.

2. Let the other person speak.

3. Get some objectivity—ask yourself, Is there a sound reason for my reaction, or am I jumping to conclusions?

4. Ask clarifying questions, rather than ones that sound
   judgmental or hostile.

This intentional change in Jack's typical overreaction response
allowed him to empathize and listen, to gather information more
fully and understand it more clearly, and to have a rational dialogue instead of launching into a harangue. He didn't have to
agree with the other person, but now he gave that person a chance
to make his case.

Still, to make those changes, Jack had to learn to notice poten-
tially problematic situations in the first place. By being alert to situations that in the past have triggered our old, dysfunctional leadership habits, we're better able to choose a new, more positive
reaction.[24] Like an early-warning radar, this anticipation signals
us that we should pay more attention to what we are about to do,
and so puts our next action in the realm of conscious choice. It
gives us the chance to practice—rather than missing yet another
opportunity to change.

Jack did practice his new behaviors, again and again. He gave
his direct reports more positive feedback on work well done rather
than merely criticizing them, he reminded them that what they
did contributed to the group's mission, and he restrained himself
from micromanaging how they got their work done. Little by little, he became more of a visionary and coaching leader. Over a
six-month period, Jack made real progress. His own records showed
he'd reduced his number of flare-ups from one or more a day to
just one or two a month. The climate in the division had improved
sharply—and its numbers were starting to creep upward at last.

### A New Model of Learning

When a leader like Jack takes stock of his repertoire of leadership skills, in a sense he is assessing the sum total of a lifetime
of learning. The lessons people get in leadership start very early
in life, from observing teachers, coaches, clergy—anyone who
has been in the role of leader in their lives. These models offer the

first scaffold for people's own leadership habits, their original ideas about what a leader does. Then, as they begin to step into their first leadership roles in clubs, teams, student government, or as leaders in their peer groups, they put those models into practice. In their jobs, they encounter new leaders and try out new leadership behaviors, adding on to that early initial scaffolding that they had built.

Virtually none of these lessons involves explicit instruction in elements of leadership—they arise naturally in the course of life. But they lay down the brain circuitry for leadership habits, determining what a person will automatically tend to do in similar situations throughout life. Each time an individual heads a team, for instance, he'll most readily repeat what he did before as a team leader—and each time he repeats it, the neural connections for that habit become stronger. Cognitive scientists call such automatic strengthening of a habit *implicit* learning, as opposed to the explicit variety provided in school courses.

For the most part, the brain masters the competencies of leadership—everything from self-confidence and emotional self-management to empathy and persuasion—through implicit learning. You'll recall that implicit learning occurs not in the topmost layers of the neocortex—the thinking brain—but rather toward the bottom of the brain in the basal ganglia. In the case of leadership, that learning occurs presumably through connections to the prefrontal–limbic circuits of emotional intelligence.[25] This primitive section of the brain picks up and masters the habits we constantly rely on, continually learning how to perform the basic tasks of our lives —everything from stringing a sentence together to running an effective meeting.

All this learning goes on tacitly, most of the time without people even being aware that they are mastering such lessons, in what amounts to stealth learning. It's an elegant system, for the most part. The problem, though, is that people pick up their leadership habits rather haphazardly over the course of life through repeating what they see their models do, or through repeating their own attempts at leading. If that first manager who so impressed one was a frantic pacesetter, then that may become the model emulated as a leader; if he was a superb coach, what one will learn follows quite a different route. The net result: People end up with a mixed bag of leadership skills, akin to having mastered a few golf strokes but being a terrible putter.

Still, as we've seen, it's possible to improve if you do three things: Bring bad habits into awareness, consciously practice a better way, and rehearse that new behavior at every opportunity until it becomes automatic—that is, until mastery has occurred at the level of implicit learning.

Improving an emotional intelligence competence take months, rather than days, because the emotional centers of the brain are involved—not just the neocortex, the thinking brain where technical skills and purely cognitive abilities are learned. As we've mentioned before, the neocortex learns very quickly, even on a first hearing. But the basal ganglia and its links to the emotional centers learn differently: To master a new skill, they need repetition and practice.[26]

That's why it's hard to learn leadership abilities effectively in a classroom. A teacher can't instruct your brain circuits that carry old habits of leadership to relearn new habits. What's needed is practice: The more often a behavioral sequence repeats, the stronger the underlying brain circuits become. People thereby literally rewire their brains: Learning new habits strengthens pathways between neurons, and may even foster neurogenesis—growth of new neurons.[27]

For example, to overcome his pacesetting habit and broaden his leadership repertoire, Jack will have to practice repeatedly. The more settings in which he practices these new ways of thinking, feeling, and acting, the more flexible and strong the new circuits will become. At that point someone like Jack would find himself going through the paces of leadership, effortlessly controlling his emotional reactions while listening with empathy. This marks the moment the new neural pathways have become the brain's default option.

And that level of mastery lasts for years, if not an entire lifetime.

## All Performance, No Practice

Jack wouldn't have gotten far in developing his coaching style, however, without trying new ways of acting, particularly pausing to listen and ask questions. It was not easy. When a problem arose, every muscle in his body prepared for him to jump in, take over, and try to solve the problem himself. For Jack, that tendency was as automatic as knowing how to ride a bicycle—a reaction every bit as unconscious and powerful.

That's why experimentation with more positive alternatives is crucial. The new way of thinking, feeling, or acting feels unnatural at first, something like putting on someone else's clothes. At the neural level, a person is forcing the brain to go along a path less traveled. Small wonder that Jack was filled with self-doubt during the first week or so he was trying to listen to others rather than jumping in and taking over. It just didn't feel natural—at first.

Great athletes spend a lot of time practicing and a little time performing, while executives spend no time practicing and all of their time performing, as Jim Loehr and Tony Schwartz observed in the *Harvard Business Review*.[28] No wonder leaders so often recycle their problems: In the rush to achieve their goals and complete their tasks, they short themselves on learning to lead better. Often, a leader will try a new approach once or twice, and then apply it—without giving himself the chance to *practice* it.

The key to learning new habits for leaders lies in practice to the point of mastery. Otherwise they invite a relapse, a return to old habits. If you've ever played a musical instrument, you know that when you rehearsed your sheet music just enough so you made no mistakes, you were practicing to the point of comfort; you could wing it when playing for your teacher. But under the stress of a recital, you might forget parts of the piece. Professional musicians, however, go a crucial step further: They rehearse and rehearse, and then rehearse some more. They practice until the fingering of their instrument or breathing is automatic. They practice until they can play it without thinking about it and can just feel it.

Similarly, to master a leadership skill, you need to change the brain's default option by breaking old habits and learning new ones, which requires an extended period of practice to create the new neural pathway and then strengthen it.[29] You know that the new habit has been mastered when you're able to sustain that new response long into the future—not just for a week or a month.

The self-regulation competencies, particularly emotional self-control—may require special effort at first to get to the point of mastery. Some research suggests that managing emotional impulses is real mental work: The stress of the intentional effort to alter one's mood can deplete the energy it takes for self-control.[30] Still, sometimes self-control is the very thing that's needed when practicing a new leadership style—say, when a leader like Jack tries to master his pacesetting or commanding urges and replace them with a more affiliative style. In that case, learning requires a special effort: holding back the tendencies to react in the old way. A person has to override his emotional impulses, which adds to the burden of learning and can make him lose his focus.

This suggests a learning strategy that at first focuses a bit more on overcoming the impulsive leadership habits you are trying to undo—before giving full attention to the new habits with which you want to replace the old. Eventually, by practicing self-control to the point of mastery, what was once an effort becomes automatic, taking the pressure off. Once you've taken this key step, then your mental energy and attention are freed up for practicing new modes of leadership.

### Stealth Learning

While much, if not most, typical leadership development takes place in seminars, during a weekend or maybe even over a week of offsite training, that time frame hardly begins the process.

So rather than, say, just going off to some kind of weekend sensitivity-training program to hone his empathy, Jack used naturally occurring situations at work with his subordinates and peers as his training arena. He also talked about his learning plan with his wife and enlisted her as an informal coach to help him become a better listener at home and with friends. By expanding his learning arena in this way, Jack leveraged more from his life activities—and maximized his learning efficiency.

The trick is to learn while doing other things, a strategy that might be thought of as "stealth learning" and that can be useful for improving emotional intelligence abilities, particularly leadership skills. In studying outstanding managers among scientists and engineers—those who, for example, regularly used competencies such as empathy—researcher Christine Dreyfus found that they had refined those talents in many settings.[31] Their abilities were particularly impressive given that they were engineers working in a technological culture that didn't often model those competencies.

As described in chapter 6 for outstanding leaders at Johnson & Johnson, most of the leaders Dreyfus studied had started experimenting with the skills as much as forty years earlier, in childhood activities such as the Boy Scouts. Then, in high school and college, they used sports, clubs, music groups, and dorm life to experiment further. Later, when they became bench scientists and engineers working on problems in relative isolation, they continued to learn and refine these abilities in activities outside of work, practicing team building in settings such as church and community organizations, or by planning conferences for professional associations. The normal pacesetting brusqueness of the engineering culture softened as they experienced other, more relationship-oriented milieus.

One engineer, for example, who'd become a strong leader, reported that he'd been able to transcend the command-and-control, pacesetting engineering culture through a somewhat surprising venue for leadership development: his church. "My church group easily lent itself to people expressing feelings and opinions," the engineer recalled. "Where, as an engineer, I usually felt the need to always have a logical flow, in the group I became more accepting of less structure. Over time, that acceptance worked its way into how I acted as a leader—less concerned with flow and content and more attuned to group process."

For most of the engineers that Dreyfus studied, early experiences of being a project leader provided their key leadership-learning laboratory in the work setting. Over the years, they took on greater management responsibility, worked with coaches, and attended training programs sponsored by their company. As they continued to refine their leadership abilities, they became models for how stealth learning can go on anywhere, anytime.[32]

### The Power of Mental Rehearsal

The more time you put into practicing, then, the greater the payoff. There's another way to expand opportunities to practice leadership abilities: by using mental rehearsal.

Let's return to our example of Jack. Following part of his learning plan, he began to spend idle moments during his drive to work thinking through how to handle encounters he would have that day. One day, driving to a breakfast meeting with an employee who seemed to be bungling a project, Jack ran through a positive scenario in his mind: He asked questions and listened to be sure he fully understood the situation before starting to solve the problem. He anticipated feeling impatient, and rehearsed how he would handle these feelings rather than resorting to his usual response of jumping in too soon.

Such mental rehearsal can greatly improve how well you learn new skills. It's a well-known fact, for example, corroborated by scientific study, that mental rehearsal enhances the performance of athletes. Olympic athletes, such as the American diver Laura Wilkinson, use it routinely. While preparing for the 2000 Olympics, Wilkinson broke three toes and was unable to go in the water. Rather than stop her preparations, Wilkinson sat for hours each day on the diving platform, repeatedly recreating in her mind a detailed vision of each of her dives. She went on to win an upset victory in the 2000 Olympics—the gold medal in the ten-meter platform competition.[33]

There are dozens of such dramatic stories of athletes using the power of mental rehearsal, envisioning their success. That kind of visioning enlists powerful biological forces. For thirty years, a growing body of research has shown that you can raise the temperature of part of your body, and slow your breathing or heartbeat, through mental training, the right feedback, and the right vision of what you want to do. Accordingly, leadership success depends on your ability to clearly picture yourself achieving your ideal state, and then maintaining that focus. This visualization has another advantage: The brain, remember, motivates us by carrying an image of where we're going and how we'll feel when we get there.

But the benefits go beyond even that. Brain studies have shown that imagining something in vivid detail can fire the same brain cells that are actually involved in that activity.[34] In other words, the new brain circuitry appears to go through its paces, strengthening connections, even as a person merely repeats the sequence in his mind. That suggests a tactic for alleviating fears that might be associated with trying out new, riskier ways of leading. If you first visualize some likely situations at work or at home, you'll feel less awkward when you actually put the new skills into practice.

Experimenting with new behaviors, then, and seizing opportunities inside and outside of work to practice them—as well as using such methods as mental rehearsal—eventually triggers in one's brain the neural connections necessary for genuine change to occur.

# The Fifth Discovery:
# The Power of Relationships

In the early 1990s, a group of women who were partners in what was then Coopers & Lybrand met to form a study group. At first they gathered monthly to discuss their careers and how to provide leadership in the firm and in a traditionally male-dominated industry. But after a few meetings, the women began to realize that they were meeting to discuss their work *and* their lives in general. They developed a strong mutual trust, and found they could rely on each other for frank feedback as they worked on strengthening their leadership abilities.

Many professional women today, seeking to be leaders or sustain leadership in their organizations, have created similar groups— and for good reason. As we pointed out in chapter 6, women, like minorities, get shorted on helpful performance feedback. And, perhaps most important, people with whom we have a sense of trust give us a safe place to experiment, to try out unfamiliar parts of our leadership repertoire in a no-risk setting.

For anyone who has gone through leadership development that works, the importance of the people who help along the way will be obvious. As one midcareer leader put it during the last meeting of a peer group that had undergone a two-year development process, it wasn't just the program that made such a difference, but rather "the people and the relationships that we have built." In fact, perhaps paradoxically, in the self-directed learning process, we draw on others every step of the way—from articulating and refining our ideal self and comparing it with the reality, to the final assessment that affirms our progress. Our relationships offer us the very context in which we understand our progress and realize the usefulness of what we're learning.[35] Like consulting a lawyer, talking with a trusted coach, mentor, or friend becomes a safety zone within which to more freely explore the painful realities of a politicized work setting or to question things that don't make sense but are imprudent to raise with your boss. Experimenting and practicing new habits require finding safe places and relationships.

We've seen many instances in which such support can offer not just the hope of change, but also the *confidence* to embrace that hope. For example, at the end of a program for executives and professionals, these already highly successful people reported a large *gain* in their self-confidence.[36] How did they account for that gain, especially when their peers already had seen them as confident before the executives began the program? In interviews, the executives explained that what had increased was their confidence that they could *change*—something they hadn't felt for a long time in their professional lives. They reported feeling that many of the people around them—people at work, even their families—had an investment in them staying the same, despite their wanting to change. But in the leadership program, they developed a new reference group—others like themselves—who encouraged that change. Moreover, we've seen that result in study after study: Positive groups help people make positive changes, particularly if the relationships are filled with candor, trust, and psychological safety.[37]

### The Stress of Leadership

For leaders, such safety may be crucial for authentic learning to occur. Often leaders feel unsafe, as if they're under a microscope, their every action scrutinized by those around them—and so they never take the risk of exploring new habits. Knowing that others are watching with a critical eye provokes them to judge their progress too soon, curtail experimentation, and decrease risk taking.

In those ways and others, leadership is intrinsically stressful. Early studies on people who had a high drive for power—the need to have an impact—showed that their very desire for that power had the same arousing effect on them as if they were under actual biological stress.[38] When a person's stress increases—or his power motives are aroused—the body reacts by secreting more adrenaline and noradrenaline, the body's stress hormones. That leads to higher blood pressure, getting the individual ready for action. At the same time, the body secretes the stress hormone cortisol, which is even longer lasting than adrenaline—and which interferes with new learning.[39]

When people feel stressed, of course, they no longer feel safe and are further inhibited in practicing new ways of acting. Instead, they become defensive, relying on their most familiar habits. There's another problem that the stress of leadership introduces: When stress is high and sustained, the brain reacts with sustained cortisol secretion, which actually hampers learning by killing off brain cells in the hippocampus that are essential for new learning.

For all these reasons, learning for leadership works best under conditions where people feel safe—but not so relaxed that they lose motivation.[40] There's an optimal level of brain arousal that helps people to learn, the state in which both motivation and interest are high. A sense of psychological safety creates an atmosphere in which people can then experiment with little risk of embarrassment or fear of the consequences of failure.

Being in a resonant group—say, one with other leaders like yourself who are venturing together to cultivate new leadership styles—offers one of the best arenas for change. When you see someone like yourself overcome his inhibitions and take a risk, it sets you free to try something a bit risky yourself.[41]

Cultivating special relationships, those whose sole purpose is to help you along your path, is crucial to continuing development. Mentors or coaches, as we've seen, help you to discover your dreams, to understand your strengths and gaps and your impact on others, and to guide you through the steps in your learning plan. But just calling someone a "mentor" or "coach" isn't enough—the relationship must be one of candor, trust, and support.

### Mentors and Coaches

When we assessed high-level leaders at a large integrated-energy company, those we found to have a healthy repertoire of leadership strengths all told us the same story: They had first cultivated the strengths early in their careers, under the guardianship of a mentor. That finding confirms studies done by the Center for Creative Leadership in Greensboro, North Carolina, that have long pointed to the power of mentoring to shape a leader's abilities.[42]

Reflecting back on their careers as leaders, the executives we interviewed felt that the most pivotal experiences in their development had been jobs where they felt the challenges were over their heads—at least, at first. It took a sponsoring mentor who asked them to take the job and then protected them from meddling by "helpful hands" at corporate headquarters. The umbrella created by the mentor was so critical that the company began referring to this mentoring competence as giving others "room to act." The mentors made it safe for these fledgling leaders to spread their wings, trying out new styles and strengths. The mentoring did more than build a core of leadership strength throughout the company—it also produced two successive CEOs, each with laudable track records.

If the goal is to work with a mentor in cultivating particular leadership strengths, it's important to make that intention explicit. Working with a mentor who knows what you are trying to do, and with whom you share your aspirations and your learning agenda, converts the mentor into a coach.

Coaches come in many forms.[43] Some may be formal executive coaches, others informal mentors, and still others can be colleagues or even friends. The CEO and founder of Instill Corporation, Mack Tilling, has a mentor who is CEO of another corporation: David Garrison of Verestar Communications. Tilling feels that talking to another executive with related experience helps him sort out issues better than a coach might.[44]

On the other hand, hiring an executive coach—and there are legions of them today—can provide the opportunity to talk more freely than one could with a boss or peer. Having a coach (or mentor, for that matter) offers benefits beyond simply honing leadership skills: It gives you another set of eyes and ears, and so can be an antidote to the peril of the information quarantine that too many leaders suffer. Coaches help you see outside of the balloon surrounding your daily experience.

Good coaches will understand the dilemmas of the organization and its culture, as well as the leader's personal strengths and challenges, and use EI themselves.[45] To be really helpful, a coach will understand the leader's dilemmas from multiple perspectives: the individual level (what's going on for the person); the team level (the group dynamics of the executive or staff teams); and the organizational level (how all of this fits with culture, systems, and strategy). A coach can tailor a leader's development program, offering the luxury of going through the entire process outlined here in a one-on-one relationship.

*Bringing the Whole Team Along*

Helping a single leader move toward greater resonance marks a beginning. But for an entire organization, the impact will be all the greater if leadership growth goes beyond the individual.

Take the case of Rozano Saad of Huntsman Tioxide, a chemicals manufacturer in Malaysia. Not long after he was promoted to general manager of operations, he received feedback from his subordinates that jolted him: He tended to be a commanding, pacesetting leader. At one level, this was not surprising—after all, Rozano was an engineer by training, and those styles were the norm in the engineering culture in which he'd operated for the past sixteen years.

The problem was that he needed to draw on a wider repertoire if he was to succeed in his job. Huntsman Tioxide had been operating at a loss for four years. Although the Malaysia plant was the company's most modern facility, it had the worst productivity and quality record in the worldwide group. As a result, the Huntsman Group, a conglomerate based in Salt Lake City, Utah, had bought the Malaysian company (previously ICI Tioxide) "for a song," as one consultant said.

To help the plant out of its predicament, Rozano used his new awareness about his leadership to set learning goals toward building visionary and coaching leadership styles. His larger aim was to dramatically improve the organizational climate, particularly when it came to people's clarity about their responsibilities and the standards expected of them. He also knew that self-awareness was not one of his strengths, and that became one of his personal learning goals.

As a way to inoculate himself from the CEO disease, Rozano made his personal learning goals known among his staff. By involving the many people with whom he interacted daily, Rozano made others part of his learning laboratory. He also brought his whole management team through the same leadership development program he was undergoing. He wanted everyone to be speaking the same language as a way to reinforce their new learning agenda, and to work together in identifying a vision of where they hoped to bring the company. His own learning agenda, for instance, pushed him to communicate the newly identified vision of excellence at every meeting with people in the plants.

Teams were formed among the managers, from which they identified a "Monthly Plan Personal Contact" (their phrase for internal coaches) for each leader to get support and monitor progress on his or her learning plan. In the monthly management staff meeting, discussions now addressed management style, organizational climate, and learning plans as well as the usual topics of performance and safety. They also formed special reference groups that met monthly and within which they could discuss their own personal learning plans, review progress, and get ongoing feedback.

Just two years later, Rozano and his managers were so encouraged by the changes that they opened their plants to tours and site visits by other executives. The whole environment shifted as well. At the beginning of this process, if you'd asked someone on the shop floor about their personal objectives, you'd have heard something vague in response, such as "to produce 50,000 tons of pigment." Now if you ask the same question, you can hear the focus on quality over quantity: "I have to ensure that samples are taken every four hours, and analyzed according to the right standards. And if there's any deviation from the acceptable parameters, I'll have to troubleshoot to reach the conformance level ASAP through. . . ."

What's more, the company began showing a strong upward trend in profitability, as well as improved productivity benchmarks. Regular climate surveys to monitor progress showed jumps of nearly 200 percent when assessed by all managers in the company (and by close to 300 percent seen by Rozano's direct reports)— particularly in the dimensions of clarity, flexibility, standards, and team commitment. In the third year after the change effort, the conglomerate's CEO reported that Huntsman Tioxide-Malaysia was one of the highest performing companies in the group, breaking productivity targets with record profits.

What had happened? The same people were there; personnel hadn't changed much during that time. What had changed was how they worked together: The climate became one that encouraged everyone to increase their use of emotional intelligence and to build their leadership talent. Each manager had the opportunity to articulate his dreams and aspirations (the first discovery), to see himself as others saw him through 360-degree feedback and identification of strengths and gaps (the second discovery), to develop a personal learning agenda (the third discovery), and to experiment and practice new habits of leadership at work (the fourth discovery). The managers did this work with each other (the fifth discovery) and created a new climate of leadership. They developed emotional resonance about their mission and development as leaders.

When it comes to leadership, you've just begun the task when you change a single leader. The rest of the job is to develop a critical mass of resonant leaders and thereby transform how people work together, and then to encourage the ongoing development of such leaders. The most effective leadership development works hand in hand with parallel transformations in the organization that those leaders guide—as we will see in the next part of this book.

# PART THREE

# BUILDING
## EMOTIONALLY
### INTELLIGENT
# ORGANIZATIONS

### CHAPTER NINE

# THE EMOTIONAL REALITY OF TEAMS

THE TOP MANAGEMENT TEAM of a manufacturing firm had accepted an important charge: to find ways to address the fact that the firm was perennially locked in what they called "flat growth." Translation: They were losing their edge. The trouble was, the team simply could not seem to make big decisions, no matter how important. In fact, the more urgent the decision, the more the team members would put off making it, careful to avoid topics on which they knew they disagreed. Worse yet, they sometimes acted as if they did agree on key issues, only to leave the meeting and, as one person put it, "quietly sabotage the decision." Meanwhile, the manufacturing firm fell more and more behind on implementing crucial strategy.

What was going on with this team? Through a leadership audit of the team members, the truth came out: Virtually every one of them was uncomfortable with interpersonal disagreements, scoring low on the conflict management EI competence. Suddenly the reason for the team's inability to make decisions was obvious. It had never come to the collective realization that open discussion and disagreements about ideas—as opposed to attacks on people who hold disparate views—sharpen decision making. Instead, the team had adopted the habit of avoiding all disputes.

For this group, recognizing that their shared gap had resulted in inefficient team habits was like a light going on. In fact, what they had discovered was an important, but invisible, force acting on the team: The ground rules regarding conflict and their collective feelings about it added up to an emotional reality that paralyzed them. With that insight, they could see what they as a team—and as individuals—needed to change; further, they recognized that beyond a behavioral adjustment, a real solution would require a shift in mindset about conflict.

We've seen repeatedly that when teams (and entire organizations) face their collective emotional reality, they begin a healthy reexamination of the shared habits that create and hold that reality in place. In fact, for leaders to extend emotional intelligence throughout their teams and organizations, that's precisely where they need to start: by taking a hard look at reality, rather than focusing first on an ideal vision. Thus the sequence of reflection and self-discovery is reversed from what it was at the individual level, described in chapter 7.

Why the reversal? It's a matter of motivation. As individuals, we feel most motivated to change when we tap into our dreams and ideal visions of our lives. That vision of our personal future gives us the energy and commitment to change our behavior. The ideal vision for a group, however, is often a much more distant concept, so it simply doesn't provide enough motivation to instigate change. A good example is the lofty language found in company mission statements, which often feels light-years away from employees' day-to-day experiences at work.

Groups begin to change only when they first have fully grasped the reality of how they function, particularly when individuals in the group recognize that they're working in situations that are dissonant or uncomfortable. It is critical that they understand this reality on an emotional, even visceral, level. Yet recognizing discomfort does not, in itself, enable change. Group members must discover the source of discontent—an emotional reality that usually goes beyond such obvious sources as "a bad boss." The root of the problem often lies with long-established and deeply embedded ground rules, or habits that govern the group. We call those rules *norms* when we talk about teams, and *culture* when we refer to the larger organization.

Once there's an understanding of the emotional reality and norms of teams and the culture of an organization, it can be used as a basis from which to develop the ideal vision for the group, which, to be truly captivating, must also be in tune with each individual's personal vision. With the reality and ideal vision understood, it is possible to identify and explore the gaps between them and consciously plan to align what's happening today with the vision of tomorrow. The more aligned the reality is with the ideal, the more the change can be counted on to persist over the long term. That type of "attuning" ideals with reality is what creates the framework for moving away from dissonance and toward an emotionally intelligent, resonant, and more effective group.

Before exploring how to make change happen, however, we'll look more closely at the concept of emotional reality. We'll first explore this in the context of teams and move later to discuss organizations, since team situations are usually closer to people's daily experience. Teams also provide a more immediate venue for change —while at the same time offering a reflection of the larger organizational reality.

## When Teams Fail: The Power of Norms

In the last few decades much research has proven the superiority of group decision making over that of even the brightest individual in the group.[1] There is one exception to this rule. If the group lacks harmony or the ability to cooperate, decision-making quality and speed suffer. Research at Cambridge University found that even groups comprising brilliant individuals will make bad decisions if the group disintegrates into bickering, interpersonal rivalry, or power plays.[2]

In short, groups are smarter than individuals only when they exhibit the qualities of emotional intelligence. Everyone in the group contributes to the overall level of emotional intelligence, but the leader holds special sway in this regard. Emotions are contagious, and it's natural for people to pay extra attention to the leader's feelings and behavior.[3] So, very often it is the group leader who sets the tone and helps to create the group's emotional reality—how it feels to be part of the team.[4] A leader skilled in collaboration can keep resonance high and thus ensure that the group's decisions will be worth the effort of meeting. Such leaders know how to balance a team's focus on the task at hand with attention to the relationships among the team members. They naturally create a friendly, cooperative climate in the room, a climate that fosters a positive outlook on the future.[5]

Accordingly, a leader who isn't emotionally intelligent can wreak havoc in a team situation. Consider the following examples.

- A division of a healthcare company was losing money hand over fist, providing inferior service while employing too many people at every level. The management team was headed by a short-sighted leader and held endless meetings to seek consensus before it would make changes regarding critical issues such as cutting staff. Unable to come to any decisions, within a few years the ailing division pulled the entire company into financial disarray.

- Janet, a brilliant leader in a large insurance company, stepped into a sleepy division with the force of a tornado—and absolute intolerance for the old ways of doing things. For people on the team who didn't agree with her plans, she had one clear and very public message: There's no room for you here; find something else to do. Little did Janet realize she had mobilized a force for a new cause in her team—to see her fail at any price. Within a matter of months, what had been a reasonably successful division began performing miserably, and within a year it was dismantled.

Unfortunately, these scenarios are all too familiar to many of us. At the root of both situations was a problem related to how the leader managed the silent language of both emotion and norms. We take norms for granted, but they are immensely powerful. Norms represent implicit learning at the group level—the tacit rules that we learn by absorbing day-to-day interactions and that we automatically adopt so they can fit in smoothly.

When all is said and done, the norms of a group help to determine whether it functions as a high-performing team or becomes simply a loose collection of people working together.[6] In some teams, contention and heated confrontation are the order of the day; in others a charade of civility and interest barely veils everyone's boredom. In still other, more effective teams, people listen to and question each other with respect, support each other in word and deed, and work through disagreements with openness and humor. Whatever the ground rules, people automatically sense them and tend to adjust how they behave accordingly. In other words, norms dictate what "feels right" in a given situation, and so govern how people act.

Sometimes norms that seem helpful, and that are even rooted in noble goals, can become destructive. That was the case with the healthcare division example recounted earlier. One of the division's most vaunted norms was a commitment to consensus in the decision-making process. But whereas consensus usually results in highly committed and motivated team members, in this division the leader had come to use it as a way to stall and even hijack decisions—especially decisions that would move things in a new direction.

In the case of the new leader of the sleepy insurance division, Janet's failure to identify the team's emotional reality and to comply with its underlying norms wrought catastrophic results. She underestimated the power of the tribe: the tight cohesion that people feel when there are long-standing collective habits and a shared sense of what they hold sacred.

Charged with transforming the division into a state-of-the-art unit, Janet came in with big dreams and a keen eye for what needed to change. Using a classic commanding leadership style, she looked around, found a few folks who looked liked "leaders" (actually they looked just like her), pulled them close, and began cleaning house—readily sacrificing people with the least power. When her new subordinates objected to her tactics, Janet wasn't fazed; she was convinced that the senior people would see the need for change and adopt her vision—or else get out.

What Janet failed to take into account were the unspoken but powerful norms that had governed the division long before she came aboard. The most important of those norms was a strong bond of loyalty among the team members, who prided themselves on taking care of each other even during hard times. They had also found ways to deal with conflict that ensured that few people were hurt. By treating people roughly, Janet violated core cultural norms. The team members found their guiding principles—collaboration, kindness, and respect for "face"—under attack, and they fought back. Within a matter of months, as people came together around their shared sense of outrage, key team members openly tried to wrest leadership from her, while many others chose to leave—leading to the division's eventual demise.

Janet is a good example of one of the biggest mistakes leaders can make: ignoring the realities of team ground rules and the collective emotions in the tribe and assuming that the force of their leadership alone is enough to drive people's behavior. Still, it happens in company after company: A leader walks into a new job—often a turnaround situation—ignores the power of the group's norms, and pretends that feelings don't matter. Rather than using resonance-building leadership styles, the leader employs a steamrolling combination of commanding and pacesetting styles. The result is a toxic and rebellious environment.

Clearly, the leaders in the previous examples lacked the emotional intelligence to address the group reality and raise team interactions to more productive levels. Leaders who have a keen sense of the group's pivotal norms, on the other hand—and who are adept at maximizing positive emotions—can create highly emotionally intelligent teams.

Collective emotional intelligence is what sets top-performing teams apart from average teams, as shown by the work of Vanessa Druskat, a professor at Case Western's Weatherhead School of Management, and Steven Wolff, a professor at Marist College's School of Management. Group emotional intelligence, they argue, determines a team's ability to manage its emotions in a way that cultivates "trust, group identity, and group efficacy" and so maximizes cooperation, collaboration, and effectiveness.[7] In short, emotional intelligence results in a positive—and powerful—emotional reality.

## Maximizing the Group's Emotional Intelligence

Not surprisingly, a group's emotional intelligence requires the same capabilities that an emotionally intelligent individual expresses: self-awareness, self-management, social awareness, and relationship management. What's different though, is that the EI competencies relate both to individuals and to the group as a whole.[8] Groups have moods and needs, and they act collectively—just think about the last time you walked into a meeting late and could actually feel the tension in the room. You could tell there had been a conflict of some sort, even before anyone said a word. The group, as a whole, was tense and poised for a fight. You also knew that the group, as a whole, needed some action to get back on track—and if it didn't happen soon, things would spiral downward. This is what we mean by group moods and needs.

As is true with individuals, in teams each of the EI abilities builds on one another in practice, becoming a kind of continuum. In other words, when team members begin to practice self-awareness, noticing the group's mood and needs, they tend to respond to one another with empathy. The very act of showing one another empathy leads the team to create and sustain positive norms and manage its relationships with the outside world more effectively.

At the team level, social awareness—especially empathy—is the foundation that enables a team to build and maintain effective relationships with the rest of the organization.

### The Self-Aware Team

An engineering firm's management team had scheduled its weekly meeting at an offsite location. Just as the meeting was about to begin, one team member stormed in, mumbling something about the meeting being held at a place and time that was inconvenient for him. Noticing how upset he was, the leader called everyone's attention to the sacrifice the team member was making and thanked him for it. The effect of that acknowledgment: no more anger.

A team expresses its self-awareness by being mindful of shared moods as well as of the emotions of individuals within the group. In other words, members of a self-aware team are attuned to the emotional undercurrents of individuals and the group as a whole. They have empathy for each other, and there are norms to support vigilance and mutual understanding. So although this team leader's gesture may have seemed simple, often just such an astute and seemingly subtle move can do more to reduce dissonance and restore resonance than an action full of bells and whistles.

Since emotions are contagious, team members take their emotional cues from each other, for better or for worse. If a team is unable to acknowledge an angry member's feelings, that emotion can set off a chain reaction of negativity. On the other hand, if the team has learned to recognize and confront such moments effectively, then one person's distress won't hijack the whole group.

That intervention in the engineer's team points to the near seamlessness between a team's self-awareness and empathy, which leads to its self-management. It also illustrates how a leader can model behavior. The leader in this case modeled an empathetic confrontation of a member's emotional reality and brought it to the group's attention. Such a caring attitude builds a sense of trust and belonging that underscores the shared mission: We're all in this together.

Team self-awareness might also mean creating norms such as listening to everyone's perspective—including that of a lone dissenter—before a decision is made. Or it can mean recognizing when a teammate feels uncomfortable in learning a task, and stepping in to offer support.

In their research on teams, Susan Wheelan of Temple University and Fran Johnston of the Gestalt Institute of Cleveland point out that very often it is an emotionally intelligent team member— not just the leader—who is able to point out underlying problems and thus raise the self-awareness of the group.[9] Such was the case at a strategic planning session at Lucent Technologies.

The meeting was going all too predictably. The reigning executive had asked, as she always did, for a "stretch goal" to set next year's numbers. The team responded with its usual bravado: "Double digit!" "We can do anything we set our minds to!" But Michel Deschapelles, currently a regional vice president for Latin America, felt frustrated. He knew that the team's norm of public bravado had long masked underlying patterns of ineffective goal setting— which went far to explain the division's slow growth—and reflected people's tendency to avoid accountability by hiding behind vague goals.

He decided to challenge his teammates: "Do you guys really mean it?" he asked. "Then let's go for 400 percent growth this year! Let's make that our goal!" You could see the reaction on people's faces: They thought he had gone mad. For a moment dismay paralyzed the group. But after a few minutes, people started to laugh: Deschapelles had called their bluff and shed light on the group's hidden norm of empty bravado.

His challenge initiated a frank discussion about how the team had hidden the truth of its performance behind meaningless phrases. Soon the team was able to have more realistic conversations about measurable goals and concrete steps to attain them, holding one another accountable for what they could achieve as a team. That proved to be a pivotal moment for business performance, creating new clarity about who was responsible for what. For the first time, financial results for the following fiscal year let the team demonstrate its value to the corporation: They helped to close over $900 million in sales.

Deschapelles's actions sparked collective mindfulness—awareness of what the team was doing, and why.[10] This level of self-awareness in a team leads to an ability to make decisions about what to do and how to do it, rather than blindly following ineffective norms or swaying with the winds of team members' (or the leader's) emotions.

### The Self-Managed Team

Cary Cherniss, chair of a well-known research group, puts team self-awareness front and center and holds group members accountable for managing how they work together. At the beginning of a day-long meeting, he passes out the day's agenda—along with a list of "process norms" that outlines how the group will carry out that agenda. For example:

*Everyone, not just Cary, should take responsibility for:*

- *Keeping us on track if we get off*
- *Facilitating group input*
- *Raising questions about our procedures (e.g., asking the group to clarify where it is going and offering summaries of the issues being discussed to make sure we have a shared understanding of them)*
- *Using good listening skills: either build on the ongoing discussion or clearly signal that we want to change the subject, and ask if that is ok . . .*

Members of this group, who come from around the world, say these meetings are among the most focused, productive, and enjoyable of any they've attended.

This example offers an excellent lesson in how a team led by an emotionally intelligent leader can learn to manage itself. Of course, Cherniss should know what he's doing—after all, he heads the Consortium for Research on Emotional Intelligence in

Organizations at Rutgers University. But none of the process norms that Cherniss passed around were out of the ordinary, in and of themselves. What was unusual was that Cherniss made sure he reminded the group of its collaborative norms—making them explicit so that everyone could practice them.

This raises an important point about team self-management: Positive norms will stick only if the group puts them into practice over and over again. Cherniss's group continually maximized its potential for interacting with emotional intelligence, raised its level of effectiveness, and produced a positive experience for all of the group members each time it met. Being so explicit about norms also helped to socialize newcomers into the group quickly: At one point, the consortium doubled its size, but did so smoothly because people knew how to mesh.

When core values and norms are clear to people, a leader does not even need to be physically present for the team to run effectively—this is of special importance to the thousands of managers who work with virtual teams and whose team members are located all over the globe. In self-aware, self-managing teams, members themselves will step up to the plate to instill and reinforce resonant norms and to hold one another accountable for sticking to them. At one research laboratory, for example, no one can remember who started what has become a tradition during meetings of R&D groups. Whenever someone voices a creative idea, the person who speaks next must take the role of an "angel's advocate," offering support. That way the prospects are better for the survival of the fragile bud of an idea, insulating the innovative thought from the inevitable criticisms. The "angel's advocate" norm does two important things: It helps to protect new ideas, and it makes people feel good when they are creative. As a result, people are more creative, and resonance is continually reinforced in the team.

So, team self-management is everyone's responsibility. It takes a strong, emotionally intelligent leader to hold the group to the practice of self-management, especially for teams not accustomed to proactively handling emotions and habits. When core values and the team's overall mission are clear, however, and when self-management norms are explicit and practiced over time, team effectiveness improves dramatically, as does the experience of team members themselves. Being on the team becomes rewarding in itself—and those positive emotions provide energy and motivation for accomplishing the team's goals.

### The Empathic Team

A team in a manufacturing plant knew that its success depended in part on getting the maintenance team to give their equipment top priority. So the manufacturing team members nominated that team for a "Team of the Quarter" award, and they wrote the letters that helped the maintenance team win. That relationship polishing helped the manufacturing team maintain its record as one of the plant's top producers.

The effect was clear: By helping to trigger a feeling of team pride in the maintenance group, the manufacturing team created goodwill between those two parts of the organization—and a desire to help the other succeed. The team used its skills to try to understand another part of the organization and how the two groups affected one another, thereby cultivating a mutually beneficial relationship. As a result, both teams succeeded better than either one would have on its own.

An emotionally intelligent team, then, has the collective equivalent of empathy, the basis of all relationship skills. It identifies other key groups in the organization (and beyond) that contribute to the team's success, and it takes consistent action to foster a good working relationship with those groups. Being empathic at the team level doesn't just mean being nice, though. It means figuring out what the whole system really needs and going after it in a way that makes all those involved more successful and satisfied with the outcomes.[11] The manufacturing team's proactive stance worked on two levels: It built resonance between the two groups, and it helped shine a spotlight on the good work of the maintenance team when it was recognized as the plant's top performer.

Empathy across organizational boundaries—team to team, for example—is a powerful driver of organizational effectiveness and efficiency. Moreover, this kind of empathy goes far toward creating a healthy emotional climate organization-wide, as well as creating a positive emotional environment in teams themselves.

## Uncovering a Team's Emotional Reality

The leader who wants to create an emotionally intelligent team can start by helping the team raise its collective self-awareness. As some of the examples discussed earlier illustrated, this is the true work of the leader: to monitor the emotional tone of the team and to help its members recognize any underlying dissonance. Only when a team can confront that emotional reality will it feel moved to change. By acknowledging a shared sentiment as simple as "I don't like how it feels around here," a team makes a critical first step in the change process.

A leader helps initiate that process by listening for what's really going on in the group. That means not only observing what team members are doing and saying but also understanding what they are feeling. Then, once a leader has helped the team uncover its less-productive norms, the group can come together around new ways of doing things.

Strategies for exposing a group's emotional reality can take myriad forms. For example, a vice president at a financial services company told us: "I always start by looking not at how I see things, but at how my team members see things. I ask myself, 'What's happening with that person? Why is he doing those awful things? What is he afraid of or angry about? Or, what is she excited about, and what makes her feel secure and happy?' "

By modeling and encouraging in her team the key competency self-awareness, that vice president made her division a center of excellence. Moreover, since its group norms included empathy and a focus on others—rather than on its own wants and needs—the division was able to look beyond itself and identify leadership

## SETTING GROUND RULES: THE LEADER'S JOB

**M**ORE THAN ANYONE ELSE, it is the team leader who has the power to establish norms, maximizing harmony and collaboration to ensure that the team benefits from the best talents of each member. A leader accomplishes that by moving the group toward a higher emotional tone, using positive images, optimistic interpretations, and resonance-building norms and leadership styles, particularly visionary, democratic, affiliative, and coaching styles (see chapter 4 for more on styles).

For example, leaders can model behavior through their own actions or by positively reinforcing members who do something that builds the group's emotional capacity. One might do this by conducting a short check-in session before meetings start, to ensure that people whose mood might be "off" can express their feelings and have them soothed. As Kenwyn Smith of the University of Pennsylvania and David Berg of Yale University noted in their research, such emotions in a group are crucial signals to a leader "that the issue or event at hand should be engaged rather than avoided"—short-circuiting the trouble rather than letting it smolder.[12] For example, a leader might make a point of phoning a member whose behavior has been rude and discussing the issue, or she might make sure she asks members who have been quiet what they think about a particular decision.

Setting the right ground rules requires an emotionally intelligent leader—again, common sense, but not common practice. The best leaders pay attention and act on their sense of what is going on in the group, and they needn't be obvious about it. Subtle messages, such as quietly reminding someone not to attack ideas during a brainstorming session, are powerful too. Under such leadership, teams over time naturally accumulate a common, positive lore about how to operate with each other.

and management issues that the company as a whole needed to address. As a result, the division has hit several home runs in the programs and initiatives it has launched, including a management-assessment center that's known in the industry as best in class.

Another senior manager pays attention to the group as a whole. Aware that teams often behave differently at different points in their life cycle, this manager creates ways for members to talk about issues that are problematic in new teams.[13] When convening a project team, she'll routinely get people to talk about their strengths and about what they can contribute to the effort. Subtly, this leader is making team members aware of two aspects of the team's emotional reality: inclusion dynamics (who's in and who's out) and people's roles (who does what, and why). The openness she establishes with these team start-ups helps to create good norms—habits that will enable the team to deal with the inevitable conflicts later on.

Another way that leaders can uncover the emotional reality of the group is by observing important signals. For example, during a recent merger between two European pharmaceutical giants, one manager checked an easy barometer of her division's collective emotions: She monitored the number of cars in the parking lot.

When the merger was first announced, this manager noticed that the parking lot was always full, and that many cars remained well into the evening. She knew that people were working extra hard because they were excited about the potential opportunities that the merger represented. Then, as the change process began to hit one delay after another, the manager noticed fewer and fewer cars in the parking lot. Clearly, many people's initial excitement and commitment was dwindling—and their anxiety increasing.

But what about the cars that continued to appear in the parking lot, day after day? Several pockets of people were apparently managing to remain productive and relatively happy even during that sluggish process. At this division it was discovered that while many of those people were motivated internally—either by a deep commitment to the work itself, such as the R&D scientists, or because they were otherwise skilled in emotional self-management—most people who weathered the change were protected from the turmoil by effective leaders. Those emotionally intelligent leaders made sure that they engaged their teams in the change process, giving them as much information and as much control over their destiny as possible. They noticed how their team members were feeling, acknowledged that those feelings were important, and gave people opportunities to express those emotions.

For example, one R&D manager recognized early on that morale was tanking after a favorite leader left the company. Rather than ignoring the problem (after all, he couldn't change the situation), he talked to each of his team members individually about their sorrow and concerns. That kind of personal attention enabled him to then bring the team together so that it could refocus its energy on the more positive changes surrounding the merger. Another manager held "team closedowns." Instead of simply shuffling people on to their next job as new positions were announced, on several occasions he brought the old team together to celebrate the past, mourn the end of an era, and discuss hopes for the future.

These managers are good examples of leaders who managed their own feelings and the collective feelings in their units so that people spent a minimal amount of emotional energy deciphering—or fighting—the changes. By keeping their eyes open and monitoring the tone of their groups, the leaders captured positive energy and found constructive outlets for negative feelings.

## Discovering the Team's Emotional Intelligence

The CEO of a midsize company asked us to work with three members of an executive team who were not cooperating well together. The CEO thought the cure would be simply a matter of doing some team building to get things back on track. We decided to get more information. In our coaching conversations with team members, we looked for the emotional reality of the team and its norms, as well as themes concerning the leader's impact. We also took a snapshot of the team's emotional intelligence using the Emotional Competence Inventory (ECI), and we assessed management style and the executives' impact on the climate of their organization.[14] What we found surprised this CEO. True, the team wasn't working well together, but what it needed wasn't team building. The results of our interviews and the picture the 360-degree feedback painted about the team showed several underlying problems that required a very different kind of solution.

Not surprisingly, there were a few problems with specific team members. One team member, for example, measured very low on self-awareness. He was completely missing the clues people gave him about his style of interaction. In meetings, he would express strong viewpoints and not understand how his aggressive manner was coming across to others. When people tried to get through to him about these issues, his body language said, "Lay off."

Another team member, recently arrived from a plant halfway around the world, exhibited little understanding of organizational politics in the corporate center and was alienating teammates and subordinates alike with his countercultural behavior. What made it even more difficult for his co-workers (and the man himself) to understand was that, on the interpersonal level at least, he displayed excellent empathy and relationship-building skills—he just couldn't read the team's emotional reality, and he was always out of synch.

Most of the time, these problems and other interpersonal issues become the focus of team building. When we looked deeper, however, we found that the real problem was a combination of ineffective norms and a negative emotional tone of the team. There was little self-awareness on the part of individuals or the team as a whole about their own group process: They did not manage individual team members' emotions or the group's moods very well, and they spent a lot of time and energy managing the team's negative emotions. In essence, it did not feel good to be part of the team, and people were avoiding working together.

Part of the underlying problem was that the team had established some ineffective norms in response to the CEO's pacesetting leadership style. The CEO's high drive for achievement and his inability to show empathy were creating a dysfunctionally competitive environment within the team. Moreover, while this leader thought his vision and strategy were apparent to everyone, our data showed us that wasn't the case at all: The reason the team members were moving in different directions was because they were unsure of where the larger organization was supposed to be headed.

Obviously, off-the-shelf team building would have done little to help this executive committee. By recognizing that its collective gap in emotional intelligence had created unproductive habits of interaction, the team could then see what it really needed to change. Equally important, the team recognized that in order for it to change as a group, each member also would have to commit to change as an individual. Armed with accurate information, we were able to target change processes for both the team and its individual members.

This team snapshot illustrates the importance of getting a clear picture of the emotional reality of an environment before launching into a solution. Part of understanding the emotional reality is uncovering the particular habits ingrained in a team or organization that can drive behavior. Often these habits make little sense to people—and yet they still act on them, seeing them as "just the way we do things around here." Emotionally intelligent leaders look for signs that reveal whether such habits, and the systems that support them, work well. By exploring and exposing unhealthy group habits, leaders can build more effective norms.

The previous example of the executive team unearthing its unproductive norms and unhealthy emotional reality points to a critical requirement for larger organizational change—something we will examine in detail in the next chapter. Getting people in the top executive team together to have an honest conversation about what is working and what is not is a first critical step to creating a more resonant team. Such conversations bring to life the reality of what an organization feels like and what people are actually doing in it.

The problem is, these conversations are hot, and many leaders are afraid to start the dialogue—fearful of taking it to the primal dimension. Too often, unsure of their ability to handle the emotions that arise when people talk honestly about what is going on, leaders stick to the safe topics: alignment, coordination of team members' functional areas, and strategy-implementation plans. While these safer conversations can set the stage for the next discussion—about the team itself, the organization, and the people—most teams stop the discussion at the level of strategy and functional alignment. They find it too difficult to be honest with one another, to examine the emotional reality and norms of the team. And this causes dissonance on the team—after all, everyone can feel when the norms are dysfunctional and the emotional climate is unproductive. By not taking on the problem, the leader actually magnifies it. It takes courage to break through that barrier, and it takes an emotionally intelligent leader to guide a team through it.

The benefits of such a process at the top are threefold. First, a new and healthy legitimacy develops around speaking the truth and honestly assessing both the behavioral and the emotional aspects of culture and leadership. Second, the very act of engaging in this process creates new habits: When people in the organization see their leaders searching for truth, daring to share a dream aloud, and engaging with one another in a healthy manner, they begin to emulate that behavior. And third, when truth seeking comes from the top, others are more willing to take the risk, too.

As we have seen in this chapter, leaders cannot lead with resonance if their team's norms hold them captive. And they cannot change the team's norms unless they are willing to take on the leader's primal task—working with people's emotions and with the team's emotional reality. That truth is even more apparent at the organizational level, when norms extend to entire corporate cultures. After all, even the most courageous individual finds it hard to buck an entire system. The next step for fostering new leadership, then, is to consider the real and the ideal state of the larger organization.

### CHAPTER TEN

# REALITY AND THE IDEAL VISION

## Giving Life to the Organization's Future

F OR MANY YEARS, Shoney's restaurant chain had a close-knit group of executives at the top—people who knew each other well, shared history and beliefs, and generally thought they had it figured out when it came to how to manage the business. The problem was that there was a lot of cronyism at the top, too. It was really an old-boys' network of white, male senior executives—and there was an underlying culture that promoted from the buddy system and left people of color by the wayside.

All of that changed, however, in 1992, when the company was forced to pay $132 million to settle a class-action lawsuit from 20,000 employees and rejected job applicants, who claimed discrimination in hiring and promotion practices. Since that time, a cadre of new leaders at Shoney's has intentionally changed the company's culture, launching a decisive campaign to broaden opportunity for qualified people of color.[1] In just ten years, Shoney's has gone from an old-boys' club to one of *Fortune* magazine's "Top 50 Companies for Minorities."

None of that change happened overnight, of course. The process began with an undeniable wake-up call (the lawsuit) regarding *the reality* of the company's dissonant culture. Then the new leaders entering the scene had to identify *an ideal vision* that would guide hiring decisions in the future. And finally, the organization as a whole had to embrace that vision—become *emotionally attuned* to it—before lasting change could occur.

At Shoney's, leaders took on reality, and they led the organization into a very different future. They knew that, just as is true for teams, identifying the emotional reality and norms of an organization begins the process for change. Leaders can initiate a widespread shift toward emotional intelligence when they identify a *company's* emotional reality and habits—what people do together and how.

The real difference is that whereas the components of individual emotional intelligence competencies can translate directly to teams, organizations are more complex and thus the goal is broader: to foster emotionally intelligent leadership widely and deeply at every level, and to systematically create norms and a culture that support truth and transparency, integrity, empathy, and healthy relationships. That kind of transformation begins with leaders who are open to the truth, who can ferret out the emotional reality of the organization, and who can engage others in a compelling vision of their own future. When a company develops that kind of emotionally intelligent leadership at all levels, and when those leaders face up to reality, a transformed company can, and often must, emerge.

## When Leaders Don't Listen

That first step, uncovering the truth and an organization's reality, is the leader's primal task. But too many leaders fail to invite the truth, which can leave them prey to the CEO disease—being a leader who is out of touch and out of tune. In their most benign form, such leaders seem to have no time for important conversations, and do not build the kind of affiliative or coaching relationships that result in deep dialogue about what's working and what is not. They don't have enough real contact with people in their organizations to get a sense of what is happening, living in a kind of rarefied air that leaves them out of touch with the underlying emotional reality of day-to-day life.

Less benign are leaders who use rigid commanding and pacesetting styles and who actually prevent people from telling them the truth. These leaders are clueless, or in denial about the reality of their organizations. While they may believe that everything is fine, they have in fact created a culture in which no one dares to tell them anything that might provoke them, especially bad news. That kind of silence can come at a very high price.

Consider the estimated 100,000 deaths each year in U.S. hospitals caused by routine medical errors—such as a doctor writing the wrong orders for a patient's medicine, or the wrong bottle being attached to an intravenous tube. Often these mistakes could have been prevented if only the command-and-control culture in most medical organizations had been acknowledged and changed.[2] One physician, who belongs to an Academy of Medicine task force addressing these issues, told us: "In the culture of hospitals, a nurse who corrects a doctor—telling him he wrote too many zeroes in an order for a patient's meds—can get her head bitten off. If medicine were to adopt the zero tolerance for mistakes that sets the norm for the airline mechanic industry, we'd cut medical errors drastically."

Of course, no one tells nurses they may risk the wrath of doctors if they challenge them. Those are the kinds of lessons about organizational culture that people learn implicitly by picking up on cues in the environment, and those cultures are not easy to change. Creating a hospital culture that supported "zero tolerance" would mean, for example, building in a far greater level of systematic checks and cross-checks than the medical field has thus far accepted. It would also mean challenging the widespread pacesetting and commanding leadership styles that hierarchical cultures encourage—and, as the physician put it, making it "safe for that nurse to tell a doctor he's made a mistake."

## The Toxic Organization

When leaders operate with dissonant styles, the resulting culture is inevitably toxic. How does it feel to work in such an organization that lacks emotional intelligence? One manager we know described a leader and a toxic organization that ultimately left her physically ill and feeling as if she had lost her competence, confidence, and creativity. The cause was clear: a pacesetting leader who relied on threats and coercion to get things done.

Despite the company having public service and education as its explicit mission, the president focused instead on short-term profit. The company had very little competition, so in this leader's mind, corners could be cut on quality with no risk of losing customers. Also troubling was that he openly expressed how little he cared about employees' welfare. "Bring 'em in and burn 'em out," he liked to say. Worse, he did not respect people; he was a bully. A typical example was the day a junior staff member mentioned to a few people, including the president, that it was her birthday, and offered them a piece of cake. While everyone else smiled and said "Happy Birthday," the president said loudly to a nearby manager, "What's this bullshit? Can't you get your staff to work?" Then, turning to the junior staffer and looking her up and down, he said, "And you sure don't need the calories in that cake."

That leader's negative style underpinned a set of highly destructive cultural norms. For example, as part of their jobs, staff members were expected to be duplicitous, making the customers feel as if they were elite and highly privileged and that the (very expensive) services of the company were the best in the world. In reality, the customers were just regular folks and the services hardly above average. The staff's forced smiles barely masked the tension they felt—and customers became more and more demanding as they began to realize that the services they received were mediocre. Moreover, the high-profile personalities who were often brought in for the conferences showed up only for cameo appearances, since they didn't enjoy working with the company either—frustrating both staff (who needed them) and customers (who wanted them). Unable to reconcile reality with the fantasy that they were charged with maintaining, many of the staff found their day-to-day work meaningless and emotionally draining.

The destructive habits in this company created a culture in which people stopped questioning how and why things were done and merely tried to muddle through, day after day, driven by harmful attitudes, rules, and policies. And because the leaders in this toxic organization systematically discouraged attempts to improve the underlying culture, change was all but impossible. Today, this company's reputation has slipped considerably in the industry, and turnover is at an all-time high.

## Where Change Begins

This sad story doesn't mean toxic organizations cannot change. Quite the contrary: Change begins when emotionally intelligent leaders actively question the emotional reality and the cultural norms underlying the group's daily activities and behavior. To create resonance—and results—the leader has to pay attention to the hidden dimensions: people's emotions, the undercurrents of the emotional reality in the organization, and the culture that holds it all together.

In one large research hospital we worked with, this lesson was learned the hard way, but leadership *did* learn—and successfully transformed the culture.

The hospital reflected many of the ills experienced by U.S. health care in the late 1990s: increasing demands from patients for quality care and from insurance companies and government agencies for lower costs—demands in conflict with each other. As a result, local communities claimed that the hospital didn't serve them well, and the hospital was losing business to other health-care systems. The leadership's answer was to craft a five-year strategy to overhaul almost every aspect of how it led and managed the institution. They commissioned the design of complicated software to manage financial data. They outsourced functions that could be managed better elsewhere. They moved people around and out with an eye toward efficiency.

But this hospital's leadership team forgot about the primary foundations for change: attention to the emotional reality and to the culture.[3] They also failed to recognize how the staff felt about the change process itself. They imposed change from above—rational goals, clear mandates, and logical processes. But they ignored the force of the emotional realm: Within two years, the hospital was on the brink of spiraling downward, its vaunted new systems showing little return and turnover having doubled.

Our work with the hospital's leaders focused on helping them to recognize the dissonance in the organization—and to recognize that the price of such discord could be a failed change effort. Gradually, the leaders began to find ways to let people discuss their feelings about what was and wasn't working, through a process called dynamic inquiry. To their surprise, the leaders discovered that staff members didn't believe that the culture—or the leaders themselves—supported real change, risk taking, or learning.

For example, while people were being asked to do things in new ways, the small amount of training they received was considered old-fashioned and irrelevant. In fact, because training had been disdained historically in the organization, people felt discouraged from attending new programs, and therefore could not learn new ways of doing things. Furthermore, staff believed that the change process was hindered by long-standing cultural habits. The confrontational way in which staff routinely treated one another, for instance, often amounted to rudeness and left people feeling beaten up and on the defensive. The atmosphere was rife with back-biting, vendettas, and petty warfare—discord that undermined any positive change program.

By engaging people in a process of discovering the "real," the hospital leadership took a step in the right direction. They acknowledged that people's feelings mattered and that the culture itself might need to change, and they provided a venue for people to talk about how to do that. Accordingly, momentum picked up and the tone became more positive. As the conversations continued and the management team committed itself to making critical changes, the staff began taking responsibility for its part in creating the new culture as well. Soon, people were feeling more positive about the change process: Resonance began to grow around the vision, and people responded with enthusiasm. There was a marked increase in attendance and participation at meetings to do with the new strategy, and the atmosphere at the hospital lightened dramatically. In other words, the culture and the emotional reality of this hospital began to improve, fostering positive energy rather than resistance, and resonance rather than dissonance. Today, it's an institution that has remade itself: Organizational systems are streamlined, turnover is down and patient satisfaction is up, and the resonance-building norms that were established during the change process still foster commitment, high energy, and flexibility. Before the leadership's emotionally intelligent turnaround, the hospital was a good example of how an organization's underlying culture can kill even the best-laid plans. If the cultural norms don't support passionate action, innovation, or resonance, leaders will find themselves fighting an uphill battle.

But perhaps the most unfortunate aspect of organizational dissonance is what it does to the individuals who work there: As their passion diminishes, they can lose touch with their own best qualities. In place of excellence and self-confidence, we've seen in such companies displays of false bravado, thoughtless compliance, or open resentment. People show up for work, in body at least, day after day—but they leave their hearts and souls elsewhere.

How can an organization transform itself from a place that discourages people's best selves from making an appearance into a vibrant workplace where people feel energized and purposeful? That kind of change requires a great leap: from a thorough understanding of the reality to a profound engagement with people's ideal visions—of both themselves as individuals and as part of an organization. Sometimes, however, to create resonance, a leader first has to fight the organization's own underlying inertia. How do you do it, though? How does a leader uncover the emotional reality—and sow seeds of the dream—in a way that is motivating, not paralyzing?

## Discovering the Organization's Reality through Dynamic Inquiry

Many large companies have processes in place for systematically evaluating employee attitudes, values, and beliefs—a kind of proxy for the emotional reality. These processes can be very helpful, but the problem is that surveys measure only what they set out to measure—and they rarely tap the more subtle layer of subterranean feelings and complex norms that flow through an organization. This blind spot can result in simply measuring what people want to know, but not what they don't want known. And even when surveys do measure aspects of culture and leadership that are problematic, it takes focused effort and courage to address the issues. Too often, we see the results of such revelatory surveys just set aside.

A process called *dynamic inquiry* was developed by Cecilia McMillen of the University of Massachusetts and Annie McKee as a potent way to offset the "find what you look for" effect of most surveys and to enable leaders to begin to address the underlying cultural issues that are getting in their way.[4] This method of discovery uncovers an organization's emotional reality—what people care about; what is helping them, their groups, and the organization to succeed; and what's getting in the way. Through the process of discovering the truth about their organization, people begin to create a *shared language* about what's really going on as well as what they'd like to see—their ideal vision of the company.

Dynamic inquiry involves focused conversations and open-ended questions intended to get at people's feelings. While this may strike some leaders as a bit removed from the business issues, it is only when people talk about their feelings that they begin to uncover root causes of problems in the culture and the true sources of inspiration around them. Also, when people have authentic conversations about how they *feel* about their organization, there tends to be a very high level of agreement about what's working and what's not. As McMillen says, "People begin to paint a picture of the soul of the organization." They create a language that captures the real truth about the forces that affect people's day-to-day lives in the organization as well as their hopes for the future.

From these initial conversations (usually held with both formal and informal leaders at all levels, and with people who have a point of view), themes become apparent that are typically much more meaningful and less generic than those that usually emerge from attitude surveys or more traditional interview processes. These themes, when taken to small groups, tend to spark spirited conversations about the reality of the organization. Perhaps more important, discussions about cultural issues, the emotional reality of an organization, and how it feels to work there usually result in people feeling some ownership of the problems, the dream, and the process of getting from the real to the ideal. And, by focusing not just on what's wrong with the organization but also on what's right, people become aligned with a vision for change — and see how their dreams, and their personal contributions to the change process, fit with the big picture.

Once people are engaged in this kind of open dialogue about their culture and their dreams, it is very difficult to put the lid back on the box. Unlike surveys or one-time visioning sessions, dynamic inquiry starts a *conversation* that has momentum of its own. The creation of a shared language that is based on feelings as well as facts is a powerful driver of change. This shared language provides a sense of unity and resonance, and the resulting momentum helps people to move from talk to action. They feel inspired and empowered, willing to work together to address their collective concerns. This is exactly what happened at an Asian nongovernmental organization (NGO) when a leader we'll call Lang Chen took on a top role.

### Finding the Spirit at Work: Lang Chen and the Asian NGO

Imagine this: Your organization has 220 employees, and you serve a customer base of 150 million people. Needless to say, an organization of those dimensions will have a hefty bureaucracy to support it. That was precisely the problem when Lang Chen took the reins at the Asian division of an international nongovernmental organization.

Although this NGO's mission of improving women's and children's health around the world was inspiring and very motivating for new employees, Lang Chen noticed that typically that initial enthusiasm became lost amid the day-to-day reality of the work. Passion and creativity seemed to fall by the wayside, and this leader sensed that the way people worked together and the systems that guided them were the culprits. The mission of the organization, in fact, seemed buried under its many regulations.

Partly because of the weighty bureaucracy, the pace of work at the NGO was slow and quality mediocre, despite increased demands on the organization and increased criticism from funding agencies and governments. Nothing seemed to happen when it needed to. People displayed the dull complacency that comes with "a job for life" (a common problem in many large NGOs), and there seemed to be little connection between competence and success. There was only vague clarity about what it took to do well in one's job, and the organization had seemingly lost the capacity to evaluate itself; as long as the rules were followed, people's strengths and weaknesses went unaddressed. And, in an organization dedicated in part to the needs of women, there were very few women in the office, and fewer still in responsible positions.

Furthermore, there was a real division between the support staff and the people who actually provided the NGO's services— with the direct service providers getting all the accolades for any successes. In both groups, people were comfortable with the status quo and reluctant to change, even when sometimes urgent circumstances demanded it.

As a result of this environment, some of the NGO's core values—such as compassion and integrity—were clouded by misunderstanding and old policies. It was clear to Lang Chen that, overall, the staff felt disconnected, and the resonance that once had been a natural by-product of the compelling mission was dwindling. Chen's challenge was every leader's: to find out what was working and what was not, and lead people to solutions. But how does a leader fight the inertia of a system? How does she develop an organization's capacity to assess and monitor itself and to function well in a complex environment? How, in short, does a leader perform the alchemy that transforms an organization?

Lang Chen followed simple principles. She used an inclusive approach, employing dynamic inquiry and involving people in discovering the truth about themselves and the organization. She drew people together around their passion for the work and the dream of what could be: They saw her as visionary, and they followed. She became a model for the changes she wanted to see. Finally, she put systems in place to support new habits and ways of doing things. This last set of actions—changing the systems— was critical in sustaining the changes. As Ruth Jacobs of the Hay Group notes, creating human resource practices that foster emotional intelligence—recruiting and performance management, for instance—is key to supporting resonance and a healthy emotional climate.[5]

Emotionally intelligent leaders know that their primal task is to look first to the organizational reality, identifying the issues with the full involvement of key individuals. They take the conversation to the organization as a whole, using engaging processes to get people viscerally involved in unearthing the current reality, while tapping into individual and collective hopes for the future. Like Lang Chen, these leaders enable people to identify both the best aspects of the organization as well as its faults, and they help to create a shared language about the current reality, releasing energy for the move to a shared vision of the future.

## The Critical Shift:
## Moving from Dissonance to the Ideal Vision

Once the cultural reality has been uncovered and explored, the next stage in working toward an emotionally intelligent organization requires defining an ideal vision for the organization that is in synch with individuals' hopes and dreams for themselves. By acting from a place of emotional intelligence and modeling that behavior, leaders can help their employees embrace an ideal vision for the group. What does an organization look like whose members are attuned to a common vision? Consider Lucasfilm, headquartered in Marin County, California, and the parent company of a number of producer George Lucas's creative media companies.

Perhaps the first things that strike anyone who meets Gordon Radley, the president of Lucasfilm Ltd., are the small tattoo hash marks on his cheekbone. Those tattoos mark Radley as a member of a tribe in Malawi with whom he lived for two years as a Peace Corps volunteer in the late 1960s. Thirty years later, he still stays in touch with his friends among the Malawi tribe, even making small grants to help them put tin roofs on their wattle huts or start a small business. "It's unlike any place we on the outside know, yet it's a coherent world that stayed very much the same," says Radley, telling of a recent visit back to Malawi. "Being there put me in touch with how much I love these people. Being part of a tribe has always had some special meaning."

Likewise, that almost tribal sense of belonging to a special group, of inhabiting a unique world together, characterizes places people love to work. For Radley, one of his responsibilities as a leader is to nurture and maintain the company culture at Lucasfilm. Of the empire George Lucas created and owns, Lucasfilm is the parent company for the legendary special-effects house Industrial Light and Magic, as well as a string of other creative media companies in sectors ranging from video games to sound systems for theaters.

For Radley, the best corporate culture is not unlike the tribal feeling he experienced in the Peace Corps. Radley's mission: "How do you create that tribal feeling? It's a hard thing to do, because it's so evanescent it disappears as soon as you draw attention to it. But we want to make sure how we feel about what we do is just as important as what we do."

One way such feelings emerge can be through creating extraordinary moments, experiences people go through together that become part of the shared mythology. "A few years ago, the company was feeling some very rough edges," Radley recalls. "So I organized an all-company meeting. It had never happened before, getting everyone together in one room—we had to meet in the auditorium of a local community center. I started the meeting off in a routine way, with twenty minutes of financial results, corporate updates, and the like. And then I suddenly pulled back a curtain, and there was the cast of the Broadway musical *Stomp!* No one had been expecting anything like it."

For two hours the entire company was galvanized by the performance, an entirely nonverbal, all-percussive enactment of spontaneous attunement. *Stomp!*'s ingenious choreography shows how, using prosaic objects like brooms, buckets, mops, and plungers, a single person can initiate a rhythm that others can join and elaborate in a gorgeous, creative synchrony. It's a wordless ode to the power of a group in resonance.

"It was an electric moment," says Radley. "It bonded everyone, without a word being spoken. I did it because I wanted to bring everyone together, to create a special sense that we're all involved in working together for something bigger than just ourselves. We want to create a culture where people have compassion for each other. It's like the Peace Corps: We're serving each other. A great company culture has empathy—hopefully that becomes a shared value. You do these little symbolic things and hope they set the tone."

That moment exemplifies what Radley calls "guerrilla development," the subtle shaping of the company's culture. But the fragile nature of a group's culture means the shaping cannot be forced. As Radley says, "You set the table and hope people will come and sit down."

For instance, Radley had to struggle with his own senior leaders at an early company meeting to get the chairs put in a huge circle. "The seating itself signaled that tribal feeling," he recalls. "We had everyone introduce themselves and tell where they grew up. By the end of that introductory circle, everyone had the sense that we had come together from all over to be part of this group at this moment."

Such transitory moments of good feeling, of course, mean little if they are not matched by the ongoing workaday reality. As a company, Lucasfilm has a reputation as a very desirable place to work—the kind of reputation that gives the company an edge in attracting and retaining talent in the San Francisco Bay Area's competitive employment environment. The companies that form Lucasfilm are among the few that have shown up on "Best Companies to Work For" lists in such magazines as *Fortune* and *Working Mother*.

The degree of an organization's "tribal feel" can be a good indication of how well it has identified its ideal vision and aligned people around that common purpose. But how do leaders help their organizations to unearth an ideal vision in the first place? They begin with a close scrutiny of themselves—of their personal dreams and of their ideal visions for the organizations that they lead.

### Inspiration and the Hour of the Rat

Connecting with a vision that can build resonance starts within, as Antony Burgmans, co-chairman of Unilever, tells us. "As we launched into our growth strategy, I realized that I didn't *feel* right: something was missing, and I knew we would need to look again at our plans. I trusted my feeling—you learn to listen to that inner voice. So, I looked for the source of my uneasiness. We were doing all the right things: a new, focused strategy; shareholder support; a new organization structure; and good people in place. But something was wrong—the critical piece was missing. What I saw was that even though we had a excellent change strategy, and an inspiring vision, what was really required to bring about change at Unilever was a new culture, a new leadership mindset, and new behaviors."

Niall FitzGerald, co-chairman and co-creator of the transformation process, weighs in: "We knew where we needed to go, that was completely clear. We had all the organizational pieces in place—but it was like standing on the edge of the Grand Canyon. You know you have to get to the other side, but to do so you know you will have to take a big leap, then build a bridge. You feel anticipation, even deep uneasiness, but the excitement of the vision calls on you to build that bridge, take that leap. I paid attention to the feelings—especially the ones that let me know that something wasn't quite right, not yet. These feelings were important—for me as a leader, they led me to see what we needed to do. At Unilever, the bridge we needed to build was all about people: we needed to tap into their passion; we needed them to see their business in entirely new ways; and we needed them to develop very different leadership behaviors."

FitzGerald's and Burgmans's soul searching led to a radically fresh approach to transforming the company, starting with changing the mindset of Unilever's top leaders. Today, Unilever is in the midst of profound change—but unlike many change efforts, there is tremendous clarity throughout the organization about what is being done and why. People know they are part of the change, and they know they need to change too. In terms of financial and organizational measures, they are ahead of schedule. All this because two leaders listened to the voice within.

To connect with the kind of vision that can move a culture toward resonance, emotionally intelligent leaders start by looking inside—at what they feel, think, and sense about their organizations. They act as highly sensitive instruments to connect with the company's ideal vision and mission, and they notice the gaps between what could be and what is. This isn't intuition—it's using emotional intelligence to observe and interpret the subtle clues about what's really going on, and it offers leaders a perspective that goes beyond other kinds of data about the company.

Tapping into that kind of insight can come more easily if a leader makes a habit of retreating to a quiet place to reflect on a regular basis. Reaching into the wisdom of the unconscious mind is like trying to pump water from a deep well: It helps to keep the pump primed—in this case by regularly spending time in reflection. Often that deep wisdom comes in the middle of the night, during what we call the hour of the rat—that dark, quiet time of the night when no one is around and things start to gnaw at you. It is those times of quiet reflection that can begin to offer a leader answers to nagging questions: "What's bothering me so much that I just can't seem to let it go, even at home? What's confusing, muddled, ambiguous or just plain irritating? Where is the passion, excitement, and meaning in my work? What do I really believe in?"

By examining the sources of their anxiety and their passion—and by focusing on their own dreams—leaders can begin to identify aspects of the organization's culture, of its overarching mission and vision, and of its leadership (including their own) that need to change. Only through articulating for themselves what keeps people in the organization—beyond just "a job"—can leaders connect with the kind of resonant vision that people will be able to see and feel.

To create the vision of a company, emotionally intelligent leaders need to move beyond a solo scrutiny of an organization's vision to drawing on the collective wisdom of followers. Side by side with the rest of the organization, leaders co-create the vision that will serve to rally and energize the group as a whole. Involving people in a deliberate study of themselves and the organization—first by looking at the reality and then at the ideal vision—builds resonance and sustainable change.

Consider the examples that follow of leaders who have helped their organizations to rally around a common vision of what could be.

### Attunement, Not Alignment

- Keki Dadiseth took over as chairman of Hindustan Lever Limited (HLL) at a time of rapid change in the Indian business environment. Successful and leading edge in its management practices and results over a period of time, the company nevertheless needed to shed a culture which, in the new environment, was seen as bureaucratic, closed door, and lacking in transparency. Activities were highlighted almost as often as achievements, and cultural norms supported the hierarchy, rather than full empowerment. Thus it was often difficult to get things done speedily. Although the company had a well-defined management development process, queries were raised regarding how people were promoted or rewarded because there was a perceived lack of transparency.

Keki Dadiseth took this challenge head on: He moved toward the ideal by becoming an exemplar himself. He modeled the changes he wanted to see, involving people in the process of creating a new vision and a new reality. His concept was centrifuged leadership—that the center of gravity was not just the chairman; everyone was central to success. Within a year, the culture changed, such that people acknowledged the openness, trust, and empowerment within the company. HLL continues, as in the past, to be one of Unilever's most profitable and highly regarded businesses.

- The UNICEF immunization project in India was doing critically important work, but its Chief of Health, Monica Sharma, felt that the program itself needed a shot in the arm. While the project was inherently inspiring to the staff working closely with the health teams who immunized children in poor villages, most of the organization's 400 staff people—clerks, accountants, and administrators— were too far removed from that energizing field work to feel inspired. Monica decided to bring the excitement of the front lines into the back office, so she devised a plan and encouraged all office staff to spend several days, regularly, in a district where the real work—immunizing children— was going on. The top leadership of the office—Representative Eimi Watanabe and her two deputies, Thomas McDermott and Lukas Hendratta—were instrumental in this success because they each personally backed her fully and encouraged this initiative. As a result, staff members got to experience for themselves the mission and ideal vision that underpinned their work, and they were able to bond with each other around a more unified purpose.

- The major restructuring process that the University of Pennsylvania undertook in the 1990s—although neces- sary—was painful for many of its staff. Until the changes, most people had felt a very special connection with Penn, an Ivy League school, and considered their employment there to be a job for life. But as roles and responsibilities shifted dramatically, people were shaken out of years of complacency—and security. Mostly, they felt demoralized about losing the image they had had of themselves. To keep Penn on track with its change agenda, President Judith Rodin and Executive Vice President John Fry looked to a broader agenda for inspiration that could be shared with the entire community. It was that word— community—that got them started on a process that created resonance and engaged people both inside and outside the university around a common vision.

Leaders often talk about wanting to get their people "aligned" with their strategy. But that word suggests a mechanical image of getting all the pencils pointing in the same direction, like a mag- netic field lining up the polarity of molecules. It isn't that simple. Strategies, couched as they are in the dry language of corporate goals, speak mainly to the rational brain, the neocortex. Strategic visions (and the plans that follow from them) are typically linear and limited, bypassing the elements of heart and passion essential for building commitment.

As each of the previous examples illustrates, getting people to really embrace change requires *attunement*—alignment with the kind of resonance that moves people emotionally as well as intellectually. The challenge is in how to attune people to your vision and then to your business strategy in a way that arouses passion. Emotionally intelligent leaders know that this attune- ment requires something more than simply making people aware of the strategy itself. It requires a direct connection with people's emotional centers.

Attunement, rather than mere alignment, offers the motivating enthusiasm for an organizational vision. When this attunement takes hold, people feel the heat of a collective excitement, of many people being enthusiastic about their work. A vision that "tunes people in"—that creates resonance—builds organizational harmony and people's capacity to act collectively.

The invisible threads of a compelling vision weave a tapestry that binds people together more powerfully than any strategic plan. And people, not the business plan alone, determine the outcome. Success depends on what an organization's people care about, what they do, and how they work together.

Warren Bennis, University of Southern California professor and renowned leadership expert, has called attunement "managing attention through the vision"—something he says is the leader's fundamental responsibility, as is using the group ideal to focus people's efforts.[6] Attunement is especially important when the organization is undergoing significant change in how things are done—and is equally critical whenever a vision that built an organization's initial success grows stale and needs freshening.

Attunement starts with involving people deeply in the process of looking at gaps between the organization's emotional reality and people's ideal visions of the organization, including visions of their own interactions within it.

However, the leader must go one step further and put the people in the organization in charge of the change process itself. That's what each of the leaders in the previous examples did. Let's take a more in-depth look at each of those scenarios and see how these leaders attuned their organizations to a common vision—and brought about lasting change.

*Be the Change You Want to See:*
*Keki Dadiseth and Hindustan Lever*

Keki Dadiseth, the new chairman of Hindustan Lever Limited, took over at a time of profound change in the Indian business environment. HLL had a rich heritage of management excellence and business growth and was regarded by its peers as a company that they most wanted to emulate.

Although HLL was well regarded and successful, Dadiseth quickly realized that in the present liberalization scenario in India, the company needed to change quickly and shed an ingrained culture that the new environment saw as bureaucratic and lacking in transparency.

To make inroads into such a deeply ingrained culture and attune the company to his vision, Dadiseth knew it would take more than just talk, new policies, or even training. He needed to *demonstrate* consistently the behaviors he wished to see. A framed Japanese print in his office came to be his motto: "None of us is as smart as all of us." From the outset, he used the engaging style of affiliative leadership, backed up by a healthy dose of the democratic style—a combination that was not very common in the company. He gave up his scheduling diary and kept an open-door policy, never denying an employee request to talk with him. And he really listened when people talked: He took counsel from them, incorporating their views into the decisions that were being made. He broke down the hierarchy by eating with staff in the cafeteria, and he connected with people on a personal level. He came to know whose son was ill, and whose daughter had won a prize at school. He learned who really cared about their work, and he praised them publicly. And where he saw difficulties, he encouraged and empowered people to come up with their own solutions. He "centrifuged" decision making—pushing it as far down the organization as possible. In general, he called on people to look deeply into themselves to discover what was right for the business—and to act on it.

Although Dadiseth's new style of leadership was at first suspect, soon it became clear it was not an act: This was the real thing. He was so available, so accessible, and so transparent that no one had to speculate or try to maneuver around him. His connections with people were sincere, and the outcome of these positive, very human, relationships was mutual trust and respect. What's more, it spread: Other leaders began to see the value in redirecting people's energy toward group commitment. People began emulating Dadiseth's stance, and the norms of the culture gradually shifted toward openness and mutuality. The "managing up" mindset was broken: There was little time wasted in unnecessary speculation, and things started getting done faster and better.

Over time, as people began supporting each other through successes and difficulties alike, the cooperative spirit in the company increased. It suddenly felt safer to take on responsibility, making it easier for people to innovate and to become creative about their part of the business. From factory worker to senior manager, ideas began to flow in all parts and levels of the company, and efficiency and effectiveness increased.

While building strong, open relationships in the company, Dadiseth was careful to keep his eye on his goal: to improve the organization's performance. As he put it, "Comfort in relationship brings discomfort in accountability," and he made sure that relationships didn't get too cozy. So even as he called on the company's leadership to see their connections to employees as important to the business, he also insisted on a new sense of accountability: to the company, to one another, and to their own values.

As a result, things began to move more quickly and smoothly. Decisions that had taken weeks in the past now took hours or even minutes, even though more people were involved. Commitment to the decisions went up, partly because of the high degree of involvement, but also because people began to trust leadership more. People now found it harder to hide or to blame others. Relationships had become based more on trust and real connection, and leaders started taking more responsibility for themselves.

Within a year, performance across a range of behavioral criteria improved dramatically. The speed and effectiveness of strategy implementation were markedly increased, and the growth agenda was owned by virtually everyone in the company; people acted on it at all levels. Keki Dadiseth had led by doing. He demonstrated principles of the new organization that he and his team hoped to create: transparency, inclusiveness, honesty, rigor, and results; accurate and honest assessment of what was working and what was not;

and linking rewards to accomplishments. By essentially using the powerful symbol that his office represented in order to model change, Dadiseth had helped people to understand and act on new standards of accountability. In short, he changed the ground rules, attuned people to a new vision for the organization, and created resonance.

Throughout this organizational alchemy, Keki Dadiseth took the time needed to follow some basic rules that can trigger change:

- Focus people's attention on the underlying issues and solutions to create common ground and understanding about what needs to change and why. By helping to articulate problems and surfacing the covert, hidden habits that people take for granted, the real state of the organization becomes apparent and is a motivating force for change. Making the covert overt gives people a language to discuss what is working and what isn't in the organization, and common ground to stand on while looking to the future.

- Focus on the ideal, combining resonance-building leadership styles to get people talking about their hopes for the future and to tap into the dedication people feel for the organization. Connecting people's personal goals with a meaningful vision makes it safe to explore ways to reach the vision.

- Move from talk to action. This starts with the leader. Bringing people together around a dream, moving from talk to action, and modeling new behaviors—this is the leader's charge. And it is something that UNICEF's Monica Sharma understood as well.

### *Living the Mission: Monica Sharma and UNICEF*

In 1989, when she became Chief of Health of UNICEF's Health Section immunization project in India, Monica Sharma understood the importance of the work the organization was doing. Far too many children in that country were dying needlessly from common and preventable childhood diseases such as measles—

and her project's goal was to change that sad fact.[7] But early on, Monica sensed something that troubled her: Most of the 400 employees felt far away from the organization's mission and the inspiring work that they themselves supported in their day-to-day jobs. Because most staff worked at desks in the main office, they didn't have access to the sense of purpose that the health teams felt as they moved from village to village immunizing children.

Monica came up with a solution that would truly attune people to the common mission—by connecting them *emotionally* to their work and therefore with their own ideal visions of their purpose in the organization. "I hatched a scheme to get absolutely everyone involved in the field work of the project," Monica told us. She lobbied UNICEF's senior management to let her send every one of the over 400 office-bound staff people to work in village immunization clinics. Senior leadership supported her plan. Representative Eimi Watanabe and her deputies Thomas McDermott and Lukas Hendratta recognized that *especially* in a large bureaucracy, if there was going to be innovation and change, they needed to back the change agent. And they did.

Staff members were able to see—many for the first time—what their work was really about. They helped gather children together and bring them to the clinics; they saw, up close, the health teams at work. For the first time they were able to feel the raw emotions that underlay their daily work: excitement and hope, alongside the doubts and fears of the mothers, who themselves were scared by the syringes and were frightened for their children. Gradually, the workers in the home office came to see that each of their roles contributed to saving the life of a child, and that even seemingly unimportant or routine tasks were actually critical.

The story of one UNICEF driver is a poignant case in point. Whereas in the past he had seen his job as simply to shuttle the health team from one district to the next—never really connecting with the people in those villages—once he had spent time working in a village clinic, everything changed. He began to take a new interest in what was happening while he waited to take his passengers back to the office. He began to talk more to the workers and the village mothers. He saw the children's and their mothers' fear, and he saw how difficult it was for some mothers to comfort their children.

On his own, the driver started gathering small groups of mothers around his car, talking to them about why the immunizations were so important, reassuring them about side effects, and advising on how to calm the children down. He created his own mini-seminars, contributing palpably to the success of each clinic. The driver's impromptu work resulted in calmer, more informed parents—and clinics that ran with more ease and efficiency. Moreover, he improved how the doctors and nurses on the medical team viewed the contributions of office staff. And clearly, the driver himself felt a far deeper commitment to his work.

That deeper commitment made an enormous difference one day when he drove a team to a village where, after several hours, the vaccine still had not arrived. In the past, the driver might have shrugged and taken the team back to the office. After all, it wasn't his job to get the vaccine there, nor would he necessarily be compensated for working overtime to help with the situation. Now, however, he understood how disappointed his "class" of mothers and children would be if they didn't receive the vaccine they'd been waiting for. He set off on his own to a larger but distant village, and in a few hours he returned with the vaccine.

The driver was acting on the new cultural norms: Get involved, look for places to contribute, and live the mission. By getting people at all levels to embrace and attune to their mission, Monica Sharma fostered resonance that would far outlast any simple change program. In fact, the staff had joined her in creating that vision of their mission. Monica's visionary leadership style helped people to see how their own small contributions—whether back in the office or out on the road—actually affected the children. She realized that, in order for people to make their efforts meaningful, they need to see and feel the results of their work, to see the ways in which what they do supports what they believe.

At the same time, it was possible that a one-time visit to the field might simply fade in people's memory if the changes stopped there. But Monica understood that in order for these inspiring moments to translate into new ways of operating together—into new cultural norms that would be sustainable over time—people would need more. They would have to talk over their experiences, to share the feelings and their learning, and to tell each other the stories that would come to define their new culture.

To that end, Monica held open meetings on weekends at which people could come together to share their experiences. Then, as people began to talk about the challenges they encountered and ask for advice, Monica used a coaching leadership style to model interactions: People began to learn to coach each other. These meetings were marked by laughter, encouragement, and camaraderie. People were engaged and inspired—and felt wonderful about their work together.

Even now, years later, some of the staff in India remember Monica's initiative as a turning point—perhaps the most inspiring of their work lives. What mattered, too, was their leader's confidence in them, her belief that they could go to the districts and help, even though they were not trained. That confidence enabled many—like the driver—to go beyond their own expectations of themselves. And they remember that Monica made herself personally available to them, supporting their learning all through the process.

Of course, Monica knew exactly what she was doing: She was attuning people with the mission that exemplified UNICEF values, and providing them tangible ways to make the vision a reality. By working with people's emotions and building on their very human need for meaningful work, Monica helped to attune people's values and contributions to the greater mission. That is resonant leadership in action: engaging people's passion and connecting them with a vision of what could be. Monica Sharma fulfilled her primal task as a leader.

But what about when an organization requires adjustments that reach far beyond attitude, adjustments that involve profound changes in the way people do their jobs? In the midst of that kind of change, resonance with a vision is sometimes the one thing that holds people together, staves off exhaustion, and keeps people focused and positive. We saw this at the University of Pennsylvania as it faced a crisis in the 1990s.

*Attuning with the Community: Judith Rodin and*
*John Fry and the University of Pennsylvania*

In the mid- to late 1990s, the University of Pennsylvania underwent a major restructuring process in which staff members' roles
were completely changed, shaking many people out of years of
complacency while their seemingly secure future disappeared. People felt worried about losing their jobs, but equally important,
they felt demoralized about losing the image they had had of
themselves as "privileged" to be working at Penn, an Ivy League
school. Although the restructuring was important for the future
of the school, the process itself made people fearful and reticent.[8]

President Judith Rodin and Executive Vice President John Fry
recognized that they needed to do something to mobilize people's
energy around keeping Penn on track with its change agenda. So
they looked to a broader agenda—to the community outside the
university—for the inspiration that would engage staff members'
hearts and minds and attune them to a common vision.

Their first move was to announce that it was the university's
responsibility to contribute to its outside community, rather than
simply taking from it. It was a position that Penn—and the West
Philadelphia community that surrounded it—hadn't heard for
many years. In fact, the university and the town had long experienced a strained relationship, arguing about when and where development and construction should take place, whose job it was to
maintain a clean and safe environment, and who was responsible
for dealing with increased crime.

Rodin and Fry's vision was more than rhetoric; it led to concrete action. They worked with city officials, school teachers and
principals, and police and real estate professionals to create new,
brightly lit streets and parks, to enhance the quality of education
in the local schools, and to make it possible for residents to access
funds to restore their homes. They created a mortgage program
that encouraged Penn professors and staff to move into the area
surrounding the university, and they focused on developing new
hotels, retail stores, and services that were attractive to residents

and visitors alike. They also undertook an ambitious effort to employ local residents, and to contract with minority-owned and women-owned West Philadelphia–based businesses in construction projects and other business dealings.

As the benefits of getting onboard with this new strategy became obvious to people inside Penn, staff came together with energy and passion around the change process. Who could argue with building friendly relationships with the neighborhood? Who could argue with the new parks and lights, the dramatic decrease in crime, the attractive renovation of homes, and the chance to move to a vibrant, exciting urban area with the help of creative financing? The values driving the strategy—urban renewal and a commitment to a vibrant, diverse community—were intrinsically appealing and rewarding to people, making them feel good again about being part of Penn.

What that broad-based move did for West Philadelphia is obvious today in the way the city looks and functions. But what it did inside the university was equally impressive. By engaging people at the university in the West Philadelphia initiative, Rodin and Fry were able to also engage them in other, more difficult issues. Staff came to understand that their leaders really did believe in the values at the heart of the change process, and people began to trust them to carry through the more difficult internal change agenda with integrity. In the end, Rodin and Fry helped to create an organizational resonance in which people felt invested in the strategy because it was attuned to their personal values. That made the vision for change not only meaningful, but sustainable as well.

## Lessons: Building an Emotionally Intelligent Organization

The notion that emotional intelligence is important at work is not new, though it's only been recently that studies have begun to show how key it is to the success of any organization. Indeed, emotional intelligence and resonance in a workplace may draw on the ancient human organizing principle of the primal band—those groups of fifty to one hundred people who roamed the land with a common bond and whose survival depended on close understanding and cooperation.

In some ways, a band of hunter-gatherers on the ancient plains is not so different from the teams at Hindustan Lever, UNICEF, or Penn. In any resonant human group, people find meaning in their connection and in their attunement with one another. In the best organizations, people share a vision of who they are collectively, and they share a special chemistry. They have the feeling of a good fit, of understanding and being understood, and a sense of well-being in the presence of the others.

It is the responsibility of emotionally intelligent leaders to create such resonant organizations. These leaders involve people in discovering the truth about themselves and the organization: They recognize the truth about what is *really* going on, and they help people to name what is harmful and to build on the organization's strengths. At the same time, they bring people together around a dream of what could be, and in the process create and demonstrate new ways for people to work together. They build resonance, and then they ensure that resonance can be sustained through the systems that regulate the ebb and flow of relations and work in the organization.

There are a number of rules of engagement that our research and our work with organizations suggest will help to create a resonant, emotionally intelligent, and *effective* culture. The research produced three key findings: discovering the emotional reality, visualizing the ideal, and sustaining emotional intelligence. Each is explored in some detail in the following sections.

### DISCOVERING THE EMOTIONAL REALITY

- *Respect the group's values and the organization's integrity.* Visions change, but as the vision evolves, the leader needs to be sure that the "sacred center"—what everyone holds as paramount—remains intact. That's the first challenge: knowing what the sacred center actually is—from the perspective of others, not just oneself. The second challenge is seeing clearly what *must* change, even when it is held dear, and getting other people to see it too. If core beliefs, mindsets, or culture really need to change, people need to drive that change themselves. It cannot be forced, so when people enter into such a change process, they need to be personally and powerfully motivated—preferably by hope and a dream, not fear. A visionary leader can impact this process positively by honoring the feelings and beliefs of the people around him, while steadfastly demonstrating the benefit of moving toward the dream.

- *Slow down in order to speed up.* A target-shooting coach we know tells his students, "If you're in a combat situation, you can't miss fast enough to save your life." So too with building resonance and an emotionally intelligent organization—the shotgun approach to change doesn't work. The process of slowing down and bringing people into the conversation about their systems and their culture is one we don't see enough in organizations but that nevertheless is critical. Processes such as dynamic inquiry require a supportive, coaching approach and democratic style: The leader must really listen to what people have to say about the culture and the emotional reality of the organization. Both the coaching style—where a leader deeply listens to individuals—and the democratic style—where a group in dialogue builds consensus—can ensure that people are brought into the change process in a way that builds their commitment. Emotionally intelligent leaders rely on these styles as a way to slow things down enough to get a strong sense of exactly what's needed to give people the support they need to flourish.

- *Start at the top with a bottom-up strategy.* Top leadership *must* be committed to facing the truth about the emotional reality of the organization, and they must be committed to creating resonance around a vision of the ideal. But that's not enough: A bottom-up strategy is needed as well, because resonance only develops when everyone is attuned to the change. This means engaging formal and informal leaders from all over the organization in conversations about what is working, what is not, and how exciting it would be if the organization could move more in the direction of what *is* working. Taking time out to discuss these kinds of issues is a powerful intervention. It gets people thinking and talking, and shows them the way. Once the excitement and buy-in builds, it's more possible to move from talk to action. The enthusiasm provides momentum. But the movement needs to be directed: toward the dream, toward collective values, and toward new ways of working together. Transparent goals, an open change process, involvement of as many people as possible, and modeling new behaviors provide a top-down, bottom-up jump-start for resonance.

### VISUALIZING THE IDEAL

- *Look inside.* To formulate a vision that will resonate with others, leaders need to pay attention, starting by tuning in to their own feelings and the feelings of others. The facts alone—for instance, what is happening in the market-place—do not provide enough information to create a meaningful vision that will touch people's hearts. To do that, a leader needs to "see" at the level of emotion, then craft a meaningful vision with which people can identify on a deep and personal level.

- *Don't align—attune.* For a vision to be compelling, it needs to touch people's hearts. People need to see, feel, and touch the values and the vision of the organization to make these abstractions meaningful. Tuning people in to a meaningful vision has integrity at its heart: People need to feel as if they can reach for the organization's dream without compromising their own dreams, their own beliefs, and their values.

- *People first, then strategy.* Leaders who use resonance-building styles model norms that support commitment, involvement, active pursuit of the vision, and healthy, productive work relationships. They create connection by focusing on what people really want and need, and by deliberately building a culture that supports good health in the tribe. When a leader focuses on people, emotional bonds are created that are the ground in which resonance is sown—and people will follow that leader in good times and bad. Resonance creates an invisible but powerful bond between people based on a belief in what they are doing and a belief in one another. For that to happen, people need to connect with one another in real time—not just online—around their work. They need to talk, laugh, share stories, and—just perhaps—build a dream together.

### SUSTAINING EMOTIONAL INTELLIGENCE

- *Turn vision into action.* At every opportunity, leaders need to demonstrate what the vision looks like, what it feels like, and how people can live it today as well as in the future. They use themselves as instruments of discovery and change, get close to the process, and don't let go until they reach the goal. Ideally, in each interaction, each decision, leaders act consistently with their own values and with the values of the organization they intend to create. They lead through coaching, vision, democracy, and respect for the people around them. And they call on others to live up to their own values and the mission of the organization.

  In addition to the primal leader's stance, there are other necessary steps for turning vision into action: changing organizational structures and job designs, changing relationship norms, reshaping systems and performance expectations to better match the vision, and making what people do fit better with the organization's mission.

- *Create systems that sustain emotionally intelligent practices.* People matter, but so do systems, rules, and procedures. Reminders of what is acceptable and what is not are powerful drivers of behavior, be these policies and procedures (that are actually enforced) or attention to the right leadership behaviors. Specifically, for an organization to sustain emotionally intelligent practices, the rules, regulations, and human resource practices have to be totally in synch with the desired outcomes. There's no sense hoping for emotionally intelligent leadership when in fact it is not recognized in the performance management systems or reward systems—so change the rules, if need be, to reinforce the vision.

- *Manage the myths of leadership.* Myths and legends withstand the vagaries of the day-to-day grind—and the upheaval of change. When the right myths are in place— that is, those that support emotional intelligence and resonance—people have an easier time holding on to a positive emotional climate, even in the face of adversity. Leaders have an enormous impact on the overall emotions of an organization, and they are often at the center of the organization's stories. Managing the myths, the legends, and the symbols of the office can be a powerful driver of change. By using the symbolic power of their role to model emotional intelligence, leaders can create new, positive myths through even small gestures and actions.

Creating organizations that are emotionally intelligent is ultimately the leader's responsibility. It is up to leaders to help the organization identify its reality—including the cultural norms that hinder it—and then to explore the ideal vision of what could be and to help members of the organization uncover their own roles in that vision. And it is leaders who attune people to the vision and begin taking action toward change.

Emotionally intelligent leaders who use resonance-building leadership styles and create norms that foster healthy, effective working relationships (rather than using styles that breed fear and cynicism) will release a powerful force: the collective energy of the organization to pursue any business strategy. These kinds of leaders build with positives: They craft a vision with heartfelt passion, they foster an inspiring organizational mission that is deeply woven into the organizational fabric, and they know how to give people a sense that their work is meaningful.

### CHAPTER ELEVEN

# CREATING SUSTAINABLE CHANGE

OW DOES A LEADER create resonance in an organization that is sustained over time? It's a challenge, but it can be done by ensuring that the entire fabric of the enterprise is interwoven with emotionally intelligent leadership. After all, if it takes emotionally intelligent leadership to create resonance in an organization, then the more such leaders there are, the more powerful that transformation will become.

In any large organization there will naturally be some pockets of resonance and some pockets of dissonance. The overall ratio of resonance to dissonance, we propose, determines that organization's emotional climate and relates directly to how it performs. The key to shifting that ratio in the right direction lies in cultivating a dispersed cadre of leaders who will create emotionally intelligent groups.

By their very nature, however, organizations don't readily encourage new learning.[1] In fact, leaders who wish to instill widespread change need to first recognize that they're working against a paradox: Organizations thrive on routine and the status quo. Professionals in organizations rely on the established systems in order to carry out their jobs with minimal resistance and stress. As a result, most people in companies today have not challenged themselves to learn something really different for a long time.

Developing a new leadership style often means fundamentally changing how one operates with other people. But the paradox of trying to introduce new learning in organizations makes that a difficult task at best, and not one accomplished only in the classroom. Sadly, most executive education and leadership development efforts fall far short of the mark, not only because of how they are done, but also because of what they do *not* do. Even the best development processes—those based on exploring the five discoveries—will not help to change the *organization* if they focus only on the person and do not take into account the power of the emotional reality and the culture.

Consider the situation described in the following section, in which the leadership's intentions were good, but the outcome of organization-wide learning was little more than a few people changed and lots of time and energy wasted.

## When Leadership Building Fails

The CEO of a Pacific Rim bank wanted to put his top 600 executives through leadership development after he himself had worked with an executive coach on emotional intelligence competencies, had gone through a 360-degree feedback process, and had dramatically changed his leadership style. He instructed his head of human resources to design a program for his top executives so that they could receive similar development opportunities. But when the HR department posted the program offering, few people signed up. Only the inquisitive and the courageous went through it, rather than those who might have benefited most.

The problem was that the program just didn't seem relevant to people in this organization. Culturally, training was considered a waste of time, and going to a workshop was certainly not a priority—for anyone. One important way to ensure that learning *does* feel important is to make it a mandate that the top leader is driving personally. To succeed, leadership development needs to be *the* strategic priority of the enterprise, an issue that is galvanized and managed at the highest levels—by the executive committee or governing board.

That is what the CEO of the Pacific Rim bank failed to recognize. In fact, he was shocked when so few people seemed interested in receiving the same kind of coaching and feedback that had changed his own leadership style in such obvious ways. Where before this CEO had been a compulsively focused, pacesetting leader, he had now expanded his leadership repertoire, becoming more affiliative, more visionary, and more of a coach. He had begun to have coaching sessions with his direct reports, and asked his staff to brief him on key events in his employees' lives. One example of his transformation came when he stopped a project meeting to send home a staff member whose husband, he had heard, had suddenly become very ill—a simple gesture of human kindness that would not have occurred to him before.

Even so, the leadership development program he made available at the bank was sparsely attended because it was perceived as unimportant to top management's overall agenda. The CEO had indeed had a transformational experience—but he'd kept the process itself quiet. Sure, people could see changes in him, but no one really understood the learning experience that he'd undergone—the coaching, the feedback, his development plan. So the new leadership program appeared as just another in an expanding menu of the company's HR offerings. By funneling the program through his HR training director, the CEO sent the unintended message that it was a low priority.

For leadership development to succeed, top management needs to demonstrate that commitment comes from the top. Unfortunately, what we've observed in most companies—as we saw at the Pacific Rim bank—is the opposite: Leadership development typically becomes the mandate of human resource departments.

## EXECUTIVE COACHING

L EADERS NEED to balance learning—which by definition means becoming vulnerable—with managing their image as leaders. One good way to do this is to work with an executive coach, a relationship in which it is safe to explore and where leaders can have an opportunity to talk more freely than they may have done with anyone, ever, about their own dreams and their business challenges. In the context of executive coaching, leaders can talk about things that they feel pain and passion about—and really get at the core issues for themselves, their teams, and the organization. Of course, the sheer level of emotion in these conversations is far beyond what typically occurs in business, so the coaching relationship must be trusting, totally confidential, and almost sacrosanct.[2]

Most executive coaching processes involve leadership assessment and an ongoing focus on development. They also include work on the broader organizational issues—especially those in the people realm, such as the leader's challenges with his or her team, the organizational climate, culture, and politics, and how all this fits with the business strategy.

Leadership assessment and feedback can be done in a number of different ways, but the best practice starts with a series of interviews and observations by a professional executive coach. The interviews should look and feel much like conversations a good part of the time, with the intention of building a strong, confidential relationship between the leader and the coach. Typical processes include conversations about the leader's career and life history, discussions of current managerial and leadership challenges, and discussions of the organizational-level issues as well, including things such as climate, politics, and systems. In addition, this phase often includes observation of the leader in action at meetings, when giving speeches, and when engaging in one-on-one performance reviews, among other things.

One such process called "A Day in the Life" was developed by our colleague Fran Johnston of the Gestalt Institute of Cleveland.[3] The coach spends a typical day with the leader, literally following her around, attending meetings and one-on-one sessions with staff, even sitting in on phone calls. Of course, all of this is done with a clear explanation to employees—with the added benefit that the leader is seen to be actively involved in learning and leadership development.

More structured assessment is also usually a part of the coaching process, and will often include behavioral event interviews and 360-degree feedback on emotional intelligence, managerial style, climate, and other factors pertinent to the particular leader and her organization. When it comes to coaching on team and organizational issues, it helps for the coach to have more than just the leader's perspective. Whether or not the leader is really suffering from CEO disease, it is a fact of executive life that much information is filtered, and many issues are softened or disguised before they reach the top. Through interviews, observation, and assessment, and even a mini–dynamic inquiry process, a coach can gather information about what's really going on in an organization that can be truly helpful to the leader. Of course, for this process to work over the long term, the coach needs to honor the confidentiality of all relationships—even with those people interviewed to gather information about the leader—which means that the coach presents the leader with only general themes, not specifics.

Coaching enables a leader to further her own learning quickly, while getting a different—and sometimes more accurate—picture of what's happening in the organization, especially with respect to how people experience the leader and the leadership team.

But despite their technical expertise and, in many cases, their contribution to the strategy, HR people cannot, on their own, drive significant change in behavior or culture. Even the best HR professionals will admit that they operate under a cloud in which people perceive their work as out of touch with day-to-day managerial issues. Although this appraisal may be unfair, it points to the importance of an organization's top leaders being actively involved in any leadership development process.

There's yet another reason that commitment must come from the top: Change of the sort we are talking about requires effort, support, and resources—and not just money. New leadership means a new mindset and new behaviors, and in order for these to stick, the organization's cultures, systems, and processes all need to change too. In the development of resonance-building leaders, we are talking about tapping into—and changing—the emotional reality of the organization itself, the culture, as well as deep-seated behaviors. Because most groups and organizations revolve around the status quo, fighting off anything that threatens it, this level of change requires courageous leadership, stamina, and unswerving commitment.

### You Can't Ignore Culture

Even a mandate from the highest levels of the organization doesn't guarantee that a leadership development initiative will bring about needed changes. Consider the case of a professional services firm we worked with. The top managers of this large company recognized that given the changing nature of their business, unless they encouraged people to behave in very different ways, the company would lose its competitive edge. Rather than attempting to change the collective habits of the whole organization, which felt too daunting, the leadership decided that if enough individual managers learned new competencies, the culture would change itself. Several years later, however, it's become clear that all efforts at change in the company have failed miserably. Leadership practices are a mess, morale is down and turnover is at an all-time high, and the company is being sold against the management's will.

At first, top management did everything right. They made it clear that leadership development was a critical strategic priority. They did the research and crafted a pristine competency model in which most of the competencies related to emotional intelligence. They designed a state-of-the-art development process, focusing explicitly on the five discoveries, and they selected highly motivated people to participate.

In short, the company's management crafted a comprehensive change process. They even began to revamp the HR processes to hire and promote for the new leadership competencies. Intuitively the leadership knew that the organization reinforced negative cultural norms. They could see that old habits were out of synch with what new clients, vendors, and partners were expecting. But they weren't exactly sure how the culture could change, and since changing the deeply ingrained habits and underlying culture of the entire organization seemed like an impossible task, management decided instead to focus on developing individual leaders. Hopes for a ripple effect throughout the enterprise diminished quickly when one major glitch became apparent: Some new leadership competencies went so against the cultural grain that when people began to use them, they got into trouble.

For example, one of the new competencies called on people to have courage when attempting to do the right thing for the business, even when that meant standing up to senior management. One manager, encouraged by the top's apparent willingness to foster this kind of risk taking, put himself on the line over what he saw as a business—and an ethical—issue. As he began to discuss this issue in the leadership program, he came to see this as an opportunity to practice a new behavior and, he thought, to help the company do the right thing. Given the hype about the new competencies, his boss's response wasn't too surprising, only very disappointing: When the manager confronted his boss, the boss did what he knew was expected of him and praised the manager for his courage in standing up for what he believed. But then, behind closed doors, that same boss laid out a plan to get rid of the guy—he was just too dangerous.

We saw similar scenarios play out again and again in this organization. Even when it was clear that leadership behaviors needed to change, and even when people knew what they should do, they could not act in new ways. The pockets of resistance were too widespread, the inertia in the culture too powerful. Individual leaders alone cannot change a culture. For a new vision to take hold, it must spread throughout every level. In an organization as enormous as this one, it would have taken hundreds of converts to bring about a wholesale cultural change.

The lesson is that you can't ignore culture—and you can't hope to change it one leader at a time. By ignoring the big picture and focusing instead on developing leaders one by one, this company's leadership failed to bring about critically needed changes that would have helped the organization succeed. Although people tried to do things differently, basic patterns didn't change, making it next to impossible for individual leaders to achieve key learning goals they'd set for themselves. Powerful drivers of behavior were never addressed—and they ultimately stalled the entire change program.

As research shows, there are a number of reasons why leadership development initiatives fail. A primary reason, as we saw in chapter 6, is that many development programs do not focus on the whole person or on the discoveries that lead to sustainable change, such as finding one's own dream and tying development to it. Other programs fail to take into account the power of the culture when they do the following:

- Ignore the real state of the organization, assuming that if people learn what they should do and be, systems and culture will automatically support them in the change process.

- Attempt to change only the person, ignoring the norms of the groups they work in every day and the larger surrounding culture in play.

- Drive the change process from the wrong place in the organization. Leadership development that transforms people *and* organizations must start at the top and be a strategic priority.

- Fail to develop a language of leadership—meaningful words that capture the spirit of leadership by symbolizing ideas, ideals, and emotionally intelligent leadership practices (a notion that we will examine later in this chapter).

Naturally, programs that fail to take these issues into account create frustrated individuals, cynicism, and wasted time, energy, and money.

## Succeed with a Process—Not a Program

Let's say that, as a leader, you get it: You've already set the stage by assessing the culture—examining the reality and the ideal at the organizational level. You've created resonance around the idea of change, and you've identified the people who will take top leadership roles in the future. The next step is to design a process that continually builds leadership that gets results. This process will include helping your organization's leaders uncover their own dreams and personal ideals, examine their strengths and their gaps, and use their daily work as a laboratory for learning. What else can you do?

For one thing, avoid the traps of many leadership development programs that we've seen. Too often they are simply executive education classes, focused on engaging people in learning topical content from experts: strategy, marketing, finance, general management, and similar abstractions. While all of these academic areas are of great importance to many leaders, no discrete program focused on them will add up to transformation of the person or the company.

And, although we've sometimes referred to leadership development "programs" in these pages, in fact what many organizations need aren't just one-time programs but a *process* built as a holistic system that permeates every layer of the organization. The best of these leadership development initiatives are based on an understanding that true change occurs through a multifaceted process that penetrates the three pivotal levels of the organization: the individuals in the organization, the teams in which they work, and the organization's culture. Based on the principles of adult learning and individual change, such processes take people on intellectual *and* emotional journeys—from facing the reality to implementing the ideal. We've found that the design of this kind of leadership development differs in fundamental ways from what one typically finds in most business schools or executive training centers.

The best development processes create a safe space for learning, making it challenging but not too risky. Moreover, in order for leaders to truly learn something new, they need experiences that are both relevant *and* frame breaking. The experiences have to be different enough to capture people's imagination but familiar enough to seem relevant. As our colleague Jonno Hanafin of the Gestalt Institute of Cleveland often cautions, "When attempting to bring about change in a person—or a company—you've got to be careful to manage your 'perceived weirdness index.'"[4] In other words, break the rules but don't scare people away.

Strong leadership development processes are focused on emotional *and* intellectual learning, and they build on active, participatory work: action learning and coaching, where people use what they're learning to diagnose and solve real problems in their organizations. They rely on experiential learning and on team-based simulations, where people engage in structured activity that they can use to examine their own and others' behavior. Exemplary processes are multifaceted, using a bold mixture of learning techniques; they are conducted over a period of time; and they take the culture head on.

### Building Culture Change into Leadership Development

When team members at Unilever began to design a new leadership development initiative for top management, they were nervous. They knew that the global company needed something to help it become a more enterprising and competitive industry leader. Their proposal, therefore, was intended to fundamentally change leadership behaviors and create an entirely new, enterprising company culture. Overall, the process would span years, levels, geographies, and businesses. It would call on leaders to rethink everything from their personal dreams to their visions for their businesses and how to execute leadership. It was a big, bold proposition.

As leaders began to paint a picture of the seminars and retreats planned for the company, they used unusual words such as *passion, emotionally charged, vulnerability, risk,* and *personal vision.* In many conversations over a period of months, they watched people's faces for reactions and pushed on, certain that their framework for individual and organizational change was good and that executives needed to be emotionally engaged in the process if it was to be successful.

This was the plan: First, the top 100 leaders in the company would participate in a kick-off retreat, led by chairmen Niall FitzGerald and Antony Burgmans. There, they would explore in a personal way habits of the past, as well as personal beliefs and their dreams for the future. It would be held in a place sure to inspire and certain to get the top team out of its comfort zone. It would present physical challenges while simultaneously taking people on an emotional journey with their colleagues—a chance to get to know each other and develop a level of trust and openness heretofore unthinkable; a chance to be honest. It would be an experience that touched people's hearts and became relevant to them in their lives once they returned. The ultimate goal was to take these new behaviors, the new mindset, and new ways of working together back to the business.

After that first retreat, the second phase would begin, when the top 500 leaders company-wide would attend a series of seminars designed to put into practice the new norms of the culture, turn vision into action, and drive change in the businesses. Then, over several years, around the world, business units one step below

# ACTION LEARNING

A SENIOR VICE PRESIDENT of a U.S. telecom listened intently as people in his company, who'd just completed a year-long, multifaceted executive development process, each made their action learning presentations. When they were finished, the senior vice president said, almost in disbelief: "These people are leaders. I had no idea we could find this in our company. Here we are struggling to find a few key leaders, and there are twenty of them here today. Twenty! I wish people would speak at all our meetings the way they have today. They showed leadership, and they showed courage."

Why was this vice president surprised? After all, he should have expected greatness: He had just spent several hundred thousand dollars on this leadership development initiative, which had been conducted for high-potential women and people of color. At this concluding event, he'd expected to encounter maybe a few outstanding people and to hear some mildly interesting presentations about their action learning projects. Instead, he'd heard all four groups, and all twenty people, discuss key strategic issues and how to deal with them. He had heard people present creative, powerful, and viable plans for addressing some of the issues that were keeping him up at night and causing no end of concern for leaders all over the company. And he'd heard the participants talk directly about the "unspeakables"—those issues that the organization never addressed because they were so loaded politically.

The action learning projects that were part of this company's executive development process could be thought of as active experimentation with a purpose.[5] The method enables participants to practice what they're learning, drawing on real-life challenges in the organization's business as the starting point for team projects among participants. With learning as a primary objective and achieving outcomes as a secondary purpose, each team works on its specific organizational challenge during the length of the course.[6]

Some principles to consider when engaging in action learning include the following:

➤ *The projects must be strategic in nature, multidimensional, ambiguous (i.e., there really is no one answer), and new, meaning no one is currently working on the issue in the organization.*

➤ *There must be active executive-level sponsorship in determining the projects and working with the teams.*

➤ *Teams must work on the projects, not individuals, and the teams need support throughout the duration of the project in creating a healthy climate, maintaining functional norms and emotional intelligence, dealing with conflict, focusing on learning rather than achievement, and so on.*

➤ *The process of learning needs to be examined, and this exami- nation needs to be expected as part of the outcome.*

➤ *The projects should be highly visible.*

➤ *Resources must be dedicated to the teams, and in particular people need to be released, to some extent, from normal duties to work on the projects.*

---

top management would mirror the process: engaging people's dreams and passion, and then turning these toward the business.

As the ideas caught on and leaders started to get excited about the prospects, conversations became more specific and focused on what people would actually *do* in these seminars. For example, executives would engage in deep reflection and conver- sation with one another about important and meaningful aspects of personal *and* business life—values, relationships, vision, hopes and dreams for the future, the regrets and high points of the past. They would chart their successes—and their failures—focusing on what they personally bring to each new challenge. They would speculate about how to overcome personal and organizational shortcomings and create a collective vision of the future. Through this important work of emotional engagement, they would create a learning community—teams of people who took the process of development and business growth seriously and who would challenge each other to change.

The idea of close, connected conversations about what the executives hoped to be and do in the future was appealing and energizing. In discussions, people often chimed in with even more ways to encourage executives to reflect deeply, move beyond platitudes, and talk straight with one another about life, about change, and about the business. They talked about how to build on the passion this process would spark and they talked about how to direct this new energy toward a hopeful future for Unilever.

But, occasionally, the design process got bogged down. This usually happened when more traditional, familiar leadership and strategy sessions were suggested. Energy would simply drain from conversations when more typical processes were considered: Heady discussions of stakeholders, objectives, and "blasting obstacles to success" usually brought to mind the many strategic planning programs the Unilever managers had attended over the years, and as good as they may have been, this was not what was needed now. In one such discussion, a top Unilever manager couldn't stand it anymore. Quietly, but with passion, he said, "People, we must be very careful here. Our leaders have done every kind of strategic planning exercise in the book, facilitated by the best business school professors and management gurus. They don't need another strategy, and the last thing they need is another stakeholder analysis!" His point was that these executives *understood* the strategy—now it was time to engage it passionately, while developing a different mindset and new leadership behaviors in order to turn vision into reality.

When leaders engage *only* on an intellectual level with the strategy, it's virtually impossible to maintain energy and commitment, and learning suffers. So what did the company's leaders need most? "To become emotionally engaged with their own passion and their dreams—with each other *and* with the strategy," said this executive, "and to connect with the possibilities of the future, to be given a chance to do something about it."

For most leaders, and even most managers, it is not more clarity about the strategy that will make the difference. It is not yet another five-year plan, and it is not another mundane leadership program. What makes the difference is finding passion for the work, for the strategy, and for the vision—and engaging hearts and minds in the search for a meaningful future. One more intellectual planning exercise is not going to get people engaged, and it certainly won't change a culture. Even the best leadership development programs, if conducted in a vacuum, do little to foster the kind of change that organizations need today.

What leaders must do is find a way to get executives emotionally engaged with each other and with their visions, and see to it that they begin to act on those visions. People change when they are emotionally engaged and committed. Fortunately, at Unilever the planning process for leadership development hit on this key to successful change and development. The design team made sure it kept the focus on passion—and discovered ways to turn that passion toward real action in the business. And the fact that senior leaders were guiding the process from the start ensured that people would be held accountable for change. It was a process that truly would build cultural change into leadership development.

### Creating Buzz

By design, the process employed at Unilever had lots of people thinking about leadership, speculating on their own organizational culture, and considering change. But for leadership development to take hold, one needs to create buy-in throughout the organization—which, as we've seen, begins with a mandate from the top. Leaders need to attend to the process themselves, as chairmen Niall FitzGerald and Antony Burgmans have done at Unilever. Moreover, to really draw people in, the process itself must be made emotionally rewarding.

For example, make sure people understand that their inclusion in the initiative is a sign of admiration for their abilities. At

Unilever, being invited into the process was considered an honor, a mark of prestige, and a sign that the company had spotted the participant as making a difference to the business. Seeing the program as giving themselves an advantage in career advancement, executives sought out the chance to be included.

That didn't happen by accident—it was a strategy. Roles for point people were scripted, letters were written, and seeds were deliberately planted in informal conversation—all designed to create an audible buzz about developing leadership capabilities and changing the culture of the company. Key leaders spoke with people personally about why they were being selected and what it could mean to be a leader in the new organization they were trying to build.

But Unilever also knew it needed to keep candidate selection clean. If there were politics involved it would be obvious to everyone, and the process would lose credibility. We saw this happen at a European manufacturer, where three kinds of people ended up in their high-potential program: those who deserved to be there, those who needed the education in order to catch up to the younger leaders, and those who top leadership felt were entitled to the perk because of long years of service. Imagine the dynamics: Everyone knew who was in which category!

Organizational leaders need to create a selection process that allows for the paradox of involvement: The best of the best get in, and everyone has a chance. All this means having real conversations, not merely releasing a memo or a voicemail telling people when and where to show up for a new leadership program. It's more effort, yes—but worth it: Attending to the entry process can determine the success of the entire initiative.

Once the leadership development process is under way, developing and using a language of leadership is a powerful way to create the buzz important to people's continued involvement. For example, the Unilever executives' kick-off retreat was held in Costa Rica (something that, for maximum emotional impact, was kept secret from the participants until they arrived in that country). That retreat, which included physical journeys and intensive interpersonal and group-level conversations, fundamentally changed the way the leaders felt about themselves, each other, and the company. Through this simple but profound series of conversations, held in the context of a magnificent and fragile ecology, people learned new ways of communicating with one another that would translate to new ways of operating together as a business.

When they returned home and began to apply their learning to themselves and the company, "Costa Rica" came to be a phrase that referred to the genuine kinds of conversations and emotional connection that participants experienced—and wanted to continue back at the home office. Indeed, in the first year and a half of the change process, words such as *authentic relationships*, *integrity*, *accountability*, and *empowerment* came to symbolize a host of new leadership behaviors. And although those are common words, at Unilever they've taken on special meaning as a result of the processes in which its leaders have participated.

Today, several years into the change agenda, leadership development at Unilever is fundamentally affecting how business is conducted and relationships are managed. Business leaders are being held accountable for results and for supporting the new mindset and the new emotional reality. Human resource systems such as succession planning, compensation, and performance management are becoming aligned with the change strategy, focusing deliberately on supporting the new culture.

Developing leaders involves more than just the people themselves. As we've seen, it also involves the organizational culture and systems that drive and constrain people's behavior, the groups and teams in which people spend their time, and more obvious issues such as the current state of the organization and the external challenges it faces. Using leadership development to address all of these levels builds greater resonance in the organization.

A good example is the multifaceted effort to develop leadership at Merrill Lynch's U.S. Private Client business.

### Getting Bullish on Leadership

Already a highly successful business with a long history of solid, experienced leadership, Merrill Lynch's U.S. Private Client business unit was confronting new challenges. Throughout the industry, competition was coming from unexpected sources. Clients' demands for services were becoming markedly more insistent, the global marketplace was now a reality, and the e-commerce revolution was threatening the very core of the business itself. To ensure that leadership strengths would grow with the business unit's changing needs, First Vice President Linda Pittari worked with Tim McManus, director of leadership development and training, to create a more systematic method for developing leaders—with a focus on emotional intelligence competencies.

"We knew that the challenges of the coming few years were going to be different from anything we'd faced before," Pittari told us. "We wanted to be sure our leaders were learning how to operate in a new environment."

The process began with identifying people in the field—as well as the home office—who had management potential. As time went on and the initiative progressed, Pittari and her team coached these managers in their first few critical years on the job. The experiences that managers had in the field, coupled with good mentoring, enabled the company to develop good leaders. But one of the main reasons that Pittari's leadership development initiative worked so well was that she went beyond a focus on people. She understood the importance of looking broadly at the business's underlying culture and how it supported or inhibited leadership. That is a dramatic difference from most development programs—which begin and end with the individual.

Linda Pittari began with a keen sense of what the pivotal norms were in the culture and set about exploring which of those were actually helpful to a new kind of leadership and which got in the way. Using the process of dynamic inquiry that we discussed in chapter 10, she and her team interviewed key leaders to get a sense of the cultural box they lived in. In essence, they asked: What's allowed here? What behaviors and values were expected? Which management styles were smiled upon and which panned? Which competencies were developed and which ignored?

But that was just a start. Pittari and her team also began to peel back the onion, looking for root issues and the deep-seated reasons why people succeeded or failed in the context of the culture.[7] They explored the depth of commitment to core principles, and why leaders behaved the way they did. And they asked people about the leadership of the company and what was and wasn't working—a key to understanding how to position leadership development later on. Armed with this information, the team was able to see which aspects of the culture were hampering leadership effectiveness, and which habitual leadership practices needed to change. They could also see what they needed to preserve.

For example, in this company, which after all was grounded on relationship building with clients, people relied on the affiliative leadership style. The warm relationships that managers established with their direct reports were powerful drivers of loyalty and dedication—resulting in lifelong commitment, hard work, and strong, trusting relationships. That affiliative style also meant, however, that these managers hesitated to expose areas where people needed to improve, and it made real coaching difficult to pull off. Although managers tried to compensate by using elaborate performance-management systems and holding people accountable for the numbers, often people would still go for years without receiving direct feedback about how to improve or develop themselves for the next step.

Using the dynamic inquiry process as a foundation, as well as a thorough review of individuals who were seemingly very effective in this new environment, Pittari's team was able to construct an agenda for leadership development that was designed to counteract some of the old culture while supporting the values, norms, and systems that were positive and helpful to new leaders. They identified skills and competencies that people would need to develop, such as how to give and receive developmental feedback, how to achieve the right balance of good judgment and risk taking, how to foster innovation, and how to manage an increasingly diverse workforce. They also identified areas of business acumen that needed enhancing.

Today, several years after Pittari and her team initiated this leadership development process at the Merrill Lynch business, 40 percent of the people who participated in the process have been promoted and are in significantly more responsible positions than they were a few years ago. Perhaps more important, the change effort focused the top level's attention on management, leadership, and cultural practices that really needed to change, and they have continued the work. Succession planning is now more systematic—with more attention paid to those individuals who exemplify leaders of the future.

By understanding that the initiative would have to do double duty—exemplifying the individual change model while also working on cultural issues—Pittari's team crafted a process that changed both the culture and the lives of individuals who worked in the company every day.

### Maximizing the Half-Life of Learning

In sum, the best leadership programs are designed for culture, competencies, and even spirit. They adhere to the principles of self-directed change and use a multifaceted approach to the learning and development process itself that focuses on the individual, team, and organization. Excellent processes include the following elements:

- A tie-in to the culture—and sometimes culture change— in an organization
- Seminars built around the philosophy and practice of individual change
- Relevant learning about emotional intelligence competencies—not just business acumen
- Creative and potent learning experiences with a purpose
- Relationships that support learning, such as learning teams and executive coaching

We look at developing leaders in terms of maximizing the half-life of learning. The idea is to develop a process that has "stickiness" so that there's continuing learning.

In the best processes, people have learned how to learn and are focused in a new and sustained way on reaching for their dreams together. They have a road map that makes sense to them— and the road map is as good a guide in their current job as it will be in the next one. It has been drawn with the person's values, beliefs, hopes, and dreams as the backdrop. Competency development for any given job is just a piece of it: The real issue is ensuring that a development process leaves its mark on people, the culture, and the systems that support change, development, and effective norms. And one payoff should be continuous learning and an enhanced capacity for change.

People can and will change when they find a good reason to do so. Leadership change takes people to the point of understanding what they want to change and how. In order for this kind of learning to have lasting impact on an organization, one needs to go beyond the individual and think about what needs to happen in groups—and in the organization at large—that will encourage the development of EI leaders.

## Toward Resonant Work and Resonant Lives

As our journey ends, we want to look into the future and expand the implications of what we have said thus far.

First, consider our argument. We make the case that emotions matter enormously for leadership—that primal leadership is a crucial dimension, one that largely determines whether a leader's other efforts take off or go awry. We've reviewed the underlying neurology—particularly the open loop for emotions—that makes creating resonance the primal task for any leader.

We've shown that emotional intelligence offers the essential competencies for resonant leadership, and that these abilities can be cultivated and strengthened—both for the individual and for an entire team. Such resonant leadership can be distributed throughout an entire organization. And, as ample data demonstrate, there are hard payoffs in organizational effectiveness and business performance.

We've done more than just offer a new theory of leadership—we've gotten down to the question, How can I act on this Monday morning? The first practical application comes in upgrading a leader's EI abilities. We've outlined the steps that our research has shown lead to lasting improvements in the crucial EI competencies for leadership.

Then we turned to how to make a group, team, or entire organization more resonant. Raising the collective emotional intelligence of an entire group can have far greater business impact than cultivating it only in a given individual within that group. But doing so demands an astute leader who understands how to take the emotional pulse of the group and transform the norms or culture in the right direction. And finally, organizations themselves can become incubators for resonant leadership, thus making a crucial difference for those who work there—and for the bottom line.

### Now More Than Ever

Why does all this matter so much, not just today, but going into the future?

Leaders everywhere confront a set of irrevocable imperatives, changing realities driven by profound social, political, economic, and technological changes. Our world, not to mention the business world, is in the midst of transformational change, calling for new leadership. In our businesses, we face continual increases in computing power, the spread of e-commerce, the rapid diversification of the workforce, the globalization of the economy, and the relentless ratcheting upward of the pace of business—all at an ever-accelerating rate of change.

These business realities make primal leadership ever more crucial. Consider, for instance, the implications of the fact that so many business strategies viable today will be irrelevant tomorrow. "Half the business models won't work in two to five years time," the CEO of an information services company lamented. "In our case, we now sell information that may be available free on the Internet in a few years—so our focus has to be finding new ways to market our information." And, as an investment banker put it, "Most companies perish while their management is frozen with terror."

Whether a company proves nimble enough to survive tomorrow's surprises depends to a large extent on whether its leaders—particularly the top team—have the ability to manage their own emotions in the face of drastic change. As market share erodes or profits plummet, leaders can panic, their fears fueling denial—the futile ruse that "everything is fine"—or poorly conceived knee-jerk solutions. They can turn, for example, to cost-cutting measures that focus on the people cheapest to lose rather than those vital to retain. Anxiety debilitates the brain's ability to understand and respond; when fear cripples leaders' decision making, an entire organization can crash and burn.

Emotionally intelligent leaders know how to manage their disruptive emotions so that they can keep their focus, thinking clearly under pressure. They do not wait for crisis to catalyze a needed change; they stay flexible, adapting to new realities ahead of the pack rather than just reacting to the crisis of the day. Even in the midst of vast changes, they can see their way to a brighter future, communicate that vision with resonance, and lead the way.

Consider, too, how companies that once did well enough by being among the best in a small market niche now find that their competitors come from around the world. As more and more businesses find themselves fighting it out in global markets, the standards for a leader's performance are changing. Where results at a given level might have made a company best in class for its industry in one region or country, the global reality means that to be among the best now demands a world-class performance. And that demand drives a need for the resonance that spawns continuous improvement—not just in a leader, but in the whole organization.

## Excellence Redefined

There's another reason primal leadership will matter more going into the future. The old model of leadership had a functional focus, one without regard to the emotional or personal dimension;

people were seen as interchangeable parts. Such impersonal leadership increasingly fails today. Resonant leaders shatter the old leadership mold that was cast in the image of the captains of industry, those old-fashioned lead-from-the-top figures of authority who led largely by virtue of the power of their position.

Increasingly, the best of breed lead not by virtue of power alone, but by excelling in the art of relationship, the singular expertise that the changing business climate renders indispensable. Leadership excellence is being redefined in interpersonal terms as companies strip out layers of managers, as corporations merge across national boundaries, and as customers and suppliers redefine the web of connection.

Resonant leaders know when to be collaborative and when to be visionary, when to listen and when to command. Such leaders have a knack for attuning to their own sense of what matters and articulating a mission that resonates with the values of those they lead. These leaders naturally nurture relationships, surface simmering issues, and create the human synergies of a group in harmony. They build a fierce loyalty by caring about the careers of those who work for them, and inspire people to give their best for a mission that speaks to shared values.

An emotionally intelligent leader does each of these at the right time, in the right way, with the right person. Such leadership creates a climate of enthusiasm and flexibility, one where people feel invited to be at their most innovative, where they give their best. And such a working climate, given today's business realities, creates added value through the essential human ingredients for organizational performance.

Such leaders are more values-driven, more flexible and informal, and more open and frank than leaders of old. They are more connected to people and to networks. Most especially, they exude resonance: They have genuine passion for their mission, and that passion is contagious. Their enthusiasm and excitement spread spontaneously, invigorating those they lead. And resonance is the key to primal leadership.

# EI VERSUS IQ

## A Technical Note

I N RECENT YEARS, we have analyzed data from close to 500 competence models from global companies (including the likes of IBM, Lucent, PepsiCo, British Airways, and Credit Suisse First Boston), as well as from healthcare organizations, academic institutions, government agencies, and even a religious order.[1] To determine which personal capabilities drove outstanding performance within these organizations, we grouped capabilities into three categories: purely technical skills such as accounting or business planning; cognitive abilities such as analytic reasoning; and traits showing emotional intelligence, such as self-awareness and relationship skill.

To create some of the competency models, psychologists typically asked senior managers at the companies to identify the competencies that distinguished the organization's most outstanding leaders, seeking consensus from an "expert panel." Others used a more rigorous method in which analysts asked senior managers to use objective criteria, such as a division's profitability, to distinguish the star performers at senior levels within their organizations from the average ones. Those individuals were then extensively interviewed and tested, and their competencies were methodically compared to identify those that distinguished star performers.

Whichever method was used, this process resulted in lists of ingredients for highly effective leaders. The lists usually ranged in length from a handful to up to fifteen or so competencies, such as initiative, collaboration, and empathy.

Analyzing all the data from hundreds of competence models yielded dramatic results. To be sure, intellect was to some extent a driver of outstanding performance; cognitive skills such as big-picture thinking and long-term vision were particularly important. But calculating the ratio of technical skills and purely cognitive abilities (some of which are surrogates for aspects of intelligence quotient, or IQ) to emotional intelligence in the ingredients that distinguished outstanding leaders revealed that EI-based competencies played an increasingly important role at higher levels of organizations, where differences in technical skills are of negligible importance.

In other words, the higher the rank of those considered star performers, the more EI competencies emerged as the reason for their effectiveness. When the comparison matched star performers against average ones in senior leadership positions, about 85 percent of the difference in their profiles was attributable to emotional intelligence factors rather than to purely cognitive abilities like technical expertise.[2]

One reason has to do with the intellectual hurdles that senior executives jump in obtaining their jobs. It takes at least an IQ of about 110 to 120 to get an advanced degree such as an MBA.[3] There is thus a high selection pressure for IQ in order to enter the executive ranks—and relatively little variation in IQ among those who are in those ranks. On the other hand, there is little or no systematic selection pressure when it comes to emotional intelligence, and so there is a much wider range of variation among executives. That lets superiority in these capabilities count far more than IQ when it comes to star leadership performance.[4]

While the precise ratio of EI to cognitive abilities depends on how each are measured and on the unique demands of a given organization, our rule of thumb holds that EI contributes 80 to 90 percent of the competencies that distinguish outstanding from average leaders—and sometimes more. To be sure, purely cognitive competencies, such as technical expertise, surface in such studies—but often as threshold abilities, the skills people need simply to do an average job. Although the specifics vary from organization to organization, EI competencies make up the vast majority of the more crucial, distinguishing competencies.[5] Even so, when those specific competencies are weighted for their contribution, the cognitive competencies can sometimes have quite significant input too, depending on the specific competence model involved.

To get an idea of the practical business implications of these competencies, consider an analysis of the partners' contributions to the profits of a large accounting firm. If the partner had significant strengths in the self-management competencies, he or she added 78 percent more incremental profit than did partners without those strengths. Likewise, the added profits for partners with strengths in social skills were 110 percent greater, and those with strengths in the self-management competencies added a whopping 390 percent incremental profit—in this case, $1,465,000 more per year.

By contrast, significant strengths in analytic reasoning abilities added just 50 percent more profit. Thus, purely cognitive abilities help—but the EI competencies help far more.[6]

# EMOTIONAL INTELLIGENCE

## Leadership Competencies

**SELF-AWARENESS**

- *Emotional self-awareness.* Leaders high in emotional self-awareness are attuned to their inner signals, recognizing how their feelings affect them and their job performance. They are attuned to their guiding values and can often intuit the best course of action, seeing the big picture in a complex situation. Emotionally self-aware leaders can be candid and authentic, able to speak openly about their emotions or with conviction about their guiding vision.

- *Accurate self-assessment.* Leaders with high self-awareness typically know their limitations and strengths, and exhibit a sense of humor about themselves. They exhibit a gracefulness in learning where they need to improve, and welcome constructive criticism and feedback. Accurate self-assessment lets a leader know when to ask for help and where to focus in cultivating new leadership strengths.

- *Self-confidence.* Knowing their abilities with accuracy allows leaders to play to their strengths. Self-confident leaders can welcome a difficult assignment. Such leaders often have a sense of presence, a self-assurance that lets them stand out in a group.

### SELF-MANAGEMENT

- *Self-control.* Leaders with emotional self-control find ways to manage their disturbing emotions and impulses, and even to channel them in useful ways. A hallmark of self-control is the leader who stays calm and clear-headed under high stress or during a crisis—or who remains unflappable even when confronted by a trying situation.

- *Transparency.* Leaders who are transparent live their values. Transparency—an authentic openness to others about one's feelings, beliefs, and actions—allows integrity. Such leaders openly admit mistakes or faults, and confront unethical behavior in others rather than turn a blind eye.

- *Adaptability.* Leaders who are adaptable can juggle multiple demands without losing their focus or energy, and are comfortable with the inevitable ambiguities of organizational life. Such leaders can be flexible in adapting to new challenges, nimble in adjusting to fluid change, and limber in their thinking in the face of new data or realities.

- *Achievement.* Leaders with strength in achievement have high personal standards that drive them to constantly seek performance improvements—both for themselves and those they lead. They are pragmatic, setting measurable but challenging goals, and are able to calculate risk so that their goals are worthy but attainable. A hallmark of achievement is in continually learning—and teaching—ways to do better.

- *Initiative.* Leaders who have a sense of efficacy—that they have what it takes to control their own destiny—excel in initiative. They seize opportunities—or create them— rather than simply waiting. Such a leader does not hesitate to cut through red tape, or even bend the rules, when necessary to create better possibilities for the future.

- *Optimism.* A leader who is optimistic can roll with the punches, seeing an opportunity rather than a threat in a setback. Such leaders see others positively, expecting the best of them. And their "glass half-full" outlook leads them to expect that changes in the future will be for the better.

### SOCIAL AWARENESS

- *Empathy.* Leaders with empathy are able to attune to a wide range of emotional signals, letting them sense the felt, but unspoken, emotions in a person or group. Such leaders listen attentively and can grasp the other person's perspective. Empathy makes a leader able to get along well with people of diverse backgrounds or from other cultures.

- *Organizational awareness.* A leader with a keen social awareness can be politically astute, able to detect crucial social networks and read key power relationships. Such leaders can understand the political forces at work in an organization, as well as the guiding values and unspoken rules that operate among people there.

- *Service.* Leaders high in the service competence foster an emotional climate so that people directly in touch with the customer or client will keep the relationship on the right track. Such leaders monitor customer or client satisfaction carefully to ensure they are getting what they need. They also make themselves available as needed.

### RELATIONSHIP MANAGEMENT

- *Inspiration.* Leaders who inspire both create resonance and move people with a compelling vision or shared mission. Such leaders embody what they ask of others, and are able to articulate a shared mission in a way that inspires others to follow. They offer a sense of common purpose beyond the day-to-day tasks, making work exciting.

- *Influence.* Indicators of a leader's powers of influence range from finding just the right appeal for a given listener to knowing how to build buy-in from key people and a network of support for an initiative. Leaders adept in influence are persuasive and engaging when they address a group.

- *Developing others.* Leaders who are adept at cultivating people's abilities show a genuine interest in those they are helping along, understanding their goals, strengths, and weaknesses. Such leaders can give timely and constructive feedback and are natural mentors or coaches.

- *Change catalyst.* Leaders who can catalyze change are able to recognize the need for the change, challenge the status quo, and champion the new order. They can be strong advocates for the change even in the face of opposition, making the argument for it compellingly. They also find practical ways to overcome barriers to change.

- *Conflict management.* Leaders who manage conflicts best are able to draw out all parties, understand the differing perspectives, and then find a common ideal that everyone can endorse. They surface the conflict, acknowledge the feelings and views of all sides, and then redirect the energy toward a shared ideal.

- *Teamwork and collaboration.* Leaders who are able team players generate an atmosphere of friendly collegiality and are themselves models of respect, helpfulness, and cooperation. They draw others into active, enthusiastic commitment to the collective effort, and build spirit and identity. They spend time forging and cementing close relationships beyond mere work obligations.

# NOTES

PREFACE

1. A note on the use of *we* in this book: For the sake of fluidity of style, and to emphasize that we speak in a collective voice, we use the term in the most liberal sense. *We* as used here refers not just to the three of us together but to work undertaken by any one of us, as well as by our close professional associates.

CHAPTER 1

1. The BBC news division: Like most of the other vignettes we use in this book, this incident was recounted by one of the people we interviewed (who in this case was an eyewitness to these events). If vignettes are from a secondary source, credits are given in endnotes. In cases where people spoke to us in confidence, identifying details of the incident have been disguised.

2. The comforting effect: Lisa Berkman et al., "Emotional Support and Survival after Myocardial Infarction," *Annals of Internal Medicine* (1992).

3. Stress and death: Anika Rosengren et al., "Stressful Life Events, Social Support and Mortality in Men Born in 1933," *British Medical Journal* 207, no. 17 (1983): 1102–1106.

4. Limbic regulation: Thomas Lewis, Fari Amini, and Richard Lannon, *A General Theory of Love* (New York: Random House, 2000).

5. Emotional mirroring: Robert Levenson, University of California at Berkeley, personal communication.

6. Expressiveness transmits moods: Howard Friedman and Ronald Riggio, "Effect of Individual Differences in Nonverbal Expressiveness on

Transmission of Emotion," *Journal of Nonverbal Behavior* 6 (1981): 32–58.

7. Groups have moods: Janice R. Kelly and Sigal Barsade, "Moods and Emotions in Small Groups and Work Teams," working paper, Yale School of Management, New Haven, Connecticut, 2001.

8. Work teams share moods: C. Bartel and R. Saavedra, "The Collective Construction of Work Group Moods," *Administrative Science Quarterly* 45 (2000): 187–231.

9. Nurses and accountants tracking moods: Peter Totterdell et al., "Evidence of Mood Linkage in Work Groups," *Journal of Personality and Social Psychology* 74 (1998): 1504–1515.

10. Sports teams: Peter Totterdell, "Catching Moods and Hitting Runs: Mood Linkage and Subjective Performance in Professional Sports Teams," *Journal of Applied Psychology* 85, no. 6 (2000): 848–859.

11. The leadership ripple effect: See Wallace Bachman, "Nice Guys Finish First: A SYMLOG Analysis of U.S. Naval Commands," in *The SYMLOG Practitioner: Applications of Small Group Research*, eds. Richard Brian Polley, A. Paul Hare, and Philip J. Stone (New York: Praeger, 1988).

12. The leader's emotional impact in work groups: Anthony T. Pescosolido, "Emotional Intensity in Groups" (Ph.D. diss., Department of Organizational Behavior, Case Western Reserve University, 2000).

13. Leaders as the managers of meaning: Howard Gardner, *Leading Minds: An Anatomy of Leadership* (New York: Basic Books, 1995).

14. Informal leaders: V. U. Druskat and A. T. Pascosolido, "Leading Self-Managing Work Teams from the Inside: Informal Leader Behavior and Team Outcomes." Submitted for publication, 2001.

15. Moods, contagion, and work performance: Sigal Barsade and Donald E. Gibson, "Group Emotion: A View from the Top and Bottom," in *Research on Managing Groups and Teams*, eds. D. Gruenfeld et al. (Greenwich, CT: JAI Press, 1998).

16. Smiles the most contagious: Robert Levenson and Anna Ruef, "Emotional Knowledge and Rapport," in *Empathic Accuracy*, ed. William Ickes (New York: Guilford Press, 1997).

17. Laughter is involuntary: Meredith Small, "More Than the Best Medicine," *Scientific American*, August 2000, 24.

18. Laughter is "brain to brain": Robert Provine, *Laughter: A Scientific Investigation* (New York: Viking Press, 2000), 133.

19. Laughter episodes: Ibid.

20. Good moods in a leader mean lower voluntary turnover: See, for example, Jennifer M. George and Kenneth Bettenhausen, "Understanding

Prosocial Behavior, Sales Performance, and Turnover: A Group-Level Analysis in Service Context," *Journal of Applied Psychology* 75, no. 6 (1990): 698–706.

21. Sober mood and high-risk decisions: R. C. Sinclair, "Mood, Categorization Breadth, and Performance Appraisal," *Organizational Behavior and Human Decision Processes* 42 (1988): 22–46.

22. Anger and leadership: Jennifer M. George, "Emotions and Leadership: The Role of Emotional Intelligence," *Human Relations* 53, no. 8 (2000): 1027–1055.

23. Moods perpetuate themselves: A voluminous literature shows the self-reinforcing effect of moods. See, for example, Gordon H. Bower, "Mood Congruity of Social Judgments," in *Emotion and Social Judgments*, ed. Joseph Forgas (Oxford: Pergamon Press, 1991), 31–53.

24. Distressing emotions hijack attention: See, for example, Jacqueline Wood, Andrew Matthews, and Tim Dalgleish, "Anxiety and Cognitive Inhibition," *Emotion* 1, no. 2 (2001): 166–181.

25. The Yale study of mood and performance: Sigal Barsade, "The Ripple Effect: Emotional Contagion in Groups," working paper 98, Yale School of Management, New Haven, Connecticut, 2000.

26. Bosses and bad feelings: John Basch and Cynthia D. Fisher, "Affective Events–Emotions Matrix: A Classification of Job-Related Events and Emotions Experienced in the Workplace," in *Emotions in the Workplace: Research, Theory and Practice*, ed. N. Ashkanasy, W. Zerbe, and C. Hartel (Westport, CT: Quorum Books, 2000), 36–48.

27. Distress impairs empathy and social skill: Jeffrey B. Henriques and Richard J. Davidson, "Brain Electrical Asymmetries during Cognitive Task Performance in Depressed and Nondepressed Subjects," *Biological Psychiatry* 42 (1997): 1039–1050.

28. Emotions reflect quality of work life: Cynthia D. Fisher and Christopher S. Noble, "Affect and Performance: A Within Persons Analysis" (paper presented at the Annual Meeting of the Academy of Management, Toronto, 2000).

29. Job satisfaction is not the same as feeling good while working: Cynthia D. Fisher, "Mood and Emotions while Working: Missing Pieces of Job Satisfaction?," *Journal of Organizational Behavior* 21 (2000): 185–202. See also Howard Weiss, Jeffrey Nicholas, and Catherine Daus, "An Examination of the Joint Effects of Affective Experiences and Job Beliefs on Job Satisfaction and Variations in Affective Experiences over Time," *Organizational Behavior and Human Decision Processes* 78, no. 1 (1999): 1–24.

30. Mental benefits of good moods: See A. M. Isen, "Positive Affect,"

in *Handbook of Cognition and Emotion,* eds. Tim Dalgleish and Mick J. Power (Chichester, England: Wiley, 1999).

31. Good moods and performance: See C. D. Fisher and C. S. Noble, "Emotion and the Illusory Correlation between Job Satisfaction and Job Performance" (paper presented at the second Conference on Emotions in Organizational Life, Toronto, August 2000).

32. Insurance sales: Martin E. Seligman and Peter Schulman, "The People Make the Place," *Personnel Psychology* 40 (1987): 437–453.

33. The impact of humor on work effectiveness: The findings are reviewed in R. W. Clouse and K. L. Spurgeon, "Corporate Analysis of Humor," *Psychology: A Journal of Human Behavior* 32 (1995): 1–24.

34. CEOs and their top management team: Sigal G. Barsade, Andrew J. Ward, et al. "To Your Heart's Content: A Mode of Affective Diversity in Top Management Teams," *Administrative Science Quarterly* 45 (2000): 802–836.

35. Improvement in service climate drives increase in revenue: Lyle Spencer, paper presented at the meeting of the Consortium for Research on Emotional Intelligence in Organizations (Cambridge, Massachusetts, 19 April 2001).

36. Mood affects cardiac care unit. Benjamin Schneider and D. E. Bowen, *Winning the Service Game* (Boston: Harvard Business School Press, 1995).

37. Mood, customer service, and sales: George and Bettenhausen, "Understanding Prosocial Behavior."

38. Leaders' positive mood predicts sales performance: See also Jennifer M. George, "Leader Positive Mood and Group Performance: The Case of Customer Service," *Journal of Applied Psychology* 25, no. 9 (1995): 778–794.

39. Poor customer service rep morale and decline in revenues: Schneider and Bowen, *Winning the Service Game.*

40. The analysis linking climate to business performance: David McClelland, "Identifying Competencies with Behavioral-Event Interviews," *Psychological Science* 9 (1998): 331–339; Daniel Williams, "Leadership for the 21st Century: Life Insurance Leadership Study"(Boston: LOMA/Hay Group, 1995).

41. More technically, the styles were found to account for 53 to 72 percent of the variance in organizational climate. See Stephen P. Kelner Jr., Christine A. Rivers, and Kathleen H. O'Connell, "Managerial Style as a Behavioral Predictor of Organizational Climate" (Boston: McBer & Company, 1996).

42. Much the same argument has been made in George and Bettenhausen, "Understanding Prosocial Behavior"; and in Neal M. Ashkanasy

and Barry Tse, "Transformational Leadership as Management of Emotion: A Conceptual Review," in Neal M. Ashkanasy, Charmine E. J. Hartel, and Wilffred J. Zerbe, *Emotions in the Workplace: Research, Theory and Practice* (Westport, CT: Quorum Books, 2000), 221–235.

CHAPTER 2

1. We are by no means the first to argue that the key to group or organizational cohesion is shared emotions. See, for example, B. E. Ashforth and R. H. Humphrey, "Emotion in the Workplace: A Reappraisal," *Human Relations* 48 (1995): 97–125; and Edward Lawler, "Affective Attachment to Nested Groups: A Choice-Process Theory," *American Sociological Review* 57 (1992): 327–339.

2. We see resonance and dissonance as the two major poles of EI leadership. These dimensions can be thought of in terms of two dimensions: emotional tone and empathic synchrony. One dimension tracks the emotional tone and impact of a leader's actions, positive or negative. The other dimension reflects empathy: whether or not people are in synchrony with the leader's emotional tonality, and the leader with theirs.

3. Yelling at work: Survey results reported in Vivian Marino, "It's All the Rage at Work, Too," *The New York Times*, 12 November 2000, Money & Business section, 3.

4. The physiology of arguments: The research, by John Gottman of the University of Washington, was done with married couples, but the physiology of response should apply whenever the two people involved have close and emotionally important relationships with each other, such as a boss and employee. For details, see John Gottman, *What Predicts Divorce: The Relationship between Marital Processes and Marital Outcomes* (Hillsdale, NJ: Lawrence Earlbaum Associates, 1993).

5. Inept criticism: Robert Baron, "Countering the Effects of Destructive Criticism," *Journal of Applied Psychology* 75, no. 3 (1990): 235–246.

6. Stress hormones circulate for hours: See, for example, Dolf Zillman, "Mental Control of Angry Aggression," in *Handbook of Mental Control*, eds. Daniel Wegner and James S. Pennebaker (Englewood Cliffs, NJ: Prentice Hall, 1993).

7. Dementors: J. K. Rowling, *Harry Potter and the Prisoner of Azbakan* (London: Bloomsbury, 1999), 187.

8. The dark side of ambition: See, for example, Michael Maccoby, "Narcissistic Leaders: The Incredible Pros, the Inevitable Cons," *Harvard Business Review*, January–February 2000, 69–75.

9. The specifics of the neurology described throughout this chapter are

far more complex than indicated here. In the interests of clarity, we have simplified the picture, focusing on key structures within the intricate web of circuitry always involved in any complex behavior.

10. When we use the term *amygdala*, we refer to the structure itself along with the web of circuitry that integrates the amygdala with other parts of brain. See Joseph LeDoux, *The Emotional Brain* (New York: Simon & Schuster, 1996).

11. Cognitive abilities intact, but EI impaired in patients with prefrontal–amygdala lesions: Neurological patients with damage to the bilateral areas of the amygdala, the ventral-medial area of the prefrontal lobe, and the right somatosensory and insular cortices show deficits on tests of emotional intelligence, whereas patients with damage to other brain areas, such as those in other areas of the neocortex, do not. These areas appear critical for being aware of our own emotions, for regulating and expressing them, and for being aware of the emotions of others. Antonio Damasio, University of Iowa College of Medicine, personal communication; Reuven Bar-On, personal communication on preliminary data collected with Antoine Bechara and Daniel Tranel, associates of Dr. Damasio.

12. The main tasks of a leader: See, for example, Gary Yukl, *Leadership in Organizations* (Upper Saddle River, NJ: Prentice Hall, 1998).

13. For details see Fabio Sala, *ECI Technical Manual* (Boston: Hay Group, 2001).

CHAPTER 3

1. Laughter and leadership: Fabio Sala, "Relationship between Executive's Spontaneous Use of Humor and Effective Leadership" (Ph.D. diss., Boston University Graduate School of Arts and Science, 2000).

2. Competencies independently established as superior: David C. McClelland, "Identifying Competencies with Behavioral-Event Interviews," *Psychological Science 9* (1998): 331–339. Several of the EI competencies most strongly tied to humor were in the social awareness or relationship skill domain, as one might expect, since these are the most visible socially. These included empathy, organizational awareness, influence, and team leadership. But humor also had strong associations with competencies in the self-management area (initiative, the drive to achieve) and with self-confidence, which reflects self-awareness. This suggests that for these gifted leaders the expression of many or most EI competencies often came via the artful use of humor—and that this was in itself one basis of their success as leaders.

3. A radical proposal: David C. McClelland, "Testing for Competence

Rather Than Intelligence," *American Psychologist* 28 (1973): 14–31. When McClelland wrote this article, Richard Boyatzis and Daniel Goleman were his graduate students in psychology at Harvard.

4. Lyle Spencer, "The Economic Value of Emotional Intelligence Competencies and EIC-Based HR Programs," in *The Emotionally Intelligent Workplace*, eds. Cary Cherniss and Daniel Goleman (San Francisco: Jossey-Bass, 2001).

5. While average branch managers had annual sales of $17 million, these outstanding leaders had sales 75 percent higher—on average, $29.8 million—plus a 106 percent higher return on sales.

6. James C. Collins and Jerry I. Porras, *Built to Last: Successful Habits of Visionary Companies* (New York: HarperBusiness, 1994).

7. The Johnson & Johnson leadership research was led by Dottie Brienza of the Consumer Companies division and by Kathy Cavallo. Findings were presented at a meeting of the Consortium for Research on Emotional Intelligence in Organizations (Cambridge, Massachusetts, 3 November 2000).

8. The ECI-360 assesses the full spectrum of emotional intelligence–based leadership competencies. For more information, see http://www.eisglobal.com.

9. The differences were statistically significant for all twenty of the EI competencies. The ECI correlated more highly with high potentials than did the company's own leadership competence model.

10. We streamlined the EI competence model from five domains to four by folding "motivation" into "self-management." Statistical analyses have also led us to combine several of the EI competencies—for instance, "leveraging diversity" has become part of "empathy"—so that where there used to be twenty-five competencies on the list, there are now just eighteen. New thinking has also led us to rename some competencies to emphasize the features most significant for EI leaders: "Trustworthiness" has become "transparency," and "leadership" has become "inspirational leadership." Beyond that, we have dropped "conscientiousness," which is not as crucial for leaders who can delegate details to an able assistant. And we have combined "communication"—an influence tool—with the "influence" competence.

11. EI competencies and the brain: For a more detailed explanation of the links of EI competencies to the brain, see Daniel Goleman, "Emotional Intelligence: A Theory of Performance," in *The Emotionally Intelligent Workplace*.

12. For the basic theory, see Goleman, *Working with Emotional Intelligence* (New York: Bantam, 1998). In this book we extend that theory.

13. The critical mass of strengths in EI competencies was found both by Richard Boyatzis, *The Competent Manager: A Model for Organizational Effectiveness* (New York: Wiley-Interscience, 1982) and by David C. McClelland, "Identifying Competencies with Behavioral-Event Interviews," *Psychological Science 9* (1998): 331–339.

14. Motivation and the left prefrontal cortex: Richard Davidson, D. C. Jackson, and Ned H. Kalin, "Emotion, Plasticity, Context and Regulation: Perspectives from Affective Neuroscience," *Psychological Bulletin* 126, no. 6 (2000): 890–909.

15. Emotions and decision making: Antonio Damasio, *Descartes' Error* (New York: Putnam, 1994).

16. Intuitive decision making in entrepreneurs: Ann Graham Ettinger, *Make Up Your Mind* (Santa Monica, CA: Merritt Publishing, 1995).

17. Predicting the weather: Barbara Knowlton, Jennifer Mangels, and Larry Squire, "A Neostriatal Habit Learning System in Humans," *Science* 273 (1996): 1399–1402.

18. The basal ganglia and implicit learning: Matthew D. Lieberman, "Intuition: A Social Cognitive Neuroscience Approach," *Psychological Bulletin* 126 (2000): 109–137.

19. The circuitry involved: Ibid.

20. Gut feeling: Damasio, *Descartes' Error*.

21. The inhibitory function of the prefrontal areas is an active research focus, with some evidence pointing to connections from the prefrontal cortex having inhibitory effects on neurons in the amygdala. Dr. Richard Davidson, University of Wisconsin, personal communication.

22. In other publications, we've used the term *trustworthiness* for this competence. Here we use *transparency* to emphasize the importance of this aspect of the competence for leadership.

23. "Cool": Lewis MacAdams, *Birth of Cool: Beat, Bebop and the American Avant-Garde* (New York: Free Press, 2001).

24. The amygdala and prefrontal zones' role in empathy: See, for example, Paul J. Eslinger, "Neurological and Neuropsychological Bases of Empathy," *European Neurology* 39 (1998): 193–199.

25. Limbic resonance: Thomas Lewis, Fari Amini, and Richard Lannon, *A General Theory of Love* (New York: Random House, 2000).

26. The importance of vision for leadership: See, for example, Warren Bennis and Burt Nanus, *Leaders: Strategies for Taking Charge* (New York: Harper and Row, 1985); Jay Conger, *The Charismatic Leader* (San Francisco: Jossey-Bass, 1989); and John P. Kotter, *Leading Change* (Boston: Harvard Business School Press, 1996).

27. The product director: Quoted in Matthew Mangino and Christine Dreyfus, "Developing Emotional Intelligence Competencies" (paper presented to the Consortium for Research on Emotional Intelligence in Organizations, Cambridge, Massachusetts, 19 April 2001).

### CHAPTER 4

1. The database was compiled by the Boston consulting firm of McBer & Company (now The Hay Group) and originally analyzed by Stephen Kelner Jr. See Stephen P. Kelner Jr., Christine A. Rivers, and Kathleen H. O'Connell, "Managerial Style as a Behavioral Predictor of Organizational Climate" (Boston: McBer & Company, 1996). The sample was international, including leaders from Europe, Africa, North America, Australia, and the Pacific Rim; half were American. The measure of climate was developed by McBer & Company, based on the original work of George Litwin. See G. H. Litwin and R. A. Stringer Jr., "Motivation and Organizational Climate" (Boston: Division of Research, Graduate School of Business Administration, Harvard University, 1971). It assesses six specific indicators of climate, based on the pioneering work of Litwin and Stringer, as refined by David McClelland and his colleagues at McBer.

2. Bob Pittman at Six Flags: Quoted in Alden M. Hayashi, "When to Trust Your Gut," *Harvard Business Review*, February 2001, 59–65.

3. Transformational leaders: James McGregor Burns, *Leadership* (New York: Harper & Row, 1978). So, too, with "charismatic" leaders, who articulate a strategic vision informed by a sensitivity to stakeholders' needs; see Jay A. Conger, *The Charismatic Leader: Behind the Mystique of Exceptional Leadership* (San Francisco: Jossey-Bass, 1989).

4. Shelley Lazarus and David Ogilvy: "A Job and a Life Intertwined," *The New York Times*, 23 May 2001, C3.

5. The sweetness of success at stretch tasks: Cynthia Fisher and Christopher S. Noble, "Affect and Performance: A Within Persons Analysis" (paper presented at the Annual Meeting of the Academy of Management, Toronto, 2000).

6. James C. Collins and Jerry I. Porras, *Built to Last: Successful Habits of Visionary Companies* (New York: HarperBusiness, 1994).

7. Anxious affiliation: Stephen P. Kelner, "Interpersonal Motivation: Cynical, Positive and Anxious" (Ph.D. diss., Boston University, 1991).

8. Lou Gerstner on the 1993 IBM turnaround: Quoted in Steve Lohr, "IBM Chief Gerstner Recalls Difficult Days at Big Blue," *The New York Times*, 31 July 2000, C3.

CHAPTER 5

1. *Business Week*, "The Best Performers," 29 March 1999, 98.

2. SEC report and analyses of Al Dunlap's tenure as CEO of Sunbeam: Floyd Norris, "S.E.C. Accuses Former Sunbeam Official of Fraud," *New York Times*, 16 May 2001, 1.

3. The question of leadership narcissism, or "ego": See, for example, Michael Maccoby, "Narcissistic Leaders: The Incredible Pros, the Inevitable Cons," *Harvard Business Review*, January–February 2000, for a view of the positive and negative sides of such leadership.

4. See Jim Collins, "Level 5 Leadership," *Harvard Business Review*, January 2001, 66–76.

5. The insurance company study: Hay Group research team, led by John Larrere with Martin Leshner, David Baker, and Stephen Kelner, for LOMA. See Daniel Williams, "Leadership for the 21st Century: Life Insurance Leadership Study" (Boston: LOMA/Hay Group, 1995).

6. Marcus Buckingham and data on workers leaving bad bosses: Quoted by Amy Zipkin in "The Wisdom of Thoughtfulness," *The New York Times*, 31 May 2000, C1.

7. David McClelland, "Identifying Competencies with Behavioral-Event Interviews," *Psychological Science* 9 (1998): 331–339.

8. United Kingdom school leadership: See "Research into Headteacher Effectiveness" (report by The Hay Group to the U.K. Department for Education and Employment, 2000).

CHAPTER 6

1. The CEO disease: First described with this title by John Byrne in "CEO Disease," *Business Week*, 1 April 1991, 52–59.

2. Feedback is less consistent for managers: James Conway and Allen Huffcutt, "Psychometric Properties of Multi-source Performance Ratings: A Meta-analysis of Subordinate, Supervisor, Peer and Self-Ratings," *Human Performance* 10, no. 4 (1977): 331–360.

3. Women and minorities get less feedback than others: A number of studies and management scholars report that women and members of visible minority groups receive less and less useful feedback than others. See, for example, Peggy Stuart, "What Does the Glass Ceiling Cost You?" *Personnel Journal* 71, no. 11 (1992): 70–80; Ann M. Morrison, Randall P. White, Ellen Van Velsor, and The Center for Creative Leadership, *Breaking the Glass Ceiling: Can Women Reach the Top of America's Largest Corporations?* (Reading, MA: Addison-Wesley, 1987); and Taylor Cox Jr., *Cultural*

*Diversity in Organizations: Theory, Research, and Practice* (San Francisco: Berrett-Koehler Publishers, 1993).

4. The poorest managers exaggerate their ability the most: J. Kruger and D. Dunning, "Unskilled and Unaware of It: How Difficulties in Recognizing One's Own Competence Lead to Inflated Self-Assessments," *Journal of Personality and Social Psychology* 77, no. 6 (1999): 1121–1134.

5. CEOs of best-performing healthcare companies: Eric Harter, "The Quest for Sustainable Leadership: The Importance of Connecting Leadership Principles to Concepts of Organizational Sustainability" (EDM diss., Case Western Reserve University, 1999).

6. Top-performing versus low-performing leaders: Analysis by Michele Burckle, in Fabio Sala, *ECI Technical Manual* (Boston: Hay Group, 2001).

7. The honeymoon effect: John P. Campbell, Marvin D. Dunnette, Edward E. Lawler III, and Karl E. Weick, *Managerial Behavior, Performance, and Effectiveness* (New York: McGraw Hill, 1970) reviewed various studies and came to this conclusion. More recent meta-analytic studies and utility analyses confirm that significant changes can and do occur, but not with the impact that the level of investment would lead us to expect nor with many types of training. See Charles C. Morrow, M. Quintin Jarrett, and Melvin Rupinski, "An Investigation of the Effect and Economic Utility of Corporate Wide Training," *Personnel Psychology* 50 (1997): 91–119; Timothy Baldwin and J. Kevin Ford, "Transfer of Training: A Review and Directions for Future Research," *Personnel Psychology* 41 (1988): 63–105; and Michael J. Burke and Russell R. Day, "A Cumulative Study of the Effectiveness of Managerial Training," *Journal of Applied Psychology* 71, no. 2 (1986): 232–245. Furthermore, when a change has been noted, a question about the sustainability of the changes is raised because of the relatively short time periods studied.

8. Few studies show impact of training on behavior: Some studies have shown that training can have a positive effect on job or life outcomes, which are the ultimate purpose of development efforts. But showing an impact on outcomes, although desired, may also blur *how* the change actually occurs. Do the person's actions and habits change, or do other factors in the situations account for the change? A global literature search by the Consortium on Research on Emotional Intelligence in Organizations found only fifteen programs that improved emotional intelligence. Most of them showed impact on job outcomes (such as number of new businesses started) or life outcomes (such as finding a job or satisfaction). These are reviewed in Cary Cherniss and Mitchell Adler, *Promoting Emotional Intelligence in Organizations:*

*Make Training in Emotional Intelligence Effective* (Washington, DC: American Society for Training and Development, 2000).

9. Studying the effect of training: A quality research design would include pre- and post-training testing of the desired behavior, as well as some way to compare it with other programs, such as by comparison groups or through a time-series design. The lack of these elements in the relatively few attempts to evaluate training means that many results are not as useful as they could be.

10. The effect of communications training: Preston E. Smith, "Management Modeling Training to Improve Morale and Customer Satisfaction," *Personnel Psychology* 29 (1976): 351–359. Written responses to typical customer problems were coded both before and after the training for the trained group, and for comparison groups, as measures of their communications skills. The percentage improvement in this study reflects behavior after the training as compared with before the training.

11. The effect of training months later: In what is often considered a classic study, educational administrators showed improvement of only 8 percent on a broad array of these skills three months after training. Raymond A. Noe and Neal Schmitt, "The Influence of Trainee Attitudes on Training Effectiveness: Test of a Model," *Personnel Psychology* 39 (1986): 497–523. Behavioral change was assessed through a 360-degree type of measure. The training participant's immediate work supervisor, two teachers (i.e., subordinates or peers), and two support staff members rated the trainee before and after the training on six scales assessing behaviors such as sensitivity toward others, leadership, and decisiveness. The percentage improvement drawn from this study reflects behavior after the training as compared with before the training.

In another study, the social awareness and social skills of managers in a steel company improved by 9 percent three months after training, and dropped a little to a 7 percent improvement eighteen months after training. Herbert H. Hand, Max D. Richards, and John W. Slocum Jr., "Organizational Climate and the Effectiveness of a Human Relations Training Program," *Academy of Management Journal* 16, no. 2 (1973): 185–246. The behavior was assessed by groups of the participants' work subordinates using a questionnaire regarding such areas as concern and sensitivity for others, self-awareness, and initiative. These data were collected for those going through the training and for comparison groups. The percentage improvement in this study reflects behavior after the training as compared with before the training.

In several other studies where behavior of people who were trained was compared with others not trained (or not given the same type of training), but in which no pretraining testing was involved, the results were similar: an 11 percent comparative increase in social skills two months after training first-level supervisors in a large urban medical center. K. N. Wexley and W. F. Memeroff, "Effectiveness of Positive Reinforcement and Goal Setting as Methods of Management Development," *Journal of Applied Psychology* 60, no. 4 (1975): 446–450. Subordinates of the participants in the training and comparison groups completed a questionnaire regarding their supervisors that assessed behaviors such as consideration and sensitivity toward others, conflict resolution, cooperative spirit within the work group, and initiating and communicating expectations. The percentage improvement in this study reflects behavior after the training of those in the training groups as compared with those in the comparison groups. The "post-test only" comparison is a legitimate approximation because participants were randomly assigned to the training and control groups.

In another study, first-level supervisors showed an 18 percent improvement in a variety of EI-related behaviors one year after training. Gary P. Latham and Lise M. Saari, "Application of Social-Learning Theory to Training Supervisors through Behavioral Modeling," *Journal of Applied Psychology* 64, no. 3 (1979): 239–246. Supervisors of those in the training and comparison groups assessed the participants three months and one year following the training on factors such as emotional control, supervision, and interactions with others. The percentage improvement in this study reflects behavior after the training of those in the training groups as compared with those in the comparison groups. The "post-test only" comparison is legitimate because participants were randomly assigned to groups.

Another study showed an average increase of 8 percent improvement following the development of a plan for change. Dianne P. Young and Nancy M. Dixon, *Helping Leaders Take Effective Action: A Program Evaluation* (Greensboro, NC: Center for Creative Leadership, 1996). Executives and managers attending the LeaderLab program were assessed by co-workers about five and a half months after the program and retrospectively one year earlier. The behaviors studied included flexibility, self-confidence, interpersonal relationship skills, and coping with emotional disequilibrium. Percentage improvement in this study reflects co-workers' assessments at the time of evaluation minus their views of the person one year earlier, divided by the earlier scores.

12. The overall impact of training: The 10 percent figure represents the average percentage improvement on the multiple or composite EI behaviors from the five studies reviewed. It does not include the one study on communications

skills, because it looked at only one specific competency. If you include that study, the overall average is still only 15 percent. The lack of studies, difficulty in determining comparability of measures, and lack of consistency in research designs conspire to make a precise calculation impossible.

There are, undoubtedly, other studies that were not found and reviewed, or that were not available through journals and books and were therefore overlooked. We do not claim this is an exhaustive review, but it is suggestive of the percentage improvement as a rough approximation of the real impact. This approximation is offered to help in the comparison of the relative impact of management training, management education, and self-directed learning. Unfortunately, many of the more recent meta-analyses and review articles use statistical techniques reporting effect sizes and other associational data. Although this helps a researcher determine the statistical significance of the findings, it does not allow for comparison of percentage improvement. In addition, the lack of research with more than a one-year to eighteen-month follow-up period makes it difficult to comment on the sustainability of the changes observed following training.

13. The half-life of knowledge: L. Specht and P. Sandlin, "The Differential Effects of Experiential Learning Activities and Traditional Lecture Classes in Accounting," *Simulations and Gaming* 22, no. 2 (1991): 196–210.

14. People develop EI competencies throughout life: Matthew Mangino and Christine Dreyfus, "Developing Emotional Intelligence Competencies" (presentation to the Consortium for Research on Emotional Intelligence in Organizations, Cambridge, Massachusetts, 19 April 2001). The pattern of the natural acquisition of EI competencies fits with an earlier study of managers at NASA by Christine Dreyfus, "Scientists and Engineers as Effective Managers: A Study of Development of Interpersonal Abilities" (Ph.D. diss., Case Western Reserve University, 1991).

15. EI competencies improve with age: Scores from self-assessment as well as others' assessment of the competencies were significantly correlated with age for all clusters of the EI competencies. This was not a function of managerial level; the correlation with job level only appeared for the relationship management skills cluster. Sala, *ECI Technical Manual*.

16. Extinguishing of training effects: This does not include changes induced, willingly or not, by chemical or hormonal changes in one's body. But even in such situations, the interpretation of the changes and behavioral comportment following it will be affected by the person's will, values, and motivations.

17. Importance of extended practice: Thomas Lewis, Fari Amini, and

Richard Lannon, *A General Theory of Love* (New York: Random House, 2000).

18. Impact of mindfulness training: The research, as yet unpublished, is cited in Tara Bennett-Goleman, *Emotional Alchemy: How the Mind Can Heal the Heart* (New York: Harmony Books, 2001).

19. Brain plasticity of London taxi drivers: Eleanor A. Maguire, David G. Gadian, Ingrid S. Johnsrude, Catriona D. Good, John Ashburner, Richard S. J. Frackowiak, and Christopher D. Firth, "Navigation-Related Structural Change in the Hippocampi of Taxi Drivers." *Proceedings of the National Academy of Sciences* 97, no 8 (2000): 4398–4403. Available online at http://www.pnas.org/cgi/content/full/97/8/4398.

20. Using neural connections over and over strengthens them: Gerald M. Edelman, *Neural Darwinism: The Theory of Neuronal Group Selection* (New York: Basic Books, 1987), 58.

21. Strengthening of neural connections: Researchers at Case Western Reserve University, notably Professor James E. Zull, have noted that when nerve networks connecting nerves to muscles were stimulated vigorously, new branches and connections were made. James E. Zull, *The Art of Changing a Brain: Helping People Learn by Understanding How the Brain Works* (Sterling, VA: Stylus Publishers, 2002). Professor Elizabeth Gould of Princeton University, studying neurogenesis, has shown that learning new things stimulated new nerves to survive in primates, while lack of learning new things resulted in the loss of new nerve cells (summarized in Sandra Blakeslee, "A Decade of Discovery Yields a Shock about the Brain," *The New York Times*, 4 January 2000, D1).

22. It takes a limbic connection to change skills: Lewis, Amini, and Lannon, *General Theory of Love*, 177.

23. The course on competency development: This course is described in Richard Boyatzis, "Stimulating Self-Directed Learning through the Managerial Assessment and Development Course," *Journal of Management Education* 18, no. 3 (1994): 304–323; and chapter 4 in *Innovations in Professional Education: Steps on a Journey from Teaching to Learning*, eds. Richard E. Boyatzis, Scott S. Cowen, and David A. Kolb (San Francisco: Jossey-Bass, 1995). The earliest version of this course was developed for the American Management Association in 1979 as part of its fledgling Masters in Management program. Other variations on this type of course were developed in parallel by the faculty at Alverno College in Milwaukee (for a description, see Marcia Mentkoswki and associates, eds., *Learning That Lasts: Integrating Learning, Development, and Performance in College and*

*Beyond* [San Francisco: Jossey-Bass, 2000]) and by David A. Whetton and Kim S. Cameron for original use at the University of Michigan (see the fourth edition of their textbook, *Developing Managerial Skills* (Reading, MA: Addison-Wesley, 1998). The course was chosen as a model program in developing emotional intelligence by the Consortium for Research on Emotional Intelligence in Organizations, as reported in Cary Cherniss and Mitchell Adler, *Promoting Emotional Intelligence in Organizations: Make Training in Emotional Intelligence Effective* (Washington, DC: American Society for Training and Development, 2000).

24. Outcome assessment studies: Since 1987, starting even before the course was required of all students, Richard Boyatzis has directed a series of follow-up studies to document the course and program's long-term impact. The studies measured improvements from self-reports and from behavioral coding of "critical incident" audiotapes and videotapes of the students tackling typical work challenges. Data collection began when students started the course, and assessments were made when they graduated and when they were at work. For details of the studies, see Richard E. Boyatzis, Ann Baker, David Leonard, Kenneth Rhee, and Lorraine Thompson, "Will It Make a Difference?: Assessing a Value-Based, Outcome Oriented, Competency-Based Professional Program," in *Innovating in Professional Education: Steps on a Journey from Teaching to Learning*, eds. Richard E. Boyatzis, Scott S. Cowen, and David A. Kolb (San Francisco: Jossey-Bass, 1995); Richard E. Boyatzis, David Leonard, Kenneth Rhee, and Jane V. Wheeler, "Competencies Can Be Developed, but Not the Way We Thought," *Capability* 2, no. 2 (1996): 25–41; and Richard E. Boyatzis, Jane V. Wheeler, and R. Wright, "Competency Development in Graduate Education: A Longitudinal Perspective," *Proceedings of the First World Conference on Self-Directed Learning* (Montreal: GIRAT, in press).

25. Studies of the impact of other MBA programs: The studies were done for the American Assembly of Collegiate Schools of Business (AACSB) in 1979 and the 1980s and are reported in Richard Boyatzis and Mike Sokol, *A Pilot Project to Assess the Feasibility of Assessing Skills and Personal Characteristics of Students in Collegiate Business Programs. Report to the AACSB* (St. Louis: AACSB, 1982) and *Development Dimensions International (DDI), Final Report: Phase III. Report to the AACSB* (St. Louis: AACSB, 1985). The baseline studies of the Weatherhead School of Management in the late 1980s used tests for their comparisons and are reviewed in Boyatzis, Cowen, and Kolb, *Innovating in Professional Education*. The percentage improvement reported was calculated by dividing the change in students' graduating scores from their entering scores by their entering scores.

The first two programs were analyzed with assessment centers, so the data reported are about student's behavior shown in simulations. The other programs included tests that were shown to assess EI behaviors but were not direct measures of the participants' behavior.

26. Comparison of percentage improvement in EI: The percentage improvement shown and the comparison to other programs involved observed behavior (not tests) as assessed by coding of work samples, "critical incident" interviews, videotaped assessment center exercises, or 360-degree assessment by others of a person's behavior. The percentage improvement shown for each time period is an average of the increase in frequency for each of the competencies in that cluster (i.e., graduating frequency of showing the competency minus the entering frequency, divided by the entering frequency of the behavior). To control for language difficulties, only native English speakers were included in this analysis. The reader is cautioned that the percentages refer to different samples and therefore are shown to suggest the range of impact expected over time. The samples shown in the figure are from the following cadres: The one- to two-year results reflect 163 of the full-time MBAs graduating in 1993, 1994, and 1995 (reported in the references in note 25). The three- to five-year results are from fifty-four of the part-time MBAs graduating in 1995 and 1996 reported in note 25. The five- to seven-year results reflect thirty of the part-time MBAs graduating in 1995 and 1996 studied eighteen to thirty months after graduation by Jane V. Wheeler in her dissertation, "The Impact of Social Environments on Self-Directed Change and Learning" (Ph.D. diss., Case Western Reserve University, 1999).

Jane Wheeler reported a comparison of the three- to five-year results with the five- to seven-year results for the same people in her dissertation. Her smaller sample of thirty of the part-time MBA graduates of the classes of 1995 and 1996 showed 53 percent improvement in self-awareness and self-management and 33 percent improvement in social awareness and relationship management at three to five years. These numbers are slightly different from the percentages shown for the complete sample in the graph but are still at a relatively high level compared with other management training or MBA graduate education programs.

The self-awareness and management competencies included achievement orientation, planning, initiative, conscientiousness, self-control, and self-confidence. The social awareness and relationship management competencies included empathy, social objectivity, building bonds, conflict management, influence, leadership in teamwork, and developing others.

27. It is also worth noting that the graduates of the competency-based

program, both full-time and part-time, showed significant improvement on 100 percent of the six cognitive competencies assessed. Meanwhile, the earlier non-competency-based MBA program had shown improvement on only 86 percent of the cognitive competencies in the full-time program and 57 percent of the cognitive competencies in the part-time program. Among full-time MBA students, the improvements were in 100 percent of the fourteen emotional intelligence competencies assessed as compared with gains in only 50 percent of these competencies for MBA students who did not receive the course. Part-timers taking the course also showed impressive gains: They gained in thirteen of fourteen competencies as compared with gains in only one of the twelve competencies assessed for those without the course.

28. Impact of the Professional Fellows Program: Ronald Ballou, David Bowers, Richard E. Boyatzis, and David A. Kolb, "Fellowship in Lifelong Learning: An Executive Development Program for Advanced Professionals," *Journal of Management Education* 23, no. 4 (1999): 338–354.

29. Emergence of the model of self-directed learning: Richard Boyatzis first saw the promise of this approach during his personal involvement with three streams of research, all providing convincing evidence about how people can best improve the emotional intelligence abilities that make leadership effective. His first exposure to development that works came from his work with David Kolb and their colleagues at MIT's Sloan School of Management, which showed that people who used self-directed learning could improve their performance. Early in the 1970s, students there selected a business skill to improve—and because so many had "nerdy" engineering and science backgrounds, interpersonal skills were a common choice. These studies are described in David A. Kolb, Sarah K. Winter, and David E. Berlew, "Self-Directed Change: Two Studies," *Journal of Applied Behavioral Science* 6, no. 3 (1968): 453–471; David A. Kolb, "A Cybernetic Model of Human Change and Growth," unpublished working paper 526-71, Sloan School of Management, Massachusetts Institute of Technology, Cambridge, 1971; David A. Kolb and Richard E. Boyatzis, "On the Dynamics of the Helping Relationship," *Journal of Applied Behavioral Science* 6, no. 3 (1970): 267–289; David A. Kolb and Richard E. Boyatzis, "Goal-Setting and Self-Directed Behavior Change," *Human Relations* 23, no. 5 (1970): 439–457; and Richard E. Boyatzis and David A. Kolb, "Feedback and Self-Directed Behavior Change," unpublished working paper 394-69, Sloan School of Management, Massachusetts Institute of Technology, Cambridge, 1969.

His second exposure came from his involvement (along with Daniel Goleman) with the pioneering research of David McClelland and colleagues at Harvard University in the 1960s and 1970s that first showed that the skills that make people highly successful entrepreneurs can be developed. McClelland's group developed training programs to enhance the drive to achieve—perhaps the first emotional intelligence competence to be studied in depth. The results: Those who went through the training went on to lead small-business start-ups that met with dramatic success, creating more new jobs, starting more new businesses, and generating greater revenues than comparison groups. See David C. McClelland and David G. Winter, *Motivating Economic Achievement* (New York: Free Press, 1969) and David Miron and David C. McClelland, "The Impact of Achievement Motivation Training on Small Business," *California Management Review* 21, no. 4 (1979): 13–28. Richard Boyatzis's work with David C. McClelland in power motivation training as a therapeutic program to help alcoholics maintain sobriety and regain jobs and their functioning as citizens added to this work on motivational change. See Henry Cutter, Richard E. Boyatzis, and David Clancy, "The Effectiveness of Power Motivation Training for Rehabilitating Alcoholics," *Journal of Studies on Alcohol* 38, no. 1 (1977) and Richard E. Boyatzis, "Power Motivation Training: A New Treatment Modality," *Annals of the New York Academy of Sciences* 273 (1976): 525–532.

A third source for insights remains the research of his doctoral students and colleagues at the Weatherhead School of Management at Case Western Reserve University.

Other prominent models of change are David McClelland's theory of motive acquisition and that of James Prochaska and his colleagues. See David C. McClelland, "Toward a Theory of Motive Acquisition," *American Psychologist* 20, no. 5 (1965): 321–333, and James O. Prochaska, Carlo C. Diclemente, and John C. Norcross, "In Search of How People Change: Applications to Addictive Behaviors," *American Psychologist* 47, no. 9 (1992): 1102–1114. A comprehensive review of documented programs intended to increase emotional intelligence was made by the Consortium on Emotional Intelligence in Organizations, headed by Professor Cary Cherniss of Rutgers University. The review of these model programs and the Consortium's view of the best practices are provided on their Web site and in a recent book: Cary Cherniss and Mitchell Adler, *Promoting Emotional Intelligence in Organizations: Make Training in Emotional Intelligence Effective* (Washington, DC: American Society for Training and Development, 2000).

30. Description of the model of self-directed learning: Richard E. Boyatzis, "Self-Directed Change and Learning as a Necessary Meta-competency for Success and Effectiveness in the 21st Century," in *Keys to Employee Success in the Coming Decades*, eds. R. Sims and J. G. Veres (Westport, CT:

Greenwood Publishing, 1999). See also Richard E. Boyatzis, "Developing Emotional Intelligence," in *The Emotionally Intelligent Workplace: How to Select for, Measure, and Improve Emotional Intelligence in Individuals, Groups, and Organizations*, eds. Cary Cherniss and Daniel Goleman (San Francisco: Jossey-Bass, 2001). This model describes the process as designed into the required course implemented in 1990 at the Weatherhead School of Management for the MBA program described earlier and executive education programs.

### CHAPTER 7

1. The ought versus ideal self: Charles Handy, *The Hungry Spirit: Beyond Capitalism, A Quest for Purpose in the Modern World* (London: Hutchinson, 1997), 86.

2. Impact of an ought self replacing an ideal self: Even studies showing the importance of working on the ideal often make the mistake of assuming that the profile of an outstanding performer will be the ideal image for people in a given job—see, for example, Mildred Burns, "The Effects of Feedback and Commitment to Change on the Behavior of Elementary School Principals," *Journal of Applied Behavioral Science* 13, no. 2 (1977): 159–166.

3. The study of values and value orientation: Gordon W. Allport, P. E. Vernon, and Gardner Lindzey, *Study of Values* (Boston: Houghton Mifflin, 1960); Chris Argyris and Don Schon, *Theory in Practice Learning* (San Francisco: Jossey-Bass, 1982); Clyde Kluckhohn, "Values and Value-Orientations in the Theory of Action," in *Toward a General Theory of Action*, eds. Talcott Parson and E. A. Shils (Cambridge, MA: Harvard University Press, 1951), 388–433; Florence Kluckhohn and Fred Strodtbeck, *Variations in Value Orientations* (Evanston, IL: Row, Peterson & Co, 1961); Milton Rokeach, *The Nature of Human Values* (New York: Free Press, 1973); Shalom H. Schwartz, "Universals in the Content and Structure of Values: Theoretical Advances and Empirical Tests in 20 Countries," *Advances in Experimental Social Psychology* 25 (New York: Academic Press, 1992), 1–65; Michael Hechter, "Values Research in the Social and Behavioral Sciences," in *The Origin of Values*, eds. Michael Hechter, Lynn Nadel, and Richard E. Michod (New York: Aldine de Gruyter, 1993), 1–28.

4. Assessing your operating philosophy: The Philosophical Orientation Questionnaire measures the relative dominance of each of the three operating philosophies—pragmatic, intellectual, and humanistic. Richard E. Boyatzis, Angela J. Murphy, and Jane V. Wheeler, "Philosophy as a Missing Link between Values and Behavior," *Psychological Reports* 86 (2000): 47–64.

5. The pragmatic operating philosophy emerged from pragmatism (as reflected in the works of John Dewey, William James, Charles Sanders Peirce, and Richard Rorty), consequentialism (as reflected in the works of C. D. Johnson and P. Pettit), instrumentalism (as reflected in the works of John Dewey), and utilitarianism (as reflected in the works of Jeremy Bentham and John Stuart Mill). See Boyatzis, Murphy, and Wheeler, "Philosophy as a Missing Link" for the full references.

6. Larry Ellison described: Mike Wilson, *The Difference between God and Larry Ellison: Inside Oracle Corporation* (New York: William Morrow, 1998); Stuart Read, *The Oracle Edge: How Oracle Corporation's Take No Prisoners Strategy Has Made an $8 Billion Software Powerhouse* (Avon, MA: Adams Media Corporation, 1999).

7. The intellectual operating philosophy emerged from rationalism (as reflected in the works of René Descartes, Gottfried Wilhelm Leibniz, and Benedict de Spinoza) and the various philosophers claiming rationalism as their etiological root, such as Georg Wilhelm Friedrich Hegel and Jurgen Habermas, as well as the philosophical structuralists (Claude Lévi-Strauss and Jean Piaget) and postmodernists (Friedrich Nietzsche). See Boyatzis, Murphy, and Wheeler, "Philosophy as a Missing Link" for the full references.

8. John Chambers described: Andy Serwer, "There's Something about Cisco," *Fortune*, 15 May 2000, 114–138; John A. Byrne, "Visionary vs. Visionary," *Business Week*, 28 August 2000, 210–214.

9. The humanistic operating philosophy emerged from communitarianism (W. F. Brundage), hermeneutics (Hans-Georg Gadamer), humanism (Francesco Petrarch and R. W. Sellars), and collectivism (R. Burlingame and W. H. Chamberlin).

10. Narayana Murthy described: Amit Dawra, Pinkey Jain, Ruchika Kohli, and Abhijit Rajan, "N.R. Narayana Murthy: Powered by Intellect, Driven by Value," unpublished paper, Case Western Reserve University, October 2000.

11. Peter Lynch's career change: J. Fierman, "Peter Lynch on the Meaning of Life," *Fortune*, 23 April 1990, 197–200.

12. Career changes for successful CEOs: B. D. Fromson, "Second Acts for the Top Guys," *Fortune*, 23 April 1990, 251–262.

13. Our dreams and passion drive life satisfaction: Ruth A. Schiller, "The Relationship of Developmental Tasks to Life Satisfaction, Moral Reasoning, and Occupational Attainment at Age 28," *Journal of Adult Development* 5, no. 4 (1998): 239–254.

14. A leader is a dealer in hope: *Napoleon in His Own Words*, vol. 4, comp. Jules Bertaut (Chicago: A.C. McClurg: 1916).

15. The Executive Doctorate in Management program: The seminar called Leadership to Create Human Value is part of the Executive Doctorate in Management program at Weatherhead School of Management, Case Western Reserve University. It is a three-year program designed for leaders from the industrial, not-for-profit, and public sectors who want to pursue organizational, community, and global leadership from a practitioner/scholar perspective. The students fly in for a several-day residency once a month from various cities and countries around the world.

16. Feedback on John Lauer's current style: Personal communications from Kathy Crowley, Christina Fiduccia, Michelle Lee, Chistopher Stevens, and Robert Stratton-Brown, December 2000.

17. Self-deception as a natural but costly process: Daniel Goleman, *Vital Lies, Simple Truths: The Psychology of Self-Deception* (New York: Simon and Schuster, 1985).

18. Optimism of successful people: Martin P. Seligman, *Learned Optimism: How to Change Your Mind and Your Life* (New York: Alfred Knopf, 1991).

19. Study showing the importance of evaluative feedback: Richard E. Boyatzis and David A. Kolb, *Feedback and Self-Directed Behavior Change*, unpublished working paper 394-69, Sloan School of Management, Massachusetts Institute of Technology, Cambridge, 1969.

20. Effective managers and leaders seek out feedback: Susan J. Ashford and Anne S. Tsui, "Self-Regulation for Managerial Effectiveness: The Role of Active Feedback Seeking," *Academy of Management Journal* 34, no. 2 (1991): 251–280.

21. Consequences of seeking positive feedback only: Paul A. Mabe III and Stephen G. West, "Validity of Self-Evaluation of Ability: A Review and Meta-analysis," *Journal of Applied Psychology* 67 (1982): 280–296.

22. Testing reality about yourself: In Morgan W. McCall Jr., *High Flyers: Developing the Next Generation of Leaders* (Boston: Harvard Business School Press, 1998), the author points out that people may have "powerful experiences" that could contribute to their development, but sometimes fail to realize these moments. He called these "moments of truth" when the person should ask himself or herself, "Am I about to be the person I want to be? Have I just acted like the person I want to be?" In our framework, these moments of truth are like looking in the mirror and coming to grips with your real self.

23. Assessing the real self in the context of the ideal self: Jay Conger, *Learning to Lead: The Art of Transforming Managers into Leaders* (San Francisco: Jossey-Bass, 1989) described the reaction of managers in development programs after receiving a lot of instrumented feedback—he found them feeling "ho-hum." They already knew most if not all of the feedback.

Without the context of the ideal self, there was no compelling concept as to where to go next—what to do about it or why anything should be done about it.

24. Knowing what to keep and what to change: This parallels what several scholars have suggested for organizations. See Ron Fry, "Change and Continuity in Organizational Growth," in Suresh Srivastva, Ronald E. Fry, and associates, *Executive and Organizational Continuity: Managing the Paradoxes of Stability and Change* (San Francisco: Jossey-Bass, 1993); and James C. Collins and Jerry I. Porras, *Built to Last: Successful Habits of Visionary Companies* (New York: HarperBusiness, 1994).

25. Commitment to vision can lead to less adaptability: Lisa Berlinger, "Managing Commitment to Increase Flexibility: An Exploration of Processes That Strengthen and Weaken Commitment" (Ph.D. diss., University of Texas, 1991); Russell Ackoff, *Creating the Corporate Future* (New York: John Wiley & Sons, 1981).

26. A caution: 360-degree feedback is most helpful when it is gathered in confidence. That means the results are revealed only to the person to whom they apply and to her coach, but not to others in her organization (unless she chooses to share them). Everyone should also be aware that the information will be used in the service of leadership development. When 360-degree data are used instead as part of performance management or reviews, people are less likely to be candid about their weaknesses, and more prone to overestimate their strengths. Similarly, peers and subordinates providing the information may lie to protect or attack the individual.

27. Different views of a manager from different sources of feedback: Gene Harris and Joyce Hogan, "Perceptions and Personalities of Effective Managers" (paper presented at the 13th Annual Psychology in the Department of Defense Symposium, Colorado Springs, Colorado, 16 April 1992).

28. Success versus effectiveness: Fred Luthans, R. M. Hodgetts, and S. A. Rosenkrantz, *Real Managers* (Cambridge, MA: Ballinger Press, 1988).

29. Strength of peers as a source of feedback: A review of the research on 360-degree feedback found that peers give evaluations that have better predictive power than those of bosses or subordinates—and, of course, better than a leader's own self-assessment. A. V. Lewin and A. Zwany, *Peer Nominations: A Model, Literature, Critique, and a Paradigm for Research* (Springfield, VA: National Technical Information Service, 1976); T. H. Shore, L. M. Shore, and George C. Thornton III, "Construct Validity of Self- and Peer Evaluations of Performance Dimensions in an Assessment Center," *Journal of Applied Psychology* 77, no. 1 (1992): 42–54. But other studies have found that subordinates' views are more powerful than peers' in predicting leadership. See, for example, Glenn M. McEvoy and Richard

W. Beatty, "Assessment Centers and Subordinate Appraisals of Managers: A Seven Year Examination of Predictive Validity," *Personnel Psychology* 42 (1989): 37–52.

30. The strength of subordinates' assessment: McEvoy and Beatty, "Assessment Centers and Subordinate Appraisals of Managers," 37–52.

31. Phil Stone calls these patterns a person's signature themes in his book *Your Corner of the Sky* (forthcoming).

CHAPTER 8

1. Working on goals in different life spheres: Jane V. Wheeler, "The Impact of Social Environment on Self-Directed Change and Learning," (Ph.D. diss., Case Western Reserve University, 1999).

2. Performance-oriented goals are not good guides: John F. Brett and Don VandeWalle, "Goal Orientation and Goal Content as Predictors of Performance in a Training Program," *Journal of Applied Psychology* 84, no. 6 (1999): 863–873.

3. Personal standards in learning-oriented goals: J. M. Beaubien and S. C. Payne, "Individual Goal Orientation as a Predictor of Job and Academic Performance: A Meta-analytic Review and Integration" (paper presented at the meeting of the Society for Industrial and Organizational Psychology, Atlanta, Georgia, April 1999).

4. Performance-oriented goals evoke anxiety: Gilad Chen, Stanley M. Gully, Jon-Andrew Whiteman, and Robert N. Kilcullen, "Examination of Relationships among Trait-like Individual Differences, State-like Individual Differences, and Learning Performance," *Journal of Applied Psychology* 85, no. 6 (2000): 835–847. More of the research on goal setting is reviewed in Edwin A. Locke and Gary P. Latham, *A Theory of Goal Setting and Task Performance* (Englewood Cliffs, NJ: Prentice Hall, 1990).

5. Learning-oriented goals lead to better sales: Don VandeWalle, Steven P. Brown, William L. Cron, and John W. Slocum Jr., "The Influence of Goal Orientation and Self-Regulation Tactics on Sales Performance: A Longitudinal Field Test," *Journal of Applied Psychology* 84, no. 2 (1999): 249–259.

6. Moving beyond contemplation to change: James O. Prochaska, Carlo C. Diclemente, and John C. Norcross, "In Search of How People Change: Applications to Addictive Behaviors," *American Psychologist* 47, no. 9 (1992): 1102–1114.

7. Goals are a key to self-monitoring: Roy F. Baumeister, Todd E. Heatherton, and Dianne M. Tice, *Losing Control: How and Why People Fail at Self-Regulation* (New York: Academic Press, 1994).

8. Bringing habits into awareness: John A. Bargh and Tanya L. Chartrand,

"The Unbearable Automaticity of Being," *American Psychologist* 54, no. 7 (1999): 462–479.

9. Preparation of the brain: Cameron Carter, Angus Macdonald, Stefan Ursu, Andy Stenger, Myeong Ho Sohn, and John Anderson, "How the Brain Gets Ready to Perform" (presentation at the 30th annual meeting of the Society of Neuroscience, New Orleans, November 2000).

10. Setting goals is nothing new: David A. Kolb and Richard E. Boyatzis, "Goal-Setting and Self-Directed Behavior Change," *Human Relations* 23, no. 5 (1970): 439–457.

11. Goal setting and entrepreneurs: For a review of the research, see David C. McClelland, *Human Motivation* (Chicago: Scott, Foresman, 1985). For the earlier research, see David C. McClelland, *The Achieving Society* (Princeton: Van Nostrand, 1961) and David C. McClelland and David G. Winter, *Motivating Economic Achievement* (New York: Free Press, 1969).

12. Goal setting and self-directed behavior change: David A. Kolb, Sarah K. Winter, and David E. Berlew, "Self-Directed Change: Two Studies," *Journal of Applied Behavioral Science* 6, no. 3 (1968): 453–471; David A. Kolb, "A Cybernetic Model of Human Change and Growth," unpublished working paper 526-71, Sloan School of Management, Massachusetts Institute of Technology, Cambridge, 1971; and David A. Kolb and Richard E. Boyatzis, "Goal-Setting and Self-Directed Behavior Change." Integration of McClelland's steps in motive acquisition and the Kolb and Boyatzis models resulted in a process called competency acquisition.

13. Recent research on effective goal setting: Wheeler, "Impact of Social Environment"; David Leonard, "The Impact of Learning Goals on Self-Directed Change in Education and Management Development" (Ph.D. diss., Case Western Reserve University, 1996); and Kenneth Rhee, "Journey of Discovery: A Longitudinal Study of Learning during a Graduate Professional Program" (Ph.D. diss., Case Western Reserve University, 1997).

14. Tipping points: David C. McClelland, "Identifying Competencies with Behavioral Event Interviews," *Psychological Science* 9, no. 5 (1998): 331–339. The theory was cross-validated in a longitudinal study of the financial impact of competencies used by senior partners in an international consulting firm, as reported in Richard E. Boyatzis, "Building Brilliant Organizations: Competencies, Complexity, and Consequences" (keynote presentation at the 4th International Conference on Competency Applications, London, 25 October 1999); Richard E. Boyatzis, Daniel Goleman, and Kenneth Rhee, "Clustering Competence in Emotional Intelligence: Insights from the Emotional Competence Inventory (ECI)," in *Handbook of Emotional Intelligence*, eds. Reuven Bar-On and James D. A. Parker (San Francisco:

Jossey-Bass, 2000), 343–362; and Malcolm Gladwell, *The Tipping Point: How Little Things Can Make a Big Difference* (Boston: Little, Brown, 2000).

15. Personal commitment is key to goal attainment: Howard J. Klein, Michael J. Wesson, John R. Hollenback, and Bradley J. Alge, "Goal Commitment and the Goal-Setting Process: Conceptual Clarification and Empirical Synthesis," *Journal of Applied Psychology* 84, no. 6 (1999): 885–896; Locke and Latham, *Theory of Goal Setting*.

16. Intrinsic motivation is far more powerful than extrinsic motivation: R. M. Ryan and E. L. Deci, "Self-Determination Theory and the Facilitation of Intrinsic Motivation, Social Development, and Well-Being," *American Psychologist* 55, no. 1 (2000): 68–78; T. Kasser and R. M. Ryan, "Be Careful What You Wish For: Optimal Functioning and the Relative Attainment of Intrinsic and Extrinsic Goals," in *Life Goals and Well-Being*, P. Schmuck and K. M. Sheldon (Lengerich, Germany: Pabst Science, in press).

17. Different planning styles: Annie McKee, "Individual Differences in Planning for the Future" (Ph.D. diss., Case Western Reserve University, 1991).

18. Crafting a meaningful future: Michael McCaskey, "A Contingency Approach to Planning: Planning with and without Goals," *Academy of Management Journal* 17 (1974): 281–291; McKee, "Individual Differences in Planning for the Future."

19. Specific, measurable goals: Edwin Locke, "Toward a Theory of Task Performance and Incentives," *Organizational Behavior and Human Performance* 3 (1968): 157–189; J. Hollenbeck and H. Klein, "Goal Commitment and the Goals Setting Process: Problems, Prospects, and Proposals for Future Research," *Journal of Applied Psychology* 40 (1987): 212–220.

20. Targeting specific competencies works: Leonard, "Impact of Learning Goals"; Wheeler, "Impact of Social Environment."

21. Using one's preferred learning styles works best: David A. Kolb, *Experiential Learning: Experience as the Source of Learning and Development* (Englewood Cliffs, NJ: Prentice-Hall, 1984).

22. Typical learning styles: Ibid.; and David A. Kolb, Richard E. Boyatzis, and Charalampos Mainemelis, "Experiential Learning Theory: Previous Research and New Directions," in *Perspectives on Thinking, Learning, and Cognitive Styles*, eds. Robert J. Sternberg and Li-fang Zhang (Mahwah, NJ: Lawrence Erlbaum Associates, 2001), 227–248. Other references are available at http://www.learningfromexperience.com.

23. Tests of learning styles: See, for example, the Kolb Learning Style Inventory and Boyatzis and Kolb Adaptive Style Inventory at http://www.haygroup.com.

24. Triggers to dysfunctional habits: In the field of cognitive behavior therapy, this early warning allows the identification of triggers before they have unleashed old, dysfunctional habits. See Tara Bennett-Goleman, *Emotional Alchemy: How the Mind Can Heal the Heart* (New York: Harmony Books, 2001).

25. The prefrontal cortex and limbic circuits: Matthew D. Lieberman, "Intuition: A Social Cognitive Neuroscience Approach," *Psychological Bulletin* 126 (2000): 109–137; B. J. Knowlton, J. A. Mangels, and L. R. Squire, "A Neostriatal Habit Learning System in Humans," *Science* 273 (1996): 1399–1402.

26. The need for repetition and practice in learning: Thomas Lewis, Fari Amini, and Richard Lannon, *A General Theory of Love* (New York: Random House, 2000); and Lieberman, "Intuition."

27. Strengthening of neural pathways and neurogenesis: Richard J. Davidson, Daren C. Jackson, and Ned H. Kalin, "Emotion, Plasticity, Context, and Regulation: Perspectives from Affective Neuroscience," *Psychological Bulletin* 126, no. 6 (2000): 890–909.

28. Executives spend little time practicing: Paraphrasing a point Tony Schwartz made from Jim Loehr and Tony Schwartz, "The Making of the Corporate Athlete," *Harvard Business Review*, at a presentation at the Weatherhead School of Management, 17 November 2000.

29. Practicing to create new neural pathways: Bennett-Goleman, *Emotional Alchemy*.

30. Using self-control for practice: Mark Muraven and Roy Baumeister, "Self-Regulation and Depletion of Limited Resources: Does Self-Control Resemble a Muscle?" *Psychological Bulletin* 126, no. 2 (2000): 247–259.

31. Practicing in many settings: Christine R. Dreyfus, "Scientists and Engineers as Effective Managers: A Study of Development of Interpersonal Abilities" (Ph.D. diss., Case Western Reserve University, 1991).

32. Action learning is stealth learning: In reviewing dozens of leadership development programs, offered both by consultants and in-house programs, Jay Conger and Beth Benjamin called action learning "the new paradigm for leadership development" in their book *Building Leaders: How Successful Companies Develop the Next Generation* (San Francisco: Jossey-Bass, 1999).

33. Laura Wilkinson's mental rehearsal: Jim Loehr and Tony Schwartz, "The Making of the Corporate Athlete," *Harvard Business Review*, January 2001, 120–128.

34. Visioning fires the same brain cells: Gabriel Kreiman, Christof Koch, and Itshak Fried, "Imagery Neurons in the Human Brain," *Nature* 408 (2000): 357–361.

35. Relationships as the context for learning: Kathy E. Kram, "A Relational Approach to Career Development," in *The Career Is Dead—Long Live the Career*, ed. Douglas T. Hall (San Francisco: Jossey-Bass, 1996); and Kathy E. Kram and Douglas T. Hall, "Mentoring in a Context of Diversity and Turbulence," in *Managing Diversity: Human Resource Strategies for Transforming the Workplace*, eds. Ellen E. Kossek and Sharon A. Lobel (Cambridge, MA: Blackwell Business, 1996).

36. Gains in self-confidence: Ronald Ballou, David Bowers, Richard E. Boyatzis, and David A. Kolb, "Fellowship in Lifelong Learning: An Executive Development Program for Advanced Professionals," *Journal of Management Education* 23, no. 4 (1999): 338–354.

37. Positive groups help positive change: Jin Nam Choi, Richard H. Price, and Amiram D. Vinokur, "How Context Works in Groups: The Influence of Group Processes on Individual Coping Outcomes," unpublished paper, University of Michigan, Institute for Social Research, 1999.

38. Leadership is stressful: Robert S. Steele, "The Physiological Concomitants of Psychogenic Arousal in College Males" (Ph.D. diss., Harvard University, 1973); Robert S. Steele, "Power Motivation, Activation, and Inspirational Speeches" *Journal of Personality* 45 (1977): 53–64; David C. McClelland, Richard J., Davidson, and C. Saron, "Evoked Potential Indicators of the Impact of the Need for Power on Perception and Learning," unpublished manuscript, Harvard University, 1979; and David C. McClelland, Richard J. Davidson, C. Saron, and E. Floor, "The Need for Power, Brain Norepinephrine Turnover and Learning," *Biological Psychology* 10 (1980): 93–102.

39. Stress and cortisol interfere with learning: Recent research suggests that "cortisol at persistently high levels cause[s] reduction in the branching of neurons in the brain center for conversion of short term memory to long term memory (the hippocampus). Even more dramatically, long duration of very high cortisol levels appear[s] to destroy hippocampal cells." James E. Zull, *The Art of Changing a Brain: Helping People Learn by Understanding How the Brain Works* (Sterling, VA: Stylus, 2002), 65. Prolonged stress and depression lead to reduction in the hippocampus in victims of post-traumatic stress disorder and severely depressed women. Robert Sapolosky of Stanford University and Yvette Sheline of Washington University in St. Louis as quoted in Robert S. Boyd, "Scientists Find Brain Continues to Readapt Throughout Life," *Miami Herald*, 17 May 2000; Davidson, Jackson, and Kalin, "Emotion, Plasticity, Context, and Regulation."

40. Settings that are safe but not too relaxed for learning: Kolb and Boyatzis, "Goal-Setting and Self-Directed Behavior Change."

41. Others taking risks helps us: Paul R. Nail, Geoff MacDonald, and David A. Levy, "Proposal of a Four-Dimensional Model of Social Response," *Psychological Bulletin* 126, no. 3 (2000): 454–470.

42. Mentors help early in our careers: Morgan W. McCall Jr., Michael M. Lombardo, and Ann M. Morrison, *Lessons from Experience: How Successful Executives Develop on the Job* (Lexington, MA: Lexington Books, 1988). Research is under way about mentoring by Professor Kathy Kram, of Boston University, in conjunction with the Center for Creative Leadership, building on her twenty years of research on this type of helping relationship.

43. Finding a good coach: If you decide to seek coaching for these leadership skills, be sure your coach is not just seasoned, but also familiar with the best-practice guidelines for improving a leader's emotional intelligence. Many are not. The guidelines—based on empirical data on what works and what does not—were developed by the Consortium for Research on Emotional Intelligence in Organizations. The guidelines are summarized in chapter 12 of Daniel Goleman's *Working with Emotional Intelligence* (New York: Bantam Books, 1998) and in Cary Cherniss and Mitch Adler, *Promoting Emotional Intelligence in Organizations* (Washington, DC: American Society for Training and Development, 2000).

44. Having another CEO as a mentor: Jennifer Reingold, "Want to Grow as a Leader? Get a Mentor," *Fast Company*, January 2001, 58–60.

45. Effective coaches use EI: Richard E. Boyatzis and James A. Burruss, *Validation of a Competency Model for Alcoholism Counselors in the Navy—Final Report on Contract Number N00123-77-C-0499* (Washington, DC: U.S. Navy, 1979); James A. Burruss and Richard E. Boyatzis, *Continued Validation of a Competency Model for Alcoholism Counselors in the Navy—Final Report on Contract Number N002 44-80-C-0521* (Washington, DC: U.S. Navy, 1981); Richard R. Carkhuff, *Helping and Human Relations: A Primer for Lay and Professional Helpers*, vol. I, *Selection and Training*, and vol. II, *Practice and Research* (New York: Holt, Rinehart and Winston, 1969); and Ted P. Asay and Michael J. Lambert, "The Empirical Case for the Common Factors in Therapy: Quantitative Findings," in *The Heart and Soul of Change: What Works in Therapy*, eds. Mark A. Hubble, Barry L. Duncan, and Scott D. Miller (Washington, DC: American Psychological Association, 1999).

CHAPTER 9

1. Superiority of group decision making: Alan B. Krueger, "Economic Scene," *The New York Times*, 7 December 2000, C2.

2. Brilliant teams with bad decisions: R. Meredith Belbin, *Team Roles at Work* (London: Butterworth-Heineman, 1996).

3.  Limbic regulation and paying attention to people who can affect our lives: Thomas Lewis, Fari Amini, and Richard Lannon, *A General Theory of Love* (New York: Random House, 2000).

4.  The leader's role in creating the emotional reality of the group: Some of the most extensive work on authority dynamics has been done by associates of the A.K. Rice Institute. For a thorough review of the foundational research, see Arthur D. Colman and W. Harold Bexton, eds., *Group Relations Reader 1* (Washington, DC: A.K. Rice Institute, 1975), and Arthur D. Colman and Marvin H. Geller, eds., *Group Relations Reader 2* (Jupiter, FL: A.K. Rice Institute, 1985). For a brief, more recent review of the leader's impact in a business setting, see Michel Deschapelle, "The National Conference Has Helped My Career," *Speaking of Authority*, vol. 7, no. 1 (Jupiter, FL: A.K. Rice Institute, 2000). For a discussion of the impact of a minority leader on the emotional reality of groups, see Kathy E. Kram and Marion McCollom Hampton, "When Women Lead: The Visibility-Vulnerability Spiral" in *The Psychodynamics of Leadership*, eds. Edward B. Klein, Faith Gabelnick, and Peter Herr (Madison, CT: Psychosocial Press, 1998).

5.  The leader's role in creating a climate that supports healthy relationships and a positive focus on the future: Rosamund Stone Zander and Benjamin Zander, *The Art of Possibility: Transforming Professional and Personal Life* (Boston: Harvard Business School Press, 2000).

6.  High-performing teams: Jon R. Katzenbach and Douglas K. Smith, *The Wisdom of Teams* (Boston: Harvard Business School Press, 1993).

7.  Group emotional intelligence: Vanessa Urch Druskat and Steven B. Wolff, "Group Emotional Intelligence and Its Influence on Group Effectiveness," in *The Emotionally Intelligent Workplace: How to Select For, Measure, and Improve Emotional Intelligence in Individuals, Groups, and Organizations*, eds. Carey Cherniss and Daniel Goleman (San Francisco: Jossey-Bass, 2001). See also Vanessa Urch Druskat and Steven B. Wolff, "Building the Emotional Intelligence of Groups," *Harvard Business Review*, March 2001, 81–90.

8.  Group as a whole: Leroy Wells, "The Group-as-a-Whole Perspective and Its Theoretical Roots," in Colman and Geller, eds., *Group Relations Reader 2*.

9.  When a group member leads: Susan Wheelan and Frances Johnston, "The Role of Informal Member Leaders in a System Containing Formal Leaders," *Small Group Research* 27, no. 1 (1996): 33–55. See also Susan A. Wheelan, *Creating Effective Teams* (Thousand Oaks, CA: Sage Publications, 1999).

10. Mindfulness: This term, used to describe a heightened attention about self, others, and the environment one lives in, is not often used in the business press. It is, however, considered fundamental for emotional/psychological health and effective interpersonal relationships, and foundational in our conceptualization of self-awareness. At the team level, mindfulness is a set of shared norms, manifested in behaviors such as attending to group moods, articulating unspoken concerns or hopes, or calling the group's attention to dysfunctional patterns. For interesting perspectives on the subject, see Robert Quinn, *Change the World: How Ordinary People Can Accomplish Extraordinary Results* (San Francisco: Jossey-Bass, 2000); Tara Bennett-Goleman, *Emotional Alchemy: How the Mind Can Heal the Heart* (New York: Harmony Books, 2001); His Holiness the Dalai Lama, *The Art of Happiness: A Handbook for Living* (New York: Riverhead Books, 1998); and Phil Nuerenberger, *The Quest for Personal Power: Transforming Stress into Strength* (New York: G.P. Putnam's Sons, 1996).

11. Empathy and the systems perspective: Emotionally intelligent individuals and teams pay attention to the whole system—self, interpersonal relationships, teams, intergroup relationships, organization, outside environment, the interactions of stakeholder groups, and so forth. A systems perspective enables people and teams to judge how their actions will affect multiple stakeholders; this is empathy for the different parts of the system, as well as the individuals involved. The concept is well documented in the organizational literature. See Peter Senge, *The Fifth Discipline: The Art and Practice of the Learning Organization* (New York: Doubleday, 1990). See also Anthony J. Dibella and Edwin C. Nevis, *How Organizations Learn: An Integrated Strategy for Building Learning Capability* (San Francisco: Jossey-Bass, 1998).

12. Paying attention to the undercurrents in the group: Kenwyn Smith and David Berg, *Paradoxes of Group Life* (San Francisco: Jossey-Bass, 1990).

13. Behavior and the team life cycle: The notion that teams go through stages of development is the basis for a primary stream of research on group dynamics and team effectiveness. For a review of the theory and guidance on application in business settings, see Susan Wheelan, *Group Processes: A Developmental Perspective* (Boston: Allyn and Bacon, 1994).

14. Team results using the Emotional Competence Inventory: Although the ECI is generally used as a 360-degree feedback instrument for individuals, we have found that when aggregated, individual scores on the competencies present a very interesting and useful picture of the team's overall strengths and weaknesses. We are currently researching this method of measuring a team's emotional competence; at this point, anecdotal evidence

(i.e., the many conversations we have had with executives and their teams about their data) suggests that aggregate scores point to underlying team norms as well as team competencies.

CHAPTER 10

1. Shoney's: Stephanie N. Mehta, "What Minority Employees Really Want," *Fortune*, 10 July 2000, 181.

2. Culture and behavior in healthcare organizations: Beulah Trey, "Trust in the Workplace: Taking the Pulse of Trust between Physicians and Hospital Administrators" (unpublished dissertation, University of Pennsylvania, 1998).

3. Attending to the organizational reality as part of the change process: Annie McKee and Cecilia McMillen, "Discovering Social Issues: Organizational Development in a Multicultural Community," *Journal of Applied Behavioral Sciences* 28, no. 3 (1992): 445–460. For a discussion of social reality and how it relates to the change process, see Edwin C. Nevis, Joan Lancourt, and Helen G. Vassallo, *Intentional Revolutions: A Seven Point Strategy for Transforming Organizations* (San Francisco: Jossey-Bass, 1996).

4. Dynamic inquiry: McKee and McMillen, "Discovering Social Issues." In this and other publications, we have also used the terms *cooperative inquiry* and *co-inquiry* to describe the process of investigating the underlying assumptions, norms, and emotional reality of organizations. We have adopted the phrase *dynamic inquiry* in our work with organizations to better reflect the action orientation of our methodology. Cooperative inquiry and co-inquiry are discussed in Edgar Schein, "Organization Development: Science, Technology, or Philosophy?" (transcript of an address to the Organization Development Division, Academy of Management, Washington DC, 1989); and Peter Reason, "The Co-operative Inquiry Group," in *Human Inquiry in Action: Developments in New Paradigm Research*, ed. Peter Reason (Newbury Park, CA: Sage, 1988). Another relevant stream of practice is discussed in Peter F. Sorensen Jr., Diana Whitney, and Therese F. Yaeger's chapter in *Appreciative Inquiry: Rethinking Human Organization Toward a Positive Theory of Change*, ed. David Cooperrider (Champaign, IL: Stipes Publishing, 1999).

5. Human resources and emotional intelligence: Ruth L. Jacobs, "Using Human Resource Functions to Enhance Emotional Intelligence" in *The Emotionally Intelligent Workplace: How to Select For, Measure, and Improve Emotional Intelligence in Individuals, Groups, and Organizations*, eds. Cary Cherniss and Daniel Goleman (San Francisco: Jossey-Bass, 2001).

6. Attending to the vision: Warren Bennis and Burt Nanus, *Leaders: Strategies for Taking Charge* (New York: Harper and Row, 1985).

7. Immunization in the developing world: Monica Sharma and J. Tulloch, "Commentary: Unfinished Business," UNICEF, The Progress of Nations 1996: Health, <http://www/UNICEF.org/pon96/heunfini.htm> (accessed 10 October 2000).

8. Challenges facing higher education in the United States, and fostering emotionally intelligent management to address those challenges: David Smith, "Leadership and Professional Competencies: Serving Higher Education in an Era of Change" (unpublished dissertation, University of Pennsylvania, 2000).

## CHAPTER 11

1. Organizational learning: Peter Senge, *The Fifth Discipline: The Art and Practice of the Learning Organization* (New York: Doubleday, 1990); and Sarita Chawla and John Renesch, eds., *Learning Organizations: Developing Cultures for Tomorrow's Workplace* (Portland, OR: Productivity Press, 1995).

2. Trust and confidentiality in the executive coaching relationship: David H. Maister, Charles H. Green, and Robert M. Galford, *The Trusted Advisor* (New York: The Free Press, 2000).

3. A Day in the Life: This process was developed by Fran Johnston of the Gestalt Institute of Cleveland in response to the need to expand the type of data available to a coach. The coaching process is greatly enhanced when the coach has an opportunity to see the leader in action—and has examples to draw on as part of the learning process.

4. *Perceived weirdness index* is a term coined by Jonno Hanafin, chair of the International Organization and Systems Development Program of the Gestalt Institute of Cleveland, to describe how to manage the way people take in new, intriguing, and possibly threatening information and different approaches. In the context of leadership development this means that processes—and the people facilitating them—should draw participants in through providing a unique, if slightly out of the box, approach, without being so different as to put people off.

5. Adult learning: David Kolb, *Experiential Learning: Experience as the Source of Learning and Development* (Englewood Cliffs, NJ: Prentice Hall, 1984).

6. Action learning: The principles we report here have been developed over the years in our work with leaders and organizations. For a review of general action learning processes, see David L. Dotlich and James L. Noel, *Action Learning: How the World's Top Companies Are Recreating Their Leaders and Themselves* (San Francisco: Jossey-Bass, 1998).

7. Connecting the culture with leadership development: Linda Pittari and Annie McKee, "Getting Bullish about Leadership" (presentation for Linkage, Chicago, 2001).

APPENDIX A

1. Competence models: The best competence studies use a methodology that identifies the specific capabilities that distinguish star performers from average, as described in Lyle Spencer and Signe Spencer, *Competence at Work* (New York: Wiley, 1993). Daniel Goleman's analysis of competence studies is described in his book *Working with Emotional Intelligence* (New York: Bantam Books, 1998).

2. EI competencies of outstanding leaders: See Daniel Goleman, "Emotional Intelligence: A Theory of Performance," in *The Emotionally Intelligent Workplace*, eds. Cary Cherniss and Daniel Goleman (San Francisco: Jossey-Bass, 2001).

3. IQ levels: Spencer and Spencer, *Competence at Work*.

4. EI versus IQ: These findings do not reflect the actual correlations between EI and IQ, which range from zero to mildly positive, depending on the measures of each used (according to reports by Reuven Bar-On and John Mayer at an EI conference held in London, 18 May 2000). Their findings, however, were not based on the most rigorous study possible, which would require including people across the whole range of IQ, from mental retardation to genius. But such a study would be of only academic interest when it comes to leadership. In the workplace, and particularly for leadership in executive, professional, and technical roles, those involved are at the high end of the bell curve for IQ (as selected for by the educational requirements they had to pass to enter these careers). It is only among those at the relatively high end of the IQ spectrum that organizations must make practical decisions about the relative value of EI and IQ in hiring, succession planning, and leadership development.

5. EI competencies distinguish outstanding leaders: Lyle Spencer, "The Economic Value of Emotional Intelligence Competencies and EIC-Based HR Programs," in *The Emotionally Intelligent Workplace*.

6. The incremental profit: Richard Boyatzis, Daniel Goleman, and Kenneth Rhee, "Clustering Competencies in Emotional Intelligence: Insights from the Emotional Competence Inventory," in *The Handbook of Emotional Intelligence*, eds. Reuven Bar-On and James D. Parker (San Francisco: Jossey-Bass, 2000), 343–362.

# INDEX

# ABOUT THE AUTHORS

**Daniel Goleman** is the author of the internationally bestselling books *Emotional Intelligence* and *Working with Emotional Intelligence*. A psychologist who for many years reported on the brain and behavioral sciences for the *New York Times*, he has been a visiting faculty member at Harvard University. Goleman is cochairman of the Consortium for Social and Emotional Learning in the Workplace, based in the School of Professional and Applied Psychology at Rutgers University, which seeks to identify best practices for developing emotional competence. He lectures frequently to professional groups and on college campuses.

Goleman has received many journalistic awards for his writing, including two nominations for the Pulitzer Prize for his articles in the *New York Times*, and a Career Achievement award from the American Psychological Association. In recognition of his efforts to communicate the behavioral sciences to the public, he was elected a fellow of the American Association for the Advancement of Science.

**Richard Boyatzis** is Distinguished University Professor as well as a professor in the departments of organizational behavior, psychology, and cognitive science at Case Western Reserve University. He is also an adjunct professor of human resources at ESADE. Prior to joining the faculty at Case Western, Boyatzis was president and CEO of McBer & Co. and COO of Yankelovich, Skelly & White and served on the board of The Hay Group. Boyatzis is the author of *The Competent Manager: A Model for Effective Performance* and *Transforming Qualitative Information: Thematic Analysis and Code Development* and a coauthor of *Innovations in Professional Education: Steps on a Journey from Teaching to Learning.* Along with *Primal Leadership*, which has been published in twenty-eight languages, he is coauthor with Annie McKee of *Resonant Leadership: Renewing Yourself and Connecting With Others Through Mindfulness, Hope, and Compassion* and *Becoming a Resonant Leader: Develop Your Emotional Intelligence, Renew Your Relationships, Sustain Your Effectiveness*, with Annie McKee and Frances Johnston. He is also the author of more than 150 articles on human motivation, sustained desired change, leadership, managerial competencies, and leadership and competency development.

**Annie McKee** is a senior fellow at the University of Pennsylvania Graduate School of Education and director of the Penn CLO executive doctoral program. McKee teaches at Wharton Executive Education and speaks widely to both private- and public-sector audiences. She is also cofounder of the Teleos Leadership Institute. In this role, she works with senior executives all over the world as an adviser, focusing on resonant leadership and change.

With coauthors Richard Boyatzis and Frances Johnston, McKee has published *Resonant Leadership* and *Becoming a Resonant Leader*, two bestselling books that extend *Primal Leadership*'s message and values. Her most recent solo publication is *Management: A Focus on Leaders.* She also writes for academic journals, trade and professional publications, and blogs. McKee is passionate about helping people to become the best leaders they can be, so that they can contribute meaningfully to their organizations, communities, and the world.